HEBREW ACADEMY · NORTHEAST PHILADELPHIA

9768 Verree Road
Philadelphia, PA 19115
(215) 969-3956

This page is dedicated
by Eliezer and Besie Katz
in memory of our family
who gave their lives, Al Kiddush Hashem

ZALMAN YOSEF GREENWALD

KAYLA GREENWALD

GENENDEL LAYA GREENWALD

HERSH MOSHE GREENWALD

CHANA HINDEL GREENWALD

ETTIL MIRIAM GREENWALD

MORDCHE BORUCH GREENWALD

ZVI KREBS

BASHA KREBS

D1566318

Various families associated with Hebrew Academy
wish to memorialize their loved ones,
who were so dear to them.

לזכר נשמת

LOUIS G. BARRON

IRVIN JEROME BENNO

CHAYA GITTEL MALKA BORENSTEIN

BENJAMIN ILAN BRENINGSTALL

SAMUEL FRIEDMAN

BERNHARD HEIDINGSFELD

NEIL HOROWITZ

YOSEF MODDEL

UNCLE ALTER PINCZEWSKI

SAUL S. ROSENSTEIN

SARAH ROTH-VOGEL

R' YITZCHOK AHARON ROTH-VOGEL

RABBI LEIB SCHULMAN

ZIPPORA SCHULMAN

הסטוריה

The ArtScroll History Series®

Rabbis Nosson Scherman / Meir Zlotowitz
General Editors

THE WAR OF A JEWISH PARTISAN

THE WAR OF

Published by

Mesorah Publications, ltd

A JEWISH PARTISAN

A YOUTH IMPERILED BY HIS RUSSIAN COMRADES AND NAZI CONQUERORS

by Yechiel Granatstein

Translated from the Hebrew
by Charles Wengrov

FIRST EDITION
First Impression ... March, 1986

Published and Distributed by
MESORAH PUBLICATIONS, Ltd.
Brooklyn, New York 11223

Distributed in Israel by
MESORAH MAFITZIM / J. GROSSMAN
Rechov Harav Uziel 117
Jerusalem, Israel

Distributed in Europe by
J. LEHMANN HEBREW BOOKSELLERS
20 Cambridge Terrace / Gateshead
Tyne and Wear / England NE8 1RP

ARTSCROLL HISTORY SERIES®
THE WAR OF A JEWISH PARTISAN
© *Copyright 1986 by* MESORAH PUBLICATIONS, Ltd.
1969 Coney Island Avenue / Brooklyn, N.Y. 11223 / (718) 339-1700

ISBN: 0-89906-476-0 (hard cover)
0-89906-477-9 (paperback)

Typography by CompuScribe at ArtScroll Studios, Ltd.
1969 Coney Island Avenue / Brooklyn, N.Y. 11223 / (718) 339-1700

Printed in U.S.A. by MORIAH OFFSET
Bound by SEFERCRAFT *Brooklyn, N.Y.*

To the memory

of the members of my family

who were destroyed by the Germans

with all the Jews of Poland

❧ ❧ ❧

And the memory of my

fellow Jewish partisans

who fell in battle with the enemy

and those who died at the hands

of their fellow fighters

❧ ❧ ❧

May Heaven avenge them

Table of Contents

ᴥ§ Preface

In Paris, 1950, this book was published in its original Yiddish version by the Jewish Pen Club, under the title *Ich hob gevolt lebn* ("I Wanted to Live"). By 1955 I was living in the Land of Israel, and the work appeared in a Hebrew translation by Y. Ginton (published by Moreshet, Tel Aviv), entitled *Yehudi BeYa'ar*, "A Jew in the Forest."

Over the course of the years, it has been helpful to students in various schools and seminaries in their studies of the Holocaust and Jewish resistance. For some time, however, the book has been out of print. Responding finally to many requests to make it available again, I decided to take my original Yiddish version and render it into Hebrew myself, anew, in my own language and style.

My translation was not literal. Here and there, in the course of translating and styling, I changed sentences, shortened or added, without deleting anything, however, from the contents of the original story. These changes, mainly technical and stylistic, seemed to me essential.

In the present version, as the book now appears, there are a few added chapters, which were not included in the book originally. These were written some twenty-five or thirty years ago, and appeared in the literary supplements of various newspapers in the Holy Land and abroad, in either Yiddish or Hebrew. In translating my book into Hebrew anew, I decided to include them.

❀   ❀   ❀

In the Preface to *Ich hob gevolt lebn*, I stated:

"I have written this book without any political motive whatever. My purpose has been to relate how the partisans fought the Germans, and how Jews in the forest perished from the bullets of the partisans themselves ...

"Perhaps in other forests the Jews did not suffer or were not subjected to so much suffering. In that case, my tale is only of what I myself experienced and saw with my own eyes ...

"Somewhere in this great wide world, I hope, the sixteen other Jewish partisans who were set free with me on that summer day of 1944 are alive and well. I hope and trust this book will reach them. Together with me, they remain the only witnesses to the things that happened in our forest, about which I tell in the pages that follow ..."

The first two of these paragraphs out of my original Preface were written at the request of the public Jewish body which at that time financed the publications of the Jewish Pen Club of Paris. It was explained to me that since the book describes the Soviet partisan movement in quite a negative light, it was likely to arouse unfavorable, unwelcome reactions. This public body was also apprehensive that on account of its publication — this was one of the first books about the partisans — harm might come to the rescue activities for the survivors of the Holocaust which were then going on in various countries in Eastern Europe. As a result, I was advised to write a Preface along the nature of the paragraphs that I cited above, its purpose being to soften the hostile reactions somewhat, if and when they would materialize.

Sure enough, when the book appeared, a sharp controversy developed in the Jewish press of Paris. The contents took people by surprise. Many were shaken and disturbed by the truth. In their uncritical, emotional attachment to the Soviet Union, certain known groups on the Jewish horizon attacked both the author and the book: not because they found no truth in it, but because I had the impudence, supposedly, to present the Soviet partisan movement in a distorting mirror. Other sections of Paris Jewry, and the general Jewish press, took a firm stand in defense of the author and the book.

Whatever the case, though, it was beyond me to straighten out the mirror. Had I done so, I would have distorted the truth.

❀   ❀   ❀

By now a wide-ranging literature, both documentary and research, exists on the partisan movement. And it is known that hatred of the Jews was to be found in the forest not in one location alone but in many places. Known are the names of the partisan brigades and units whose non-Jewish fighters subjected the Jews to fright and terror. They conspired against them, their own brothers-in-arms, and against the camps of Jewish families. When they encountered Jews on the roads or in villages, they would confiscate their weapons, and even kill them in cold blood.

So the Jew suffered for being a Jew, not only in the ghetto where he was confined, but also after he succeeded in escaping and reaching the forests of the partisans. There he exposed his life to danger no less than the others in the battle against the Germans. Yet his "brothers-in-arms" saw him first of all as a Jew, and this determined their relationship to him.

From this book the reader can draw his own conclusions about the general attitude to the Jews in the forest where the author served as a machine-gunner; about what they underwent, and about their tragic, bitter, rapid fate.

For the Jew was a Jew even in the forest.

ৰ§ Preface to the English edition

For many years I looked forward to the day when this book — with the cry of pain bursting from it — would reach the wider world, especially the English-speaking masses in America and elsewhere.

I had wanted as many Jews as possible to remember, and never to forget, what Amalek did to us, and to know the lot of the Jew in the Partisan forest. I am fortunate, therefore, that thanks to the Primary Cause this book is being published by ArtScroll, with the result that it can reach the English readership, including the Jew who will surely feel the agony his brethren endured during the Holocaust.

With joy I thank G-d that these lines to the reader come from Jerusalem, the Holy City, the City of G-d, in Adar, the month when Jews gained relief from their enemies, the month that was transformed from sorrow to gladness and from mourning to festivity.

I realize that this book may shock the reader somewhat, and I apologize. Nevertheless, the events in this book did not take place on a distant planet — but on this earth where we live, in our era, in the twentieth century.

And the agony and mourning will surely continue until the end of time.

Y.G.

THE WAR OF A JEWISH PARTISAN

A company of Jewish partisans in the forests of Byelorussia

CHAPTER ONE
To the Forests

IT WAS AROUND MIDNIGHT when the patrols found me and brought me to their partisan camp; there they turned me over to the partisan Michail. On a page of a notebook he wrote down all my personal details, and then quickly went off to tell the staff about me. When he returned, he stopped near a big-bellied pine tree, measured it with an expert eye, and spat out, "Tomorrow, if all is quiet, you can put up a real tent right here. With a long pole you'll peel off the pine bark, and you'll have a right proper place to live. The devil isn't going to get you; understand?"

That said, he went off in a hurry. His heavy boots trod noisily on the dry thin little branches, as though he were crunching fragments of glass. The further he went, the softer grew the echo, till it died in the silence of the night.

A little away from me, partisans lay stretched out on the ground, fast asleep. Some of them were naked from the waist up, while others had their boots on their feet, their Cossack hats on their heads, and their weapons right at hand — ready, it seemed, for an order that might come at any moment, to get up and get going.

I looked around. I wanted to convince myself that I was really now among the partisans. A terror was keening through me, a harrowing doubt that maybe I was only dreaming, seeing a vision, fooling myself blind. Maybe the Germans were still running after me, and they were certain to capture me — me, the one who was sentenced to death; and then they would take me back by force to the pits, to the doom where I really belonged.

I was bathed in a cold sweat. My body felt heavy. That terror of the Germans would not let me go. At times it even slapped me hard, either because the dark was so intense, or because frightful roars and yowls reached my ears from the depths of the forest.

Standing tall, proud, unmoving, somehow the pine trees looked to my eyes like frozen human bodies, with their feet stuck deep into the earth. I pushed my head into a thick bush so as not to see them. I avoided looking into the dark eyes of the night that surrounded me and rested on me. Nor was it any help at all when I suddenly discovered a full moon sauntering over the tree tops, peering here, peeking there, as though it was in search of someone hiding from it, someone who wanted no part of it.

Two squirrels skipped and leaped about on the pine tree I was facing. They jumped down and sprang up again, as though just prancing about. A bird that apparently couldn't sleep flew a few turns over me. It seemed to want to whisper something in my ear, but it finally disappeared among the tangled trees, and I saw no more of it.

I took off my jacket and covered myself with it. Then gunshots rang out and echoed in the empty air, and I thought I should get up and look for shelter. But I saw the partisans just sleeping on, while the horses behind the fire neighed and the cows tied to the grass went on chewing their cud. So I too spread out full length on the ground and lost myself in my thoughts. I breathed in the sharp air of the forest; my lungs seemed to expand and open wide; I wanted so much to fall asleep — and I couldn't. The events of the day, all that I had gone through, were there before my eyes, tiring me out and tormenting me without letup.

❀ ❀ ❀

In the middle of the previous night German soldiers, and others who had sold their souls to them, surrounded the house where we, 120 young Jews, had been kept. Every day we had been taken out for forced labor in the Jewish cemetery. There we were forced to break the tombstones on the graves, so that they could be used to pave the road at the edge of the city of Slonim, which had been damaged at the beginning of the war between the Germans and the Soviet Union.

Wrung out, beaten, dead tired after a day of backbreaking work, we were sleeping like mice, like every night. We woke at dawn as usual, not knowing yet that we were surrounded. The sun was shining, and over the windows of the large hall where the boards we slept on were laid out, it seemed as if pitchers of gold had been poured. Silken threads were glistening in the sunlit air of the room, reaching the pallets where our weary bodies rested. Silent, whispered conversations passed from bed to bed, from one floor to the next.

And then ...

Entirely by chance someone went over to the window, and cruel, frightening words burst from his mouth: "Fellows, it's the end! *The end has come for us!*"

Hundreds of soldiers armed from head to foot stood behind the barbed-wire fence that encircled the grounds. We almost went stark crazy. We embraced one another, kissed each other's cheeks. Some began saying *viduy*, the age-old confession of sins that a Jew says when he knows he is facing death. The older ones among us put on *tallis* and *tefillin* and began praying. Others proclaimed themselves absolutely determined to commit suicide by jumping into the toilet pits, just so that they would not fall into the hands of the Germans and their "helpers" alive.

Meanwhile some little time had passed, and nothing had happened. We saw the captors who surrounded the grounds talking quite pleasantly among themselves, and some of us even said, "Well, maybe they don't mean to do us any harm ... maybe ..."

We were really peculiar. We had already witnessed three operations of massacre — been through them ourselves. After all, we were all survivors of families that had been shot to death and thrown into pits at the edge of town; and when we saw hundreds of soldiers keeping under guard a house from which there was no escape, we could still delude ourselves with surmises that maybe there was no intention to destroy it; maybe no harm would come to us ...

Actually, they were only waiting for the vicious German commander who was in charge of us. This was the man who ruled us, and we were at the mercy of his whim and his whip. He was a little late, but he finally showed up. He quickly opened the locked iron gate, the entrance to his "living treasure." Hard on his heels the soldiers burst in over the grounds, and immediately afterward we heard the loudspeaker commanding us to go out of the building and line up in orderly rows.

Amid all the tumult and confusion and the panic that gripped everyone as we were running down the stairs to get out to the grounds, I suddenly noticed between the first and second floors a sort of space in the ceiling. We had been living in that house for two months. Like everyone else, I had gone up and down these stairs several times a day. And I had never noticed that space; it was just suddenly there, before my eyes.

"What's the use of that hole now, in these moments?" I wondered. "What good is it?" Then I put the thought out of my head, hurried down onto the grounds, and took my place in line near the fellow who always slept next to me.

With only a few glances, without any words, we said Goodbye to each other — glances filled with despair at the death that awaited us. Everywhere eyes were tearing. A silent weeping that could barely be heard welled up from the orderly rows ...

And yet ... On an impulse I left my place in the row and sped back to the staircase. I found again that space between the floors and squeezed my body into it, wriggling my bones about a bit. I was certain, though, that part of my body was still sticking out, and the whole effort seemed worthless to me. But now I hurried out to the grounds again, and ran back to my place in the line-up. I was afraid to be late for the roll call, when they would check to see if everyone was there ...

Standing in the row, I let my glance wander to the other side of the fence, to the sidewalks on both sides of the road, and to the wide river Szczara flowing out there.

The river water flowed slowly, sluggishly, as though forced to move on such a hot summer day against its will. I watched the people who filled the sidewalks passing by with a little smile on their lips. They were happy at the beautiful day that had come into the world, the sun shining so generously, the quiet that filled the early hours of the morning.

They saw us standing in our orderly rows, with the armed soldiers surrounding us. There were some who paused for a second at the fence, or slowed down their pace; and there were others who turned their heads to the other side, not to see us, not to look at us — miserable, lowly creatures who were fit only to be destroyed.

And the skies above were so blue, so clear and fresh: just like the day that had just started, all radiant with light ...

"Run back to that hole fast — to that space between the floors! Run back there, as long as you're still able to!" I felt some kind of voice within me calling me to get out of the line where I was standing. Yet I didn't rush to move. I wiped the sweat from my forehead, and tried to collect my scattered thoughts. I had to act according to logic, I told myself — according to common sense. "Where will you run?" I asked myself. "Where?" Death will get you even in that hole where you'll try to hide. There isn't room for your whole body. Your feet will stick out. Go to your fate with everybody, and that's all. That's the end of it!"

"Get out of here. Hurry, hurry! Don't wait another second! Listen to me!"

I am ready to swear by everything I hold dear that I felt a powerful hand taking hold of me and bringing me to that staircase, to the hole I had seen for the first time only this morning ...

I disappeared from my place in line, ran back to the building, toward that staircase. From the grounds the voice of the German in charge of us reached me. I heard him call out the names of the inmates of the house. The hammering sound of his voice was deafening in my ears. I also heard the response of the people standing in the rows, as they answered *Yes* to the call of their names. I imagined the expression on their faces, and the feelings in the heart of every one of them.

I made my body as small as I could. I shrank into myself. I became a knot. And still it seemed to me that the small space couldn't possibly hide me entirely. I squeezed my hands in close to me. My nose became flattened pressing close to the concrete. I couldn't move my head to either side. Nor could I know which part of my body was still protruding out of that narrow space that was squashing and pressing me hard. I was certain that the soldiers who were running up and down the stairs now, carrying down all the belongings that we had left on the beds, would have to notice me; and then they would finish me off on the spot, with a flash of bullets.

Yet it didn't happen. As our holy Bible might say, they had eyes and did not see. I heard their shrieks and their wild laughter. Up and down the stairs they went, and they were blind ...

And then ...

An outburst of gunfire shook the walls of the house. The agonizing outcries rose to the very heart of heaven ... groaning ... and the still, small sounds of dying, the ending of life. After a very little while all grew still. Silence came and held.

I did not know what to do with myself, with my bundle of bones and flesh.

"Why did I go and do this? Why was I persuaded to go and hide? What do I need my life for — this life that I snatched out of the death angel's hands? For what purpose should I go on living?"

"But what about the machine gun hidden in the garden of your house?'Have you forgotten it? Now is the time: now! It'll be useful to you."

Like a lump of clay I stayed in that hole, neither sleeping nor awake, without a single clear thought in my head.

I didn't know that outside the sun had set, and in another little while evening would come. I couldn't reckon how much time had passed, or how many hours were passing now. Time was now outside my regular order of things, or else it didn't exist for me at all.

And yet at a certain moment I took my cramped body out of that hole, to take stock of what was going on around me. Forgetting to be careful, instead of getting out I fell from that space between the two floors — fell onto the stairs and rolled down them like a broken wheel, till I came to a stop. I gathered my poor bones together. In spite of the pains I felt in every part of my body, it seemed that I was not seriously hurt. I could stand on my feet.

❦ ❦ ❦

It was a clear, starry night. I sat propped against the pine tree whose bark Michail had told me to peel off tomorrow, so that I could make myself a tent. I didn't feel hungry, even though I hadn't eaten anything for over a day; but a great thirst was tormenting me. So I decided to get up and look for water to drink, to quench my thirst.

I was careful not to go too far from the camp, as I didn't know then the paths leading to and from it. At the spot where the horses were tethered I found a pail with some water, and I gulped it all down. For all I know, it might have been left by some horse that had drunk from the pail earlier. Refreshed, I returned to my place, to that thick tree, and stretched out at its foot. The pine needles that kept falling covered me like a blanket.

❦ ❦ ❦

Like a little child afraid to take its first few steps alone, with no adult to watch him, I had made my first hesitant movements after I fell from that hole. With difficulty I dragged my feet to the grounds outside, and when I got there I collapsed. The grounds looked like a slaughterhouse, full of pools of dried blood, parts of human bodies, batches of hair, strewn clothing, hats.

I stumbled on a body. The face was as though dug out of the earth. Soil clung to it. I nudged it, and tried to identify it. It was the young carpenter, the third one from me on those beds of boards that we had slept on. He had been about twenty.

Another body, all in a puddle of blood. I shrank from going near it. The hair seemed to sprout from the earth, like some grass growing out of it, but with a strange dark color. I wanted to shout, to scream out to the sky; only my lips were shrunken and clamped shut. I burst out in a fit of weeping that I couldn't control.

Now I remembered that when I was lying in that hole I had heard the German commander calling my name. His hoarse voice had reached me, reached to that little space in which I had pressed myself. He must have lost his temper. He must have cursed and sworn. But I had escaped from his hands. I should have been the murdered Jew number 120, and instead, only 119 occupants of the house had been shot and killed ...

I knew I had to get away from there rapidly. I stole out of the grounds and inched my way down by the fences of houses, down through ditches, till I reached the grounds of our home in the ghetto. For a long time I lay stretched out on the ground near the low, open little door. I tried to follow everything going on there around me. I was curious about our neighbor the Polish house painter, the one who had joined the Germans on the day of the slaughter, and had shown them the lumber rooms where our whole family had hidden: seven human beings. I wanted to know if he had also taken possession of our home.

I was happy to find it abandoned, desolate, in ruins. Through the ditch that carried out sewage from the courtyard down to the stream at the bottom of the alley, I wormed my way to our garden. Here and there some bits of our household goods were scattered. The good, valuable items had been snatched away long ago, directly after the massacre. The bits and pieces that remained, strewn about in the garden and the courtyard, no one wanted. They weren't worth the trouble.

With a sharp leap I reached the house, and went inside. Utter ruin and destruction. The walls had been scraped and torn away, and the boards removed. They had come looking for hidden treasure, panting for silver, gold, diamonds ... and so they had spared no effort or toil.

The kitchen was completely dismantled, demolished. Blackened bricks lay scattered over the floor. On the day of the massacre we had all sat in the bunker that we had dug for ourselves under the kitchen, below the floor level. After several fire bombs had been thrown into our house, the smoke penetrated into the bunker, and we abandoned it. We were afraid that in a short while we would all suffocate. My family found a hiding place in the lumber room, but there was no space left for me, and I hid in our garden. I uprooted tomato plants that were growing there, and "camouflaged" myself with them.

Now the bunker was wide open, its cover lying at the side. I made my way into it, and groped about in every corner. I had the illusion that perhaps some member of my family had escaped on the way to the pits, and had come back here and hidden in the bunker.

Afraid to go out, he might have fed himself breadcrumbs that he had collected in a bottle — as I had done myself in a hiding place where I stayed in the days of the first massacre.

The bunker was altogether empty, and darker than the night which had just fallen. As I left, I felt my feet treading on small pieces of wood, and I trembled for joy — with good reason. Since the Germans invaded our town, I had taken to carrying such little pieces with me. I had never parted from them, day or night. According to a known family tradition, these were little pieces of wood from the chair of Rabbi Yisrael Baal Shem Tov (the founder of the chassidic movement — may his merit protect us). One of those pieces even had the letters of this holy man's name cut, or perhaps burned, into it. Every day when I went to my forced labor, those pieces had been with me. When we hid from the Germans, I always checked if I still had them. At the beginning of the third large massacre in our town, however, when we got out of the bunker bewildered, almost choking to death, I forgot my jacket in which I had always kept those little sticks of wood.

I never found the jacket — but now I picked up those little pieces with the greatest happiness and pressed them to my heart, as though they were the greatest treasure in the world.

I stole my way out of the house, back to the garden, worming along on my stomach till I reached the spot where I had hidden the machine gun. By the signs I had left at the time, I found it — still buried there safely. Weeds had sprouted and were growing all around and over it; I was dead certain that no stranger's hand had come ferreting here. Now I plunged my fingers into the soil and began digging, digging down, till I reached the lid of the container. When I lifted it, my eyes opened wide and a strong wave of heat struck me full in the face, making my head spin with dizziness. After a few seconds I got my two hands around the machine gun. Carefully I drew it out, with the bag of bullets that was attached to it.

In the dark of night I left the courtyard of our house. With cautious, measured leaps I made my way to the edge of town. I stole through a smashed Jewish house, shortening my route of escape. To my great good fortune, I met not a single living soul. In another little while I was outside the town. I reached the Jewish cemetery, located on a hill; and I breathed freely. Many pits had been created when the tombstones were pulled out to be used for paving. In one of the pits I hid myself.

Some single bullets seemed to be aimed toward the cemetery. Afraid that I might have been discovered, I loaded the machine gun's magazine with bullets, so that I could fire back if I had to defend myself. For further safety I then changed my location. I stretched out over a grave that I had chosen as a position from which I would be able to take aim.

A few minutes went by now, and all around me there was absolute silence. Slowly, slowly I went down from the cemetery to the edge of the road. Making sure that nothing whatever was moving on that road, I crossed it quickly; and on the other side I was already at the rim of the thick forest — the forest that the Germans who had guarded us during our forced labor at the cemetery had always feared so much, talking with no little exaggeration about the number of partisan fighters who were hidden in it.

I set to walking on one of the forest paths, not knowing where my feet would take me. Suddenly a small truck came out as if from between the trees, and almost ran me over. I leaped down into a nearby gully, just as I heard the stern command, "Get up! Put your machine gun down, and get your hands up!"

I murmured the words of *Shema Yisroel*. There was no time for speculation. I was mortally afraid that these were Russian army police working for the Germans, who specialized in capturing people who fled to the forests to join the partisans. Like religious Jews through the ages, facing mortal danger I found the words of *Shema Yisroel* coming instantly to my lips.

Two well-armed men were facing me, pointing their automatics at me. They got down into the gully and seized me with their hands. "Who are you? Where did you come from? What are you doing here?" Before I had time to answer, there were more questions: "The Germans sent you? You came to do spying?"

From their disreputable clothing and their questions I realized that I wasn't dealing with any militiamen. I told them how I had escaped from the general slaughter that the Germans had carried out on the morning of the previous day, and that my goal now was to reach the partisans. And, I added, they could see that I didn't come empty handed. My Russian machine gun could be used against our common enemy. Then, since I had not the slightest doubt that they knew my "race" or "nationality," I didn't wait for them to ask me but told them I was Jewish — the last survivor of a family that the Germans had exterminated. My purpose in doing this was to win their confidence, so that they shouldn't doubt my word or my reason for fleeing into the forest. And I sensed, further, that the fact that I turned up with a machine gun in my hand pleased them very much. My emphasis, though, that I was a Jew, didn't thrill them particularly ...

A few minutes later I was sitting in their old, battered truck along with them and three of their companions who had been waiting in the vehicle. The truck made its way to the camp of the partisans, where I would be turned over to the head of the night squad. The five who had picked me up sat on either side of me, singing all the way their heart-capturing Russian songs filled with such tender longing for their homeland, for the mother, wife and children who remained at home, away from the battlefront, so very far from them ...

And I ... I was dead tired, and sunk in despair. All my thoughts took me back to the town where all the Jews had been slaughtered; back to the hills of Petrolovitch at the edge of the town, at whose foot the great pits had been dug; the mass graves of my brothers, now filled with bodies.

"And the forests are so close to the town," went the choking thought round my neck, "so wide and large, so safe — no Germans, no enemies — only partisans fighting them, taking vengeance from them, rescuing, saving ...

"But why did they receive me so coldly, almost as if they didn't give a damn for me? Why? And these fellows say I'm going to be questioned. How are they going to question me there, at the partisan headquarters? What kind of interrogation will I get when we get there? What's there to question me about? What?"

I must have fallen asleep. When I opened my eyes the sun was up — or rather it was sort of leaning on a clump of pine trees, near which I was lying on the ground. I had no idea what time it was, or what day of the week. I didn't know how long I had been asleep — a day? two days?

I saw partisans moving around near the tents. One was holding a chunk of meat in his hand; another was biting into a loaf of farm bread; others were lying near the big fire, sleeping, snoring, letting out sounds like a railroad engine before setting off on a long trip.

It was Michail to whom the patrols who had found me and brought me, turned me over. He came to me now and told me to hurry up and come with him to the staff headquarters. When we came there, I saw a group of people sitting inside a tent in a circle on the grass. They asked me all kinds of peculiar questions: about life in the ghetto, and how it had been destroyed; about the Germans and the local police; and so on. Finally they asked why I hadn't come to the forest earlier, and if, now that I *had* come, I was ready to carry out any order they would give me, even if it meant risking my life.

"My life wasn't worth anything anyways," I replied, "till I came here. The danger of death doesn't frighten me anymore. But maybe I'll begin to appreciate the value of life again right here among you partisans, when I'll have the chance to take a little revenge from the

Germans, the enemy we have in common."

Not a word more did I add. I knew I had expressed everything that was in my heart.

❧ ❧ ❧

That very day I was assigned to a fighting unit of partisans that was being organized, to which they gave the name "Squad 67." I had no idea what the origin of the name was, and I didn't ask. Almost all the men who made up this squad were soldiers of the Red Army who had escaped from German imprisonment, and others who had evaded capture when the Germans suddenly invaded sectors of Poland which the Russians had taken, and their military units had disintegrated. They had taken to wandering around and staying in the forests, or else in nearby villages, protected by good-hearted farmers, till they began organizing themselves as partisans.

Michail confided in me that the only reason why I had not been settled in the Jewish family camp, located nearby, was that I had brought my machine gun with me. The heads of staff were interested in having the gun stay with the new squad that was being formed, and they wanted it to be handled by a soldier who had managed to serve in the Polish army. As he told me this, Michail put his head close and whispered in my ear that I would have no reason to be sorry about it.

That first day, when I was made a member of the partisan unit, I had no idea of what Michail was hinting at, and I didn't think to ask him to explain. In the days that followed, however, I came to understand that little hint of his only too well, especially later, after what happened to Michail himself.

CHAPTER TWO

My Friend Mischa

HE NUMBER OF PARTISANS in our forest kept growing from day to day. Young people kept coming to us from the farms and villages, either because they had been tormented by the Germans or because they dreaded that this inhuman enemy would send them off to forced-labor camps in Germany. Russian soldiers, escaped from imprisonment, also came along. They arrived after a long journey eastward out of Germany, after desperately trying to get ever closer, a little closer, to their homeland. They had moved along mostly by night, through villages and forests; and once they found partisans from their Russian homeland, they joined them.

One day a young Soviet soldier who had escaped German capture joined our unit. His name was Mischa.

When he left the staff headquarters, he began strolling through the camp, and he stopped at my tent. Having met me, he asked if he might sleep the first night right there, in my small sleeping quarters — because having spent a long time at the headquarters, he found that the day was gone before he had time to set up a tent of his own. I heartily agreed; and when we both went in for the night, we began talking. By the time we finished talking, there was only a little time left till dawn.

Only then, as we were about to finally fall asleep, my "guest" apologized and asked me to tell him my first name again. He didn't remember it, because it had sounded so strange, and he couldn't be sure how to pronounce it.

I told him again, enunciating the name clearly. Mischa opened wide his clear blue eyes and looked at me in puzzlement: "No; no, I don't understand. *Chil? Yechil?* I never heard a name like that."

I smiled — and sensed at once that my companion felt ashamed. Perhaps he thought I was playing games with him, hiding my real name from him. Only after I explained very carefully that this was my true personal name, he turned to me, still smarting from the upsurge of shame, and he burst out, "Do you know? — among us your name would have sounded like *Philip!*"

Philip? Yechiel? For the life of me I couldn't see any connection between them. I couldn't fathom what Mischa meant. But that was it. From the next morning on, I had a new name in Squad 67. All the partisans in the camp took to calling me Philip; and long after I left the forest I still couldn't get rid of it. It appeared in all my official papers and documents.

I didn't let Mischa set up a tent of his own. He remained my partner in my makeshift sleeping quarters. In the course of time our meeting by chance turned into a deep, solid, lasting friendship.

Mischa was a tall man, with a big body and bony hands. When he stood next to me, I looked like a tender, fragile twig next to a thick-branched sturdy tree. Yet I never felt inferior on account of that. He loved to spend his leisure hours with me, talking, telling stories, and also listening. And as for me, I found myself liking him for his plainness and simplicity, and for his good heart. As time went by, I became as used to him as to a brother with whom I might have been living. When he went out on a mission of sabotage and didn't return in a reasonable time, I worried over him; and when I heard his voice from afar at last, I felt a surge of happiness.

Of course, there was a price to pay: "Man and wife" they titled us later in the camp. Needless to say, "Man" meant Mischa the strong, tough guy.

We felt especially happy when, for one reason or another, the two of us remained alone in the tent at the same time. In those chilling winter days I used to bring chunks of wood and make a fire in a hole in the ground, in the middle of the tent; and we warmed ourselves at the flames. Splinters of fire used to fly out, landing sometimes on our pants, sometimes on our jackets, to burn holes in them — once in the front, once in the back — as if to let the air get in and out easily ...

In this way our conversations used to flow on and on for hours.

Mischa really had what to talk about. But above all else he had his harmonica, that he had brought with him to the forest; and he played on it whenever he was in a good mood, or whenever sadness pressed down so very strongly on the heart ...

At first sight it might have seemed silly: a harmonica in the forest in a time of war ... Yet it wasn't so at all. Only a few days before the Germans invaded Russia, Mischa bought it; and nowhere else but in Moscow, when he went to see the city for the first time in his life. It cost him a pile of money; he gave away all his savings for it; but it was worth it. What a beautiful harmonica it was: inlaid with ivory, all shining and gleaming, and so pleasant to the touch.

"Just imagine it, Philip," he told me the very first night we spent together in the tent. "I took it with me when I was taken into the army. And I never had a chance to fire off even one melody on it: because our whole division was surrounded in the first few hours of the German invasion of the area where we were stationed. We were surrounded completely, from all sides; and all of us were taken prisoner.

"In the temporary camp where they took us, I hid it as much as I could. But at night I played on it a great deal — sad songs — and then we felt so good. Even the guards who had to watch us used to gather around and listen to me playing ... till one day I became fed up with sitting in prison. I planned a way to escape, and I carried it out. I ran off to freedom, and the harmonica went with me ..."

Mischa yearned nostalgically for the quiet, peaceful days before the war. In the summer, on Sundays and holidays, the lads and young folk of the village used to gather on the spacious grounds of his house; in the winter they gathered in one of the large rooms inside; and he used to play on the harmonica of one of the villagers. The young folk listening would accompany him, singing, humming, and dancing, into the late hours of the night. This went on for years — till the Germans invaded his native land and put an end to all the goodness he had known.

Well, in the forest Mischa took up his old practice again. On Sundays those partisans who were in the camp would sit around the big fire, and if Mischa too was in the camp, he would take his harmonica — the new one, that he had bought in Moscow and kept with him during his imprisonment — and he would play songs that tugged at the heart, that recalled the home, the village, father, mother, wife and children, or the fiancée — those who had been left behind, far, far away from the front.

In these hours they would almost forget that they were living in the forest, while a vicious, terrible war was going on; that we were always surrounded by the Germans on every side and we had to wage a heavy battle against them; and every time we fought them, we suffered losses: Every time, or every day, another person fell ...

In one of the armed conflicts that we waged against the Germans, shortly after Mischa had come to the forest and we were already good friends, I almost lost him. We were lying at our positions, only a few yards from each other; yet we couldn't exchange a word between us, but only glances, winks, signals. No one could lift his head out of the grass, even to raise it an inch. The bullets came flying over our heads, whistling, looking for a victim ...

When the shooting stopped for a bit, I realized that the dawn had come up. The sky was clearing, as though washing its face in the first daylight. Like a thin, whitish, gossamer cloud the morning dew rose from the earth, from the fragant grass and the plants in the meadows. From the nearby village the lowing of the animals reached us, as they must have woken their owner or their shepherds promptly on time, out of habit, demanding to be taken out to pasture in the meadow.

And just then, during one of those beautiful minutes when the new light of morning was wiping away the last traces of night, the Germans renewed their attack. Vanished in an instant was the entire clear blue sky; the cloud of dew evaporated as though it had never been. The sounds of the animals no longer reached us. The shooting drowned out their cries, overpowering them.

Between our positions, the German bullets and ours crossed in the air. Every shot was echoed by a reply. And every bullet had its target. And sometimes it happened — we learned this well in the forest — that a bullet would strike a man just at a moment when he wasn't expecting it, and he never knew how, from where, it had come ... He never had time to blink, before it severed an arm, tore through a foot, struck through the chest — and a human life was cut off ...

This is what happened then:

Just a moment before, I had exchanged smiling glances with Mischa; and suddenly I heard him groan. His face was covered with blood; and it was impossible for me to crawl over to him and help him. The enemy fire we were getting was extremely heavy, and my machine gun had to keep answering without a stop, to defend us.

But my eyes didn't leave him. His face changed color. The sun that had come up dissolved the blood that had just hardened on his cheeks and spilled onto his clothes, and from there to the ground. I spoke to him in whispers, trying to give him courage. I prayed he should hold on till medical help could reach him. I didn't want to lose a friend. I wanted him to live. I wanted this obstinate battle to stop, that all this murder should finally end.

Mischa stayed alive. Our medical man did everything possible to save him and heal him. He was able to stitch up the lacerations in the cheeks; but Mischa's strong white teeth began falling out like ears of wheat from a ripe stalk.

A number of weeks went by, and I was also wounded — but only lightly. We both lay recuperating in the tent we shared. The blood we had shed brought us still closer together. For hours on end Mischa played his harmonica, and music helped us forget our pains a little — the wounds which under the conditions of the forest were in no hurry to heal.

Truth to tell, there were many hours when we just lay in the tent side by side, and neither of us opened his mouth to utter a word. We didn't interfere with each other's private thoughts, with the wish to be alone for a while with one's own reflections, with a longing for the days that were gone, a yearning for family, relations, friends, who were now beyond reach ...

There was a difference between us, however: Mischa had living people to long for. He knew that it was very possible that his whole family — mother, fiancée, brothers and sisters — were all alive. I knew that my heart was reaching out in memory with a painful yearning for a world that didn't exist any more, for loved ones who were no longer alive, because they had been murdered. And yet I brought them all to life in my memory. I absolutely couldn't accept that they were gone. At times I would even find myself talking to them, as though they were all there before my eyes, standing there next to me.

We both recovered from our wounds. We went out again, either together or separately, on dangerous missions, to send railroad trains flying off the tracks, and on various campaigns against the enemy. If it happened that we left the camp together, we always tried to remain near each other, whether in moments of working away quietly or in moments of nerve-racking battle, when the danger of sudden death hovered over us equally, or when we could know contentment and satisfaction — for instance, when we could both extract thirstily a few drops of water from the wet grass. Sometimes Mischa would try to help me, and at other times I was able to ease his plight when he found himself in distress and needed my help ...

CHAPTER THREE
For Sleeping at the Guard

MICHAIL AND I WENT OUT together to take our turn at sentry duty at one of the watch posts around the camp. As soon as the two we replaced had left, we found a well-hidden spot in the thick bushes, and we made a small fire with thin branches, taking care that it couldn't be seen from afar. We spread out on the ground, our weapons in our hands, and warmed ourselves by the flames.

I was happy to be out on guard with Michail. Ever since the patrols had brought me to the camp in the forest and turned me over to him, I had been looking for a chance to have a little talk with Michail, face to face: to ask him if it was true that he was Jewish, as the Russian partisans in the camp insisted. All the time till now I had not wanted to upset him or fluster him, although I strongly wished that in our Squad 67 there should be another Jew, and I should not be the only one. I had the impression that Michail avoided getting into conversation with me, so that he shouldn't reveal to me this deep secret of his. The whole time, however, the non-Jewish partisans used to tell me openly, "Philip, he's a Jew just as much as you are, and that's all there is to it. Just take a good look at his eyes, at his face, and you'll see we're right."

Michail heard what they said about him, and he denied it absolutely. He laughed at them. He was just a Soviet citizen, he insisted, and nothing more.

We were stretched out near the fire now, side by side, and our glances crossed. I began thinking, 'Well, maybe Michail knows better than I do what the partisans ought to know about him and what they had better not know. So why should I go searching and digging into his heart? On the other hand,' my mind went on, 'how wonderful it would be if he revealed the private, secret truth about himself to me; if he confessed now, as we're sitting here together, and said, *Philip, it's true: I'm as Jewish as you are.* Couldn't it happen during the long night that's ahead of us, or in the course of the whole day, when we'll be going out again and again for guard duty together, sometimes for a stretch of two hours? Is he going to leave me also in doubt?'

We heard footsteps approaching, apparently stepping on twigs. We quickly put out the fire, and I pressed my finger very lightly on the trigger of the machine gun, as Michail did the same with his automatic. We were prepared for anything, as the heavy footsteps drew closer and closer. But the dense, thick darkness made it impossible to identify anything.

"Stop! Who's there?"

We heard no answer.

"Stop or we'll shoot!"

This warning also brought no reply. Sensing that the footsteps were really close, we demanded to be told the password; and when there was still no answer, we sent a burst of bullets. The fire was not returned. Carefully we went out to see what had happened. Some two or three yards or meters from our sentry post we found a horse stretched out on the ground, fighting a losing battle with death. Before our eyes it died, and quiet returned to the thickly wooded forest.

We went back to our places and started the little fire burning again. Its lapping tongues of fire were pale as if with fear. They didn't have the strength to spring far from the bushes.

"Philip, the time has come for me to tell you what I think you've wanted to know for a long time. I'm honestly Jewish — a real Jew — the son of Jewish parents."

The words came hurtling out of his mouth just at a moment when I wasn't thinking about him at all, when it never entered my mind to get him talking about the subject. I stared hard at the fragments of wood that the fire was burning up, turning them into black char.

I felt Michail's hand on my shoulder.

"*Du veyst gornisht*" (You don't know anything), he said, suddenly beginning to talk to me in a rich, fluent Yiddish instead of Russian. "All the years, in the area where we lived, we tried hard to put down and control the plague of anti-Semitism — and it was no use. And now that vicious animal came alive again, and it runs wild with even greater force. They don't have anything to be afraid of. Hatred of the Jews is out in the open now, just as it was in the past, in the time of the Tsar. We have to do everything we can to save ourselves also from our enemies who live in the forests, who fight side by side with us against the Germans. We have to beware of them, Philip! Remember what I'm telling you. Remember!"

Glowing sparks flew out from the fire and died away in the thick bushes. From the camp we heard the sounds of partisans talking, coughing, snoring; we heard the neighing of horses and the lowing of farm animals that had just lately been brought to the camp from neighboring fields in a ransacking operation.

The night began to fold up, but in the midst of talking we hardly noticed it. Groups of soldiers passed by on the roads where we were keeping guard. Some were leaving the camp to carry out missions, while others were returning from actions that they had carried out, successfully or unsuccessfully. Some went out in vehicles, others came back on foot. We stopped them all and demanded the password; and when we received the right answer, we let them come in or leave and continue on their way.

When we remained alone, Michail went on telling me his story:

A few days before the Germans invaded his town, he had a stroke of good fortune: In an impressive ceremony he received a card of membership in the Communist Party. He became a full-fledged member, with all the duties and privileges. The event stirred him deeply, filling him with happiness ... And then, after a week in all, perhaps a bit less, the war broke out, and he rushed to sign up for the army. Together with other young folk from his native town of Shepitovka he marched, full of enthusiasm and song, down to the railroad station, to reach the front as soon as possible and thrust the Fascist invaders back ...

Together with many young people who were taken into the armed forces like him, he was sent from his native land of the Ukraine to White Russia. They were assured that they would swiftly reach Germany, to "punch the enemy in the teeth" and put the Germans to rout. With all his heart and might he was set to do so, like his six brothers, all of them older, most of them married — strong, manly fighters who were drafted or who volunteered into the Red Army, to be sent to the battlefronts.

And then everything turned out so weirdly that it could hardly be believed. The unit in which he served just disintegrated, fell apart in its first encounter with the Germans. The officers disappeared and were nowhere to be seen. Following in their footsteps, the soldiers deserted and scattered. But it soon became clear that they were surrounded by a large enemy, and the Germans were going to capture them.

In the very first days of the outbreak of war between Germany and the Soviet Union, the atmosphere in the the Soviet army had changed beyond recognition. Morning and night in the Communist Party the talk had always been of brotherly love. This was the great goal, the ideal to strive for and reach. Now it was gone. In its place appeared a hatred for the Jews, for Jewish soldiers and officers. Evidently they were looking for a scapegoat, a sacrificial "goat for Azazel," where they could put the blame for the breakdowns and failures, the catastrophe that befell the great Soviet army which everyone had praised to the skies.

This conclusion, however, Michail reached only later. In the early days, when the Jew-hatred first broke out, he was simply frustrated and bewildered. He ran to the Party officials and commanding officers who were still there, and complained. He growled at the "anti-Soviet" attitude of the non-Jewish soldiers toward their brothers-in-arms. He ranted at this "anti-Communist" phenomenon in the ranks of the army. And they? — they had no answer to give him. They didn't react. Michail had believed so strongly in the values with which he had been brought up, and now it was all breaking down before his eyes. His friends of yesterday had changed, turned alien to him, moved away from him and from other Jews, as though it was not at all the same homeland for which they had gone out to fight together.

By a dangerous stratagem (Michail continued telling his story) he managed to slip through the siege that the Germans had thrown around his battalion, and he deserted from the army. He got to a village, and was able to change his clothes. He grew a beard and kept going from one destination to another, till he reached the forests. In the daytime he subsisted on fruit that grew in the woods; and at night he would go out into the villages and show himself to the farmers as a complete Russian in every detail; whereupon he would get food supplies from them, as well as a store of information on what was happening in the area — till the partisans began to get organized.

We became aware that the night had come to an end. There was no more need for the fire, and we put it out. Down the length of the path we had been guarding we walked separately, abreast of each other. From time to time we came close to one another, we exchanged a few words, or kept silent, as if there was nothing out of the ordinary between us.

And yet there was something extraordinary between us — something that united us. We were two Jews in Squad 67: two among hundreds of non-Jewish partisans; two and no more.

Our breakfast was brought us. We had barely finished eating when a partisan from our squad appeared. He had been sent to replace Michail, who was now summoned to appear immediately before the staff. This puzzled me: why did they call him now? In any case we would soon be at the end of our period of guard duty, and would report to headquarters. Most likely, I thought, they wanted to consult him about something, since in the past he had been a junior officer in the Soviet army. Before he went, however, Michail hinted to me that he was possibly being called to headquarters about some unpleasant incident that had occurred over a week before. But, he mentioned casually, he didn't attach any particular importance to the matter, and he would tell me about it the next time we met.

For a few days I didn't see Michail, and didn't know where he was. In the meantime I learned details of the "unpleasant incident" that Michail had mentioned when I had last seen him:

A bunch of fighters, Michail among them, were on their way back from a complicated dangerous mission against the nearby German garrison. When they reached the village of Okuninovo, that was located within the forest and was considered a partisan village in every respect, the men separated and went to the farmers' cottages to rest. Tired out from the long way they had come, they were planning not only to get a good meal but to catch a good, proper bit of sleep. For greater safety they decided to sent a watch at the edge of the village, near the road. As usual in guard duty, the people set to watch were to be replaced every two hours. The first two who were given the assignment were Michail and Gregor, a young White Russian from one of the neighboring villages.

Hours went by. The two stayed on duty; and no one came to take over.

Meanwhile a group of partisans from another unit came up the path into the village, and they found Michail and Gregor sleeping. The arriving fighters took their weapons away from them, while the two never stirred. Then the partisans woke them up and marched them straight to staff headquarters.

Now another few days went by, and still no sign of Michail in the camp; I became worried about him. And then, one morning, all the members of our squad were awakened, and we received an order to dress quickly and gather, with our weapons, before the tent of staff headquarters.

When we arrived, we were told to form a large circle. After a short wait the head of the Division for Special Affairs came out of the tent, holding a sheet of paper in his hand. Behind him marched four partisans armed from head to foot; and between them came Michail and Gregor.

A new day had risen. A yellow-red sun sparkled down through a white poplar tree on our "morning activity." I sized up the man who was about to read from the sheet in his hand, and my heart was clamped by anxiety. The thought filled my mind: Those two men standing there before us may be living their last moments now. True, they had committed a serious offense; but was it right to pass such an extreme sentence on them? Were they to be put to death? Didn't the blame fall just as well on those who should have come and taken their place on guard duty — and never came? Had these two, Michail and Gregor, been any less tired out than those who went off into sweet slumber? And wouldn't it be better to let the two atone for their serious crime and make it up, by giving them difficult missions to carry out, so that they would strike the Germans harder and harder?

The two stood together, side by side, and stared at us — at all of us. 'Are they really seeing us' I wondered, 'in actual, physical reality?' When people have been sentenced to death — if this is really the verdict — can they look into the eyes of their comrades-in-arms who have been called to witness what is going to happen to them?

Somehow I reckoned that Michail's eyes were searching for me, trying to find me, because he wanted to finish his story; he wanted to tell me what he had not had time to relate about himself in those pleasant hours we spent near the little fire, when we had been out on guard duty together. And perhaps, I reflected further, he wants to take his leave from me, to bid farewell to the one who is going to remain the only, single Jew in Squad 67.

A cold sweat covered my body. I felt that in another minute I would collapse where I stood. I couldn't lift my eyes and look at Michail; and I didn't want those who stood next to me, on either side, to notice the tears that were filling my eyes.

A fit of trembling seized me, at the thought that in another moment we would be ordered to stand motionless, without a sound, while the four armed partisans would shoot these two fighting men to death: one a Jew, the other a young local farmer, a White Russian.

The chief of staff arrived, and he ordered the Commander of the Division of Special Affairs to read the verdict. His voice cut the silence that prevailed:

"The Staff of Squad 67 pronounces sentence against the two partisans, Michail and Gregor, for having been found asleep in the village of Okuninovo while they were on guard duty. Michail, sentenced to death by shooting; and Gregor, to a month's imprisonment in the stockade near staff headquarters."

Something tore in my heart. I didn't collapse. I only leaned on the partisan standing near me. I withstood it. I overcame it. Somehow I didn't break down.

A rain of bullets sliced through Michail's heart and split his body. I stood paralyzed, turned to stone. My heart seemed to have stopped beating. I couldn't look anyone in the eye, not then ...

Gregor was led away under guard to serve his prison sentence of a month; and the shattered body of Michail the Jew was thrown into a pit which had been prepared beforehand, for this purpose.

CHAPTER FOUR
The Nighttime

THIS NIGHT DRAGGED on without end. It filled the empty space of the village that we had put under attack, stretched over the straw roofs of the low huts, dug into the bushes together with us, and lay beside us without a sound ...

The exchange of bullets continued intermittently, as though without them this long night might lose its meaning.

We had organized this attack ourselves, never reckoning that it would turn into one of the first heavy battles that we would have to face. We couldn't accept the idea that the Germans should start turning up in the villages near our forests. Moreover, directly under our noses, in a village that we were accustomed to pass through when we went out on a mission and when we returned to the camp, they even dared set up a sentry post, manned by White Russians, Ukrainians, Lithuanians, and other — all Fascists who hated the Soviet Union and the Jews.

At our staff headquarters it was decided to drive them out of the village where they had stationed themselves, so that we would be able to move freely again, without interference and without grief.

We reached the location as darkness was falling. We drew close through the fields and opened up a strong, concentrated barrage of fire on the stone structure that served as a little fortress for the sentries acting under German orders. Precious hours of the night went by as the fighting continued, and the battle remained undecided.

Mischa lay on the ground near me. From time to time we exchanged a few solitary words, that sailed from my clump of bushes to his, and back. We merely wanted to find out every once in a while if either of us had been hit, and if there was still someone there to answer if the other spoke up ...

No one minute was like the next one. Some minutes were silent, when the rain of bullets stopped, and it could be imagined that the enemy soldiers had fallen asleep besides their weapons. At other moments the exchange of fire split the stillness of the dark, tearing up the night itself into shreds.

It was hopeless for the village to think of peaceful rest. At the very beginning of the battle the people who lived there scattered in all directions. They hid in the fields or fled into the forest — but not before they opened their barns and stables and drove out their farm animals by force, to go running wild over the fields, with no idea of where to go. Their lowing, mooing, wailing cries mingled with the gunshots and explosions of shells, till the night itself seemed to low and moo with them, joining them in their mournful outcries.

The dogs too were fairly deafening in their fearful shrieking. For some reason they were drawn particularily to our battle position. As they ran to and fro, they were caught in the barrage of crossfire coming from both sides of the battle, and were wounded and killed.

Like a thin blanket, the night's darkness covered somewhat the dead-tired partisans, as well as the wounded men, to whom it was almost impossible to get close and help. Perhaps their groans reached the fortified positions of the Germans and their helpers, so that they could estimate our harsh, difficult situation.

As the exchange of fire became more intense, stacks of wheat in the fields began to catch fire. Granaries and huts went up in flames, till the sky above us reddened ablaze, as though the gates of hell had opened before our eyes.

A bullet struck one of our men when he leaped ahead to change position. He writhed on the ground as if a snake had bitten him, rolled over and over, and fell into the bushes that provided cover for another partisan. Bullets kept chasing after him, trying to strike home, but missed their target. Since no help of any kind could be given him, the wounded man was soon dead in the bushes, alongside his fellow-partisan, who kept on shooting the whole time at the enemy. Life and death lay there side by side, in one clump of bushes ...

❀   ❀   ❀

I rested my chin on the large, round magazine of my machine gun, and looked out at the skies that were beginning to grow light. My gaze went across the distant fields, from which the night was beginning to peel away, to gather up the cloth of darkness with which it had covered them.

A thought suddenly crossed my mind, scorching me with its fire. Away out there, in the pits, in the huge mass graves, lay my father and mother, the members of my entire family, so many, many other Jews ... This ending night, I mused, was covering them also now. Perhaps the very hands that kept firing those bullets at us this night, trying to destroy us, had aimed their fire then at the poor helpless people whom they had brought to the pits.

There all the bullets struck home. Not one person escaped them. Those pitiable souls had nothing to defend themselves with. And here, in the battle by night that we were still fighting, granted that we had our fallen and our wounded, yet how different it was. In this heavy conflict, we were also killing some of theirs. We were taking revenge, revenge. It occurred to me that perhaps we would kill the very German who had shot dead my father, mother, brother and sister. Perhaps ...

My head spun with dizziness. I felt something graze the edge of my forehead with scalding heat, sending my hat flying off. When I saw it again, it lay two or three meters away. I had been touched by an enemy bullet.

"Thank Heaven it was nothing serious," I whispered to myself, feeling my forehead with my fingers. "Just a scratch, a skin-deep wound. What a great mercy ..." But before I could take any great comfort in this, a further batch of bullets landed around me. By now, however, my head was buried deep in the bushes, and the shots passed over my head, missing their mark.

I changed the position of my machine gun and chose a new target, aiming for the spot from which the bullets had been sent flying at me. I was full of a furious anger that those swine had tried to shoot me dead before I had had a proper chance, in the relatively short while that I had been in the forest, to take my revenge and pay our murderers back as they deserved. I fired a few outbursts toward the new target I had chosen. Immediately afterward, the "shooting dialogue" between us began subsiding, till it stopped altogether.

I closed my eyes, and failed to see the morning come up in all its splendor. All was quiet now as my reflections took me back to the giant pit in the large town. In my mind's image it seemed to have changed its location, or it had expanded out, till it reached the bushes near me. I could have sworn that I began feeling the weight of the bodies of my beloved family, covering me on all sides.

"Almighty Father in heaven," my lips whispered, "have mercy on me. Take pity on this last surviving remnant of an entire family, who doesn't know even now, when he is alive in the forest, whether he should bother bearing the burden of life, whether he should want to live, or if he ought to join all those lying there in that huge pit that I see before me now, its mouth wide open, calling to me — so that I shouldn't be any different from them all ..."

I opened my eyes. Somewhere out there a bunch of ravens were cawing in a shrill hoarseness. They had smelled the odor of death and burning, and now they must have flown off, waiting to return and eat their fill after the battle would be over.

In the end we defeated the enemy. With a shout of victory we entered the heart of the village, where we counted several dozen dead Germans and other militiamen. The dogs of the village were running all about the bodies, that lay there like beams of a house that had collapsed, to become widely strewn over the area.

From one hut the partisans extracted a group of German soldiers who had hidden there. They made an appearance of miserable frightened creatures, and not a twinge of pity did we feel for them. We bound their hands and covered their eyes with strips of cloth, and prepared for a long trip with them back to our forest.

On a few wagons we loaded our wounded men. Their outcries and groans of pain were heartrending, throwing a pall of misery over our great victory — one of the first we had in face-to-face battle with the enemy. Our doctor moved from one wagon to another, trying to help the wounded fighters with the pathetically small means that he had. Some of them wept and sobbed from their relentless pains. Others cried out and moaned piteously, cursed, prayed. There were even those who pleaded with us to shoot them, to spare them their infernal agonies of sheer hell. But the cries became swallowed up in the chattering songs and trills of the birds that accompanied us down the forest paths, and the rustling of the leaves that kept fluttering and dancing in the wind.

Someone began singing a melancholy song about a woman waiting for her husband to return from the battlefront, to be happy with their child that had born to them shortly after he had gone off to war; but he was never going to be back, because somewhere out there he had fallen like a glorious war hero, and no one even knew where he lay buried.

It was a mournful song, that depressed our already fallen spirits; and yet they all loved it. Tears stood in their eyes as they sang along in harmony, making the echoes roll through the whole forest. The melody leaped over the clusters of trees and forged a path into the day that had just risen fully, bathed in sunlight.

"Come on, Philip: sing. Sing with us together," a few of the partisans called to me, when they saw me sunk within myself.

"Sing, sing, Philip," Mischa also urged me, as he sat beside me in the wagon. "Get out of those thoughts of yours," he pleaded. "Come on, get together with us, right here, right now ..."

I couldn't. I would not even tell Mischa that it wasn't the song, echoing around us and depressing the heart, that was accompanying me on the way back to the camp, but the wholesale slaughter in the past, "out there": my own personal experience of death, the death in the pits, that would not let go of me for a minute, that never stopped peering into my eyes with its own terrified, terrifying eyes — as though it came to ask me, "What are you doing here? Go back to your place in the pits, with all of them, all of them ..."

I couldn't get free of my thoughts. They took me away from reality. I was certain that if I held out my two hands I could touch my beloved family, feel their physical presence as something real ... "No, no," went my mind, "I don't belong here, with all these people around me, riding ahead and behind me." I even wanted to tell Mischa now, "You can't see them, but I'm part of their death. I belong completely to them."

But I reckoned that even Mischa, so bright and intelligent, wouldn't really understand; so I preferred not to start a conversation with him. I remained alone, in my private isolation.

❀ ❀ ❀

Choruses of local birds were perched on the branches of the forest trees. The moment the partisans stopped singing, the birds' trills and calls could be heard. "This is their morning prayer," I mused, "to the Creator — giving thanks for the night that passed by peacefully and harmlessly for them, thanks for the new day that has risen, and thanks for the food they'll find, prepared for them by His great mercy."

"But what about you?" went my thoughts. "Where are you with your prayer? Haven't you been humbled by all the kindness Heaven has shown you till now? Go on," whispered my heart. "Join in the prayer. When praise and entreaty to Heaven come out of pain, out of agony and suffering, the thread of Heaven's loving-kindness spreads further, stronger over the whole of existence. Join in!"

A light breeze ruffled the leaves and tender branches on which the dew glistered with a pleasant, soothing freshness. Through the trees of the forest the sun pushed like a reddened, glistening head. When I became aware of it, it looked like a royal crown borne through space on a gigantic golden plate.

I stretched out full length in the wagon and watched the green leaves of the birch trees, and the tangled bushes that seemed like the tips of green hair. Ahead of me stretched a long line of wagons fully loaded with our wounded men, leaving trails of blood behind them. There was nothing to stanch the wounds, and the blood kept spurting out through the bandages, that were mostly made of torn shirts.

It was a difficult day for me. I could find no way to fight clear of the terrifying things I had seen on the grounds of the building from which I had escaped to the forest. I wanted to put far away the black woeful thoughts that kept tormenting me; and I couldn't. Then suddenly, before my mind's eye the forest became full of dead bodies. I saw them at the tops of the trees, between the branches: frozen corpses, attached and clinging to one another, embracing ...

I almost screamed: "Almighty Master of the world, be kind to me and take me to You. Take my soul, that is being tortured now by racking pain. Set me free of it. And if this isn't the verdict You want to give me, then by Your great, abounding mercy help me bear the heavy burden of life with which I've been saddled by all that murder and death away out there. *Help me!*"

I buried my head in a bundle of straw on the wagon, and listened to the sounds carried through the forest: the soughing of the wind, the rustle of the leaves falling over one another, and the pathetic heartrending cries of the wounded men.

"Join in the prayer!" I remembered the thought that had passed through my mind earlier, as I listened to the melodious chirping of the birds. I repeated the words that perhaps I had heard sounding distinctly from my own mouth: "Join in the prayer — for when it wells up out of pain and suffering, the thread of Heaven's loving-kindness spreads further over the whole of existence."

I kept repeating the words, and my heart grew quiet, more calm. My indrawn lips opened and began whispering words of age-old Jewish prayer, till I fell asleep in the shaking, bouncing wagon, at the side of my Russian friend Mischa.

CHAPTER FIVE

The Night of Rosh Hashanah

E HAD TO LIVE through another hard week. Almost every day we had clashes with the Germans. They waited in ambush for us along the roads, at the edges of the villages, besides the highways, in all sorts of places that they chose as good, strategic spots from which to attack us. And we paid them back in kind, from vantage points that were good for us. With cunning we beguiled them into chasing after us, to make a desperate attempt to overtake us as we ran from them in a carefully planned show of retreat, while our fighting men, situated in ambush, poured down a rain of bullets on them. We managed to lure them down paths that we had mined and booby-trapped beforehand, and so we could slaughter them. But our men also suffered. We had our share of dead and wounded fighters.

During this brutal week, Mischa and I were part of a group that went out on a mission to blow up a large bridge over a busy highway. We knew the Germans guarded it with gimlet eyes, and the approach to it was highly dangerous; but we had to carry out the assignment. We knew the goal was important enough ...

Close to midnight we reached the area. We had to cross the highway and reach the end of the bridge. One by one we crawled over the ground and drew close to our destination. Then, suddenly, a barrage of bullets came pouring down at us. The Germans were protected by their entrenched positions, while we were exposed and vulnerable. We simply had to work with lighting speed and iron resolution, before they could kill us out, one by one.

In the darkness we noticed some bushes. Into them Mischa and I leaped for cover, and from there we sent hand grenades flying into the enemy's positions. The exchange of fire between us continued. We couldn't retreat, and we certainly couldn't prevail against the strength of the Germans, who were well fortified there.

When the rain of fire back and forth died down a bit, I managed to ask Mischa if he knew what day of the week it was. My friend became irritated, and spat out some word that I couldn't catch. When I persisted and wouldn't let him go, he lost his temper, and unlike his usual self he shouted at me, "You idiot! The rockets are flying over our heads, their bullets are hunting for us, trying to put some holes into us, and you — damn it to hell — you have to know right now, just this minute, what day of the week it is! What in tarnation is the difference if it's Monday, Tuesday, or whatever? And tell me: What's going to happen in the next minute — that you know?"

"But ..."

"But, dear Philip, aim that machine gun of yours a little lower and a bit to the left, and send them a few rounds of ammunition; and that's all!"

I took Mischa's rebuke without a word of reply, and shot a few spurts of machine-gun fire toward the well-protected Germans. Under the cover of my shooting a few of our fighters had the courage to get still closer to the German positions, and the hand grenades they threw exploded with a deafening noise.

Directly after that we withdrew. We got away from there, without suffering any casualties. None of us were killed or wounded. When we reached the edge of the forest safely, we sat down for a little rest. And my mood improved. Finally, finally, I had managed to work out in my mind the reckoning of the days. I reconstructed it according to the mental system of calculation that I had been using all the time. Now I was certain I knew just when Rosh Hashanah would fall — the start of the Jewish new year ...

To Mischa I said not a word. I wasn't going to tell him my private thought, the secret of the single Jew left now in our squad. In my mind, though, I started concocting plans. I longed to leave the camp completely on the first night of Rosh Hashanah. I had no idea of what excuse I could give the squad leader for this strong wish of mine to be set free for the night; but in my heart there was a great yearning to be alone somewhere in the thick of the forest, somewhere far away from the camp, where I could make the time holy with my prayers — the holy Jewish prayers of Rosh Hashanah.

❀ ❀ ❀

It was *Erev Rosh Hashanah* now, the day before the holy festival of awe. I asked my commanding officer for permission to go off at dusk to the nearby village; and he gave me leave, on condition that I be back at the rise of dawn.

As the sun was setting, I left my tent. The clusters of trees glowed as if dipped in fire, caught by flames. I had hardly gone a few paces down the forest paths when the daylight began to wane. Slowly, slowly the last fragments of light gathered themselves and left. Evening fell, and with a quiet, gentle tread the first night of Rosh Hashanah came to greet me.

The truth was that originally I didn't plan to go the nearby village for the night. On the other hand, I had no clear idea of where I *did* want to go now. Walking on without a destination, for a moment I had the thought that I might have done better by staying at the camp — in my own tent, in fact — stretched out on my bed, covered by my coat. There I could have whispered in privacy the prayers that I remembered by heart. But I kept walking on, drawing further and further away from the base. I didn't even notice that my pace was quite fast, as though I was trying to run away ...

All at once I found myself beside an old birch tree that I had known for some time. It was a noble, handsome tree. The neighboring farmers told us that it was one of the first that had been planted in the forest, and because it was so magnificent in appearance, no axe had ever chopped it down. The cutters had always left it alone. The roots of the tree went wide and deep, breaking through ground here and there, looking like the bent knees of some tall, bizarrely grown figure. In the long course of the years some of the branches had taken root, and had become trees in their own right. Their heads became entwined in the necks of nearby trees, as they probed their way into them, till all grew in unison, as though grafted together — parts of one organism that couldn't be separated and set apart.

During the summer the old tree grew a dense covering of leaves, that gave us a shady resting place, especially when we were on our way back to the base from a mission of sabotage or some other assignment. When we reached it we would take off all our weapons and ammunition and hang them on its strong branches, or lean them against the thick sturdy trunk; and we would stretch out on the grass all around, eat to our hearts' content, and even catch a bit of sleep. And all the while, the tree protected us from the burning sun.

On the other hand, if we came to it on a cold, rainy morning, we would light a little fire near it, roast potatoes in their shells, and warm ourselves at the flames with the help of some strong liquor — home-made by the village farmers — which we used to get as presents, or else we took it by force, with the aid of our weapons ...

Ever since I discovered the tree, I was always drawn to it. At times when I was in a mood of misery, feeling my anguish and grief — and such times were certainly not lacking then in my life — I would disappear from my tent and come here. I would climb up on one of the thick, heavy branches and sit on it for hours, giving way to my flow of reflection and reverie, with not a soul to interfere.

No: I had not planned at all to come to this spot; but I was glad my feet had brought me to the place that gave me pleasure. I leaned against the tree trunk. All about me flew leaves that the wind had detached from their stems — leaves with a golden tinge, dim rays of light in the night's darkness. Tired of wandering aimlessly in the air, they finally settled on the ground, spread around my feet like an orange-yellow carpet ...

❧ ❧ ❧

... Rows of houses with open windows, curtains hung behind them; and lights shine through. The tables are set with glistening white tablecloths and candlesticks of silver or brass. The wax candles are burning, their flames aquiver. The streets and the lanes are filled with Jews — men, women and children — all dressed in their holiday clothes, streaming to the synagogues, to the houses of prayer.

I hold fast the hand of my younger brother, and we follow our father and mother as they walk ahead of us. We don't dare talk aloud. We whisper softly, so that our parents shouldn't hear us. We're somewhat afraid, even anxious. We have to get a good verdict when Heaven judges us. That's what the *rebbe* told us in *cheder*. And Father told us the same thing as our teacher in school: In heaven, on this solemn day, they write down human beings for a year of life, or — Heaven forbid — the opposite ... And who doesn't want to live?

In the chassidic *shtib'l*, the intimate local house of prayer, it is warm and crowded. People sit, people stand, swaying back and forth, whispering prayers, weeping ... Up front, at the eastern wall, sit the eminent, distinguished *chassidim*. One wears a *shtreim'l* (a round, fur hat flattened on top), another a round, velour hat. One has a long, narrow beard; another a short, thick one. One man's beard is very wide and well brushed, resembling fabric. Another's is sparse and twisted.

The evening prayers, *Ma'ariv*, have not begun yet. It is still too early for the prayers that will declare this solemn day holy. So the people wait. They dip into a *sefer*, a holy volume, trying to learn a bit; or they look into themselves, at the end of one Jewish year and the beginning of another. They finger and rummage through their deeds and actions in the days that are now in the past. They search, they probe, fearful of the sins they did. Already now, ahead of time, they ask the Almighty for great forgiveness and tremendous kindness, to be able to receive a good verdict at His judgment.

The faces are aglow in silent entreaty to Heaven, fiery in a mute supplication, covered with sweat in fear of Heaven's judgment. Sighs move across the air from one corner to another, from one bench to another. They rise up and return to their owners. The heart beats with emotion.

My father wears a dark-brown *shtreim'l*. His eyes are on a page of a holy volume that he is studying, but all the time he wipes his eyes with a white handkerchief. I believe my father is crying. I see tears falling from his eyes, rolling down his pale cheeks. Why is my good father weeping? Is he also frightened of this judgment day, like us, the youngsters who commit so many sins and do all sorts of bad things the whole year round?

The *ezrat nashim* (women's section) is also filled to the brim. From the candles and lamps a thick cloud hovers near the ceiling, casting something of a pall. The *shammash* (caretaker, manager) dashes back and forth among the women, checking if everyone is sitting in her right place, in the seat her husband paid for. The *shammash* is tired and weary. All the time a drop of sweat hangs at the tip of his nose, with no time to fall off.

My mother is leaning against the curtained partition between the two sections, holding her *machzor* (prayer-book for Rosh Hashanah) in her hand. Now, before the prayer of the congregation has begun, she is murmuring the *t'chinot*, the supplications in Yiddish composed especially for women, and the Yiddish translations of the regular Rosh Hashanah prayers. And she too is weeping, crying and sobbing, like my father.

When my brother and I were very young, our mother used to tell us little stories from the *machzor* (where they were printed in Yiddish, at the bottom of the pages), and we loved so much to hear them. They held us spellbound when we heard them from her. And then, more than once, tears used to come also to our eyes. When I grew a little older, I understood that when my mother wept there, in the *shtib'l,* she was pleading with the Almighty in heaven to have us written down in His Book of Life for another good year, all of us together, in which we should all stay healthy and our father should earn a good living, and they — our parents — should have *nachas,* a little Jewish happiness, from their seven children.

The hand of the *shammash* strikes down hard on the table in the men's section, and all grows still. Here and there a sigh still wafts about, not knowing how to ebb away. In some corner a groan, torn late out of an aching heart, is cut off at the start.

The prayers begin with *Bor'chu,* the call of the *chazzan* (the reader) to give blessing and praise to the Almighty. And now the chassidic house of prayer begins to resemble a ship sailing on the sea, finding its way among the stormy waves of life. Heads sway back and forth in devotion; they rise up and bend low. No one says the prayers by heart, grinding out the words mechanically. Everyone reads from his *machzor,* and the words come out whole and clear — prayer with meaning, intent, religious devoutness. They know that one stray, alien thought can tip the scales of Heaven's judgment the other way (Heaven forbid); and who wants to endanger his life?

The evening prayer begins to approach the end, as the *chazzan* chants *L'dovid mizmor* (Psalm 24). Sentence by sentence the worshipers repeat it after him. The holy ark stands opened wide, and the trembling chant of the reader evokes tears from the outpouring of the heart, an ocean of tears, A mighty outcry thrusts upward to heaven, rattling the broad windows, clinging to the panes, seeking a path to the infinity above this earth, trying to break through to His firmament, to plead before the Creator of the world that the prayers of His Jews should be accepted, so that they should win a favorable verdict for a year of life.

Why *not* weep and cry? They are heartbroken anyway. Their Polish fellow countrymen oppress and torment them. And what power do the children of the Almighty have to retaliate with? — only the power of prayer and tears, the attempt to cling to Him in devotion, through thick and thin ...

The reader and his congregation come to the end of *L'dovid mizmor;* Psalm 24 has been chanted; and from the women's section groans and sighs still come floating out. They wane into silence in one corner, and begin again in another ... until the mutual greetings and wishes of *l'shana tova* reach there; and then, only then, do all grow calm and still in the women's section. They wipe the remaining tears from the corners of their eyes, and are quiet.

The atmosphere is tranquil now, as though after breaking through a dangerous path and getting out in safety. Everyone shakes hands, as the people, with shining eyes and happy hearts, exchange their good wishes and blessings:

"May you be inscribed ..."

"... immediately ..."

"... for a good year ..."

"... for good life ..."

"... and for peace!"

"May it only be so: *l'shalom*, for peace, *l'shalom*, for peace."

❧ ❧ ❧

The faces passed right before my eyes. I saw them. I called out to them, *"L'shana tova, l'shana tova!* A good year, a good year!" I wanted them to answer me; I pleaded with them to wait for me: I wanted to go with them. "I won't stay here alone, by myself," I cried out. "I won't!"

A cold sweat covered my body. Its droplets fell from my forehead, my cheeks, the tip of my nose.

The minutes went by; perhaps a few, perhaps more. I opened my eyes and looked for the houses and the streets I knew so well; the wax candles burning in the brass and the silver candlesticks — and they weren't there — as if the earth had swallowed them up. My eyes searched the darkness for the chassidic house of prayer, for all the people who had poured out their supplications there, for all the loved ones who had just now been here with me. I could still hear their sobbing and weeping echoing in my ears. How could the whole scene vanish from my sight in an instant? How could they all disappear without a trace?

The thick darkness stood before me like a solid wall that couldn't be by-passed or broken through. At last I gathered my strength and stood up on my feet. I wiped the sweat from my face, and slowly, slowly became myself again ...

It was all there before me: trees, the forest, an ocean of leaves, and the ending of the night ...

There was grief and sorrow in my heart. I had a galling doubt if I had said at all the prayer declaring the day holy at the start of Rosh Hashanah. I couldn't remember. Finally, however, I managed to become convinced that I had *davened Ma'ariv,* I had indeed said the evening prayer — though certainly not when the night had begun. Perhaps it had been only a short while ago ... Evidently I wasn't able to do any praying earlier. "Father in Heaven, forgive me, forgive me. I was in such distress, and from my distress I called to You!"

I was reluctant to go, to leave the old, beautiful tree and return to the camp. I wished I could stay on and on and on, and just be alone there, by myself. But I knew only too well that by the order I had received I had to be back at the camp by dawn, and I had no wish to get into difficulties. "Don't go looking for trouble," I warned myself. "Be thankful that you had the whole night to yourself — yourself alone ..."

I made my way back to camp with the feeling that the first day of Rosh Hashanah was accompanying me, walking with me on the forest paths, in a world that was so strange to me, so different from anything I had known before ...

CHAPTER SIX

The German Attack

A BIRD SAT ON A LOG of wood in front of my tent, pecking away at the rotting bark. From time to time it stopped its pecking and trilled its bit of song in its sweet voice, so that we couldn't fall asleep.

From a nearby tent a partisan thrust his head out and looked all around; and when he saw not a living soul in sight, he went out and off to the side to relieve himself. I let out an audible growl, and in a confusion of fright he hurried back into his tent.

At that very moment someone gave our tent so powerful a kick that part of the walls buckled. Mischa, who generally slept very deeply, awoke at once. In the doorway of the tent stood a messenger of the staff. By orders of Nikolai Nikolaievitch, he said, we were to go out as fast as possible to the neighboring village and take the place of the men on guard — untrained partisans who had only now been taken into the unit. And, the messenger added, we should be on the alert about anything going on in the area.

I got into my winter clothing hastily, and nudged Mischa, who was still in bed half asleep. "Oh, go to the devil!" he grumbled. "I was in the middle of a dream, talking with my Marussia, my girl back home, and this dog had to come and wake me up!" A whole string of curses, connected like links in a chain, came rolling out of his mouth.

The ending of the night cast its veil over the trees. Dense grey clouds moved swiftly, revealing parts of the sky that began turning light. The cold was strong, biting. A week ago we had made plans to set up winter huts that could keep out the icy winds; and along came the frost of winter first. The water in our wells began to freeze over. A day ago, when we got up in the morning, we found one of our goats and the squad leader's white horse lying on the ground with not a trace of life left in them. They had frozen to death, said the men among us who had been farm laborers.

A dry snow began falling. At some moments it was as fine as white flour, like particles of farina. At other moments the air was filled with bits of snow like feathers plucked from chickens. We barely kept our balance in the whiteness that piled around our feet, as we held each other's hands.

For quite a while now there was talk in the camp that the Germans were planning an attack against us. The information was given us by people planted in the regional militias, who functioned, as far as anyone knew, in full, loyal cooperation with the Germans. These militiamen "helped" the Germans work out their plans and their strategy against us, and at the same time they passed along precise information on every detail, so that we could plan our own actions in advance.

"But," we asked, "who is to guarantee it that at the last moment the Germans won't change their plans? There are so many ways to penetrate through the forest. Who knows which way they'll choose to get through to us?"

"And who will give me any certainty," I asked in my own heart, without sharing my worry with Mischa as he walked beside me, "that they won't come up in force just through the spot where we have to go and stand guard?"

Meanwhile the night shrank away and vanished along with all the nights that had gone before. As our breath came steadily in the icy frost, Mischa's pointed beard, that he had started growing and cultivating only lately, resembled a stiff brush with white linen bristles. We walked a long way with the silence between us unbroken. We knew that our thoughts now, as we went, were identical. We were both afraid of what could well happen during the fighting, once the Germans attacked. What need was there for words?

Under the conditions of our existence, it was easy to meet our death just as dawn was rising. The enemy always lurked in ambush for us in the early hours of morning, when we were coming back from our night actions, tired, half asleep, seated on the wagons or striding along the narrow paths. They would hide in holes in the ground or in ditches, ready to confront us with their weapons of murder. The rising dawn, the clearing sky, the sparkling sun would leave us exposed to them; and then their rain of fire could catch us by surprise. Their hunting attacks, to ferret us out, also used to start with the first light of the day. What fate, then would this morning bring — the morning now starting out on its course? Would it be quiet? Would it be otherwise?

A thought from childhood flitted through my mind: How beautiful it would be if no human feet trampled the pure white snow that was softly piling up everywhere over the ground: over the paths, roads, fields. It would all stay so white and lovely. The snow would fall and fall, blanketing our tent, blanketing the whole forest. We could live under the snow day and night, through all of winter ... who knew till when?

❧ ❧ ❧

"Who goes there?"
"We're from our side."
"What's the password?"
"Smolensk."
"Stalingrad."

We took over the guard duty from the two sentries. Before they went off, the two partisans whom we were replacing told us that just before dawn they had heard some slight sounds of movement from somewhere nearby. Those sounds could have come from other partisans, roaming around in the vicinity. The noises might have been made by animals moving from one location to another. Or they might have been ... the devil knew what.

We sat down in the snow. We put hands to ears to cup them into funnels. We looked carefully all around us. And not a signal or sign of suspicious movement anywhere could we detect. Meanwhile, though, the frosty weather began nipping at the tips of our toes. We stood up, leaned against a sturdy pine tree, and began marching a few steps back and forth. We took out thin paper and shredded tobacco, rolled ourselves some cigarettes, and began chain-smoking ...

Then suddenly it came.

At some short distance away an almighty wail tore through the air. A few pine trees collapsed, breaking other trees as they fell. And from several directions a downpour of gunshots came flying at us. I was just able to call out "*Mischa*" before a bullet made a tear in my cotton pants. Then, as fate would have it, I suffered a light scratch in the hip. I kept running and falling flat on the ground, running and going flat on the snowy ground, each a bit by turns. And I kept wondering how, from such a slight scratch as I had suffered, that hardly hurt at all, so much blood could keep pouring out of my pants onto the pure white snow, to sully it. The bullets continued flying over our heads, and many of them stuck in the trunks of the trees. The more I kept running, the worse the pains became. I didn't know if we'd ever manage to get out of the range of the shooting. In a moment of despair I prayed for another bullet to hit me and put an end to my life, so that I shouldn't fall into the hands of the Germans.

In spite of everything, though, we succeeded in escaping our attackers and getting to a dense thicket nearby, where we hid in the tall bushes. Mischa helped me get my shirt off; he tore it into strips and bandaged my wound.

The barrage of bullets aimed at our sentry position stopped, but the general fire of our attackers continued stronger than ever. We decided that, as it seemed, the enemy's fire was now directed at our camp; and after a bit of time we actually heard echoes of explosions from that direction. But since we heard no fire being returned, we understood that our forces in the camp must have retreated at the right time, and weren't conducting any kind of battle against the attackers.

When the shooting stopped and all was completely quiet, Mischa undid my bandage. With the snow that he gathered in his hands he washed and cleaned my wound. I looked with total indifference at the chunks of blood that clung to my thigh. With my own hand I detached one of these chunks and threw it off into the distance, as I might have thrown away some strange piece of something that became attached to my body.

❧ ❧ ❧

We decided to make our way back to the base. Since it was absolutely still now in the forest, we could assume that the Germans had left the forest altogether. Only one question bothered us: Where would we find our men? How could we know where they had retreated to, and to which location they would return?

The closer we came to the camp, the more glaring became the signs of the German onslaught. Here and there we found animals in the throes of death, with missing limbs or torn bellies; and other were already dead. Along the path leading to the camp we caught sight of the deaf partisan Vanka hung from a tree, feet up, head down. A short distance from him we saw the body of another partisan, whom we couldn't identify. Evidently the Germans had tortured him before they put him to death.

Our base was totally unrecognizable. It was clear that when they failed to find our men there, because they had fled to safety, the Germans had become so furious that they set everything on fire: our tents, the barns, the barrels of food, and so on.

We didn't know where to turn to find our men. In utter despair we sat down on the scorched earth and stared at nothing. For a brief moment I forgot that Mischa was sitting beside me; and as I gazed at the little mounds of ashes here and there, I realized that along with our tent my summer jacket also was reduced to ashes; I had stowed it away under a bundle of straw that I used for a pillow. In one of the pockets I had kept a picture of my father that was precious to me. In another pocket were the little pieces of wood from the chair of the holy Rabbi Yisrael Baal Shem Tov, that I had always kept like the greatest treasure. And now all was gone.

Tears came to my eyes over the two losses. It was anguish to know that I would never again see the picture of my father, that had tied me with such a powerful, endless nostalgia to a world of mine that had been demolished. And with those hallowed bits of wood gone, I trembled with dread for my fate. I had cherished them, always thinking that more than I watched over them, they watched over me and protected me.

Night fell. The odor of burnt food, the stench of carcasses, vexed my nostrils till I felt like retching. We sat in the desolated camp without an idea of what to do. I was at the point of falling asleep when a thought struck me, and I turned to Mischa: "Come on. Let's get Vanka down from that tree. The night has only started, and we can still do it. We'll put him down on the ground and dig a grave for him, if we can manage it somehow."

The darkness had become so intense that we could find Vanka's "gallows tree" only with difficulty. Mischa climbed up first, and I, with the bandage on my thigh, followed him. With his sharp pocket-knife he cut the cord that bound Vanka's feet to the sturdy branch; but he did not have the strength to hold the suspended body fast. It slipped from his hands and landed on the ground.

But there was nothing we could use to dig a grave. The earth was frozen solid. With no choice left, we gathered boughs, logs and stones that we found there, and covered the body with them. As we were finishing, we noticed that Vanka's eyes were opened wide, fixed on us with a frozen stare. We covered the body completely; and yet, afterward I felt in my soul that those eyes didn't stop following us, that they were the one part of his body which didn't surrender to death.

Broken, close to despair, we left the destroyed camp still hoping we could somehow get on the track of our fellow-partisans, wherever they were now in the forest; that somehow, with Heaven's help, we could continue our actions against this bestial enemy, as though nothing serious had ever happened ...

We found them.

CHAPTER SEVEN
Hershele

"**I** GOT SICK AND TIRED of taking care of my rich uncle's sheep in that old village Domenyavitch. That man always turns nasty and beats me up. So I ran away from him. That's all. I want to get to the partisans."

This was the story, short and simple, of the boy we picked up as we rolled along in our wagon. His body told the rest: his face and torso were full of wounds, and he was bleeding.

From the moment we met I knew his "Semitic race" or "nationality" — and I did my best to keep the secret to myself. Looking into his eyes I saw what he was able to hide from the bunch of partisans who found him. I acted as if I didn't doubt in the least the story he told; and I didn't try to make him talk and reveal more, as my companions did.

Mischa made place for the boy on the wagon between the two of us. The boy looked at him in wonder, evidently finding it hard to believe that he was really being taken into the heart of the forest, to actually join the partisans.

He lay in the wagon with his eyes open, looking alternately at Mischa and me, then back to Mischa and so on. Not a word did he utter. Truth to tell, I was dying to sleep. We were totally exhausted, after bouncing around on the roads for days till we could return safely to our base in the forests. Vanya had taken the horse's reins to drive the wagon, but soon after he settled himself comfortably in the driver's seat he fell fast asleep and sank down in a pile of straw, letting out such raucous snores that even the birds perched on the branches of the trees flew off in fear, to look for a quieter, more peaceful perch.

Mischa too fell into a deep slumber. His head sank like a heavy burden into the mass of straw that covered almost all his body; and like Vanya, he too snored heavily, sounding like a giant bellows being opened and shut, opened and shut; and he groaned fearfully in the bargain.

We had lived through days and nights of tension, on the roads and sites we passed through. In one village we ran into Germans waiting for us in ambush at its entrance. Only by a miracle did we escape uninjured. In another village we finished off some traitors and informers, having first gathered exact information about what they had "done for us." We took everything they owned and sent it up in fire, to let others see and hear and remember, so that they should think twice before deciding to take those traitors' place.

The two last nights out we spent "having a good time" near a railroad track. One night passed by as we tensely waited for the train headed for the front. We had prepared a "lovely present" for it: a pail filled with dynamite, tenderly placed under the rails. That night, however, no train sped down the tracks that we watched. We reckoned that the partisans of some other squad must have blown up the tracks somewhere else along the line, or else they had derailed the train before it could reach us; and for this reason, in all the hours we spent there, till shortly before dawn, no train whatever moved along the tracks we were watching. We moved back, dug scattered trenches for ourselves in the nearby fields, and there we stayed hidden all day, till dusk came.

Our reward came in the small hours of our final "night out" (the night which had just passed): Shortly before the darkness began lifting, when we were already set to leave the site in bitter disappointment, the sonority of an approaching train came to our ears. From afar the sounds indicated that it was chugging heavily along. A few seconds or more later, its yellow headlamps were blinding us. Our eyes were on Mischa now, the leader of our task force. Sweat broke out on his full face, but he appeared to be in command of himself. The moment the train began its ascent on the long bridge, he sharply pulled the end of the cord that he held in his fist, and the tremendous explosion deafened our ears. A few minutes later we took our places on the wagon that was waiting for us, and started "back home," to our camp.

Now I leaned close to the boy, our new "would-be partisan," and in a whisper I asked him what his name was. He only gave me a blank stare, and I let him be, as I sank down into my own thoughts. I was fearfuly tired, yet for some reason I couldn't fall asleep. I envisioned in my mind the pleasure I would have lying near a good blazing fire, stretching and relaxing my frozen, tired bones; and I decided that when we got to the camp I wouldn't go into the tent directly but would first wash my outer clothing and the bedsheets and dry them before the big fire, so as to get free, at least for a day, from the creeping, crawling creatures that always stole our rest from us. Just reaching this decision made me feel refreshed, full of new life.

Mischa and Vanya continued sleeping. The horse knew the twisted, winding pathways to the camp gate, and it pulled us along without going off the road. Of its own accord it avoided snags and tangled bushes. I leaned close to the lad and asked him again what his name was.

Apparently he didn't know how to react. He waited, doing nothing, till at last he whispered in my ear in plain village-Yiddish, "My name is Hershele. Did they catch you also? Are they taking us to the pits? I'll run away; I'll run away right now!"

I calmed him down, assuring him that he was with real partisans now, and I was one of them. The machine gun in my hand, I told him, belonged to me; it was my own. He had nothing to be afraid of, I continued; no harm would come to him. I moved closer and whispered that since he was too young to join the fighting men, we would have to see to it that everything should be all right for him ... I knew that he didn't really understand what I meant; but I didn't try to explain.

A little blue-white cloud, like a broad linen sheet, spread out over a cluster of pine trees and became entangled with them, whereupon it wrapped itself around the pine needles, covering them like a long veil.

Our horse clip-clopped along slowly. It was tired out from pulling us on and on over such a long distance, for so many wearying hours. If we wanted to treat it decently, we should have gotten off the wagon and walked a while, to lighten the load it was dragging. But we didn't move. Mischa and Vanya went on sleeping sweetly, and I strongly wanted to chat with the lad we had picked up on the road: a Jewish boy named Hershele who had been saved from death, yet about whom I still knew nothing. I shut out of my mind the fact that the wagon was dragging along so slowly, shaking from side to side, leaning over sometimes this way, sometimes that way, or else limping along in places, as though it had lost a wheel and was trying to keep going on the three that were left.

I noticed that both Alexai and Piotr, sitting beside Vanya the wagon driver, had also fallen asleep. Only Hershele and I were now awake. There was no more need for us to talk in whispers. So I listened raptly to the boy's story:

❀ ❀ ❀

A whole day he remained in the pit of the massacre, lying altogether still. For hours on end he didn't know if he should open his eyes and live or keep them shut and wait till he expired, till he was like all the others who had to die. He was fully conscious; all his faculties were working fine; yet there were moments when it seemed to him that he was on the deck of a ship gone mad, sailing off into the horizon in a raging sea, the waves battering it on every side; and when the storm was over and the ship arrived where it was headed for, there his mother and father and two younger sisters would wake up, and they would all be together, never again to be separated. The thought made him feel so good. He was ready to hold on to it, lying where he was. Yet he realized immediately that it wasn't even a dream. His body was attached to a chunk of flesh. Freezing-cold hands held him clasped as though by iron bands.

And those hands were his dead mother's ...

He tried to free himself from them, and couldn't. Meanwhile the darkening evening spread over the pit, and a mighty terror took hold of him. Only then did he gather all his strength and wrestle free from the vise of his mother's fingers. He kissed her forehead, that was now like stone, and began crawling and grappling his way over the dead bodies, till he reached the edge of the pit. Up and out he climbed, and began running across the rain-soaked, muddy fields, with no idea of where his feet would take him.

He came to a village, and tried to enter a farm cottage, only to have people chasing him out and running after him, trying to seize him. But he managed to escape his pursuers. Yet the same thing happened to him in other villages when he passed through them.

There was only one thing he could do: During the daylight hours he found a place to hide and keep out of sight; and at night he went out to the fields to gather fruits and vegetables that were growing there. In this way he was able to reach the village of Domenyavitch. Tramping through a field, he met an old farmer. Hershele went up to him and told him a plausible story that he had prepared beforehand, whereupon the man took him into his home, and took him along in the daytime to help on the farm. Mainly, however, the old man made him the farm shepherd, to take care of the large flock of sheep.

In his first week there he went out with the sheep every morning, and spent the day with other young shepherds, young boys of the village. In the second week they began pestering him, asking all kinds of questions, to which he had to make up answers — till they finally told him: They simply refused to believe that he had come from a distant village where everything his parents owned had been burnt in the course of a battle between the Germans and the partisans, whereupon his parents had sent him to find work in some other village, so that he could earn his meals.

"Oh, you aren't even a country boy at all," they disputed him. "You don't begin to know how to take care of sheep."

They became suspicious that he was Jewish, and that he must certainly have run away from the town. Then, last morning, when he came to the meadow with his sheep, after everyone gathered around the bonfire, the other shepherd boys surrounded him on every side and wanted to investigate physically if he was Jewish or not. When they tried to seize and hold him, he struck out with his fists; but they gave him back as good as they got. Finally, however, he managed to get free of them. He left the sheep in the meadow and fled.

❧ ❧ ❧

I woke Mischa from his blissful sleep and let him in on the secret of Hershele's identity. On the spot we decided that when we passed by the Jewish family camp we would drop the boy off there. He was obviously quite intelligent for his age, and I would then explain to him what he had to do.

❧ ❧ ❧

Hershele was about thirteen then, perhaps a bit older than that. My friend Mischa took a great liking to him, and would often invite him to visit our camp. He took the boy under his wing, and took care of everything Hershele needed as far as food and clothing were concerned. And he gave the lad his promise that in the course of time he, Mischa, would have him join him, and the boy would stay in our squad.

The time came when Mischa kept his promise. To make sure that no one would complain against him for forming a bond of friendship with a youngster who didn't belong among the fighting men, Mischa kept the boy busy with various tasks, mainly by sending him on errands that were useful for our unit, and something useful for the entire squad.

One evening we were getting ready to go out on a "job" against a hostile village, as a result of a report we had received: At a wedding that was to take place at the home of the head of the village, several German officers with whom he was friendly were going to be present. They were generally accustomed to visiting him, to have a few drinks with him and receive presents of butter, eggs, lard, and similar useful items.

Mischa gave Hershele permission to come along with us. Before we had to leave the camp Hershele appeared all washed and sparkling clean, as though he had really been invited by the bride's or the groom's family to attend that wedding in the village.

On the way Hershele confided to me that some plan of action there had occurred to him, and he was prepared to tell it to me. I listened to details patiently, and when he finished I told him calmly, "It's a pretty good idea, Hershele, but this business of planning is not a job for you. You have to leave it to us to decide what to do and how to do it." I saw, however, that my words had no great effect on him. "Look," I said, "you're still only a boy and not a real, full partisan. You're liable to put your life in danger too soon, and that's not a clever thing to do. You have to grow, gain experience, and become a man. Then you can take revenge from the Germans — if the war hasn't ended by that time."

Hershele was hurt by what I said. Tears gathered at the corners of his pale green eyes; but they disappeared almost as soon as they came. I understood that he wanted to show me that he was able to overcome a momentary weakness. He wanted me to know that I was dealing with quite a mature person, and not with a young whippersnapper who wanted to get his way by shedding tears.

❧ ❧ ❧

Late at night we reached the ways of entry into the village. Sounds of music and singing echoed in the air. Slowly, slowly we made our way, behind the cottages and huts. We sidled close to their walls, till we reached the heart of the village. Talking the matter over together, we decided to send Hershele to scout around and find a suitable observation post for us.

We called him — and he didn't answer. "Where is he?" I asked the man next to me in a whisper. "Where's the boy? Where did he disappear to?"

"When?"

No one in the group had any answer to give me. My hair stood on end. How could I have failed to see him slipping away from us? What would I tell Mischa if, Heaven forbid, anything dreadful happened to such a young, vulnerable boy? I was responsible for his life, the life of a Jewish youngster whom the death pits had spat out and sent to us.

We took our stand behind a farm hut and from there we observed the place where the village head's daughter's wedding was being celebrated. Our eyes almost went out of their sockets as we kept looking and looking there for our vanished Hershele, trying to locate him among the people milling around over the grounds of the village. And we couldn't spot him.

The hours of the night were running out. We waited for the man we had sent to scout around, to come back with exact information on what was going on in the village and how many Germans and militiamen were there. We waited ... and for some reason that we couldn't fathom, the man didn't appear. Unable to find out anything more and having no wish to risk our lives further, we simply withdrew without embarking on any action, as agreed originally at the staff headquarters. We retreated to a thicket close by the village, and sat down to consider what we should do about Hershele. The decision was that we would not move from the area and not go back to the camp as long as we didn't know what had happened to him and where he was. We were agreed that no matter what the price, we would get him out of the village and bring him back with us.

Meanwhile dawn had risen. The morning light came slowly, to find us completely dejected, sunk in a black mood. No one in the group blamed anyone else for having let the boy get lost; but every one of us felt guilty that he was simply gone. I was furious with myself for not having kept a strict eye on him, for having given him the chance to slip away.

Then he came along. As soon as the sun came up he appeared on the horizon. One of the group spotted him from afar, and he shouted out, "He's here! He's here! I swear it!" His yells brought us jumping to our feet, straining to see him from afar.

There he was, walking, bent over under his load. At first we had no idea of what he was carrying. As he came closer, however, we made out the barrels of two automatic rifles — no more, no less! In his hands he held something more: two pairs of army pants ... Crawling along slowly, Hershele resembled a bent-over peddler wandering from place to place, from one village to another, to offer his poor wares for sale.

"Hershele," I railed at him the moment he came into our midst, while my heart was jumping with joy at seeing him back in perfect condition. "How could you put yourself in danger like that — going right into the village all by yourself? I told you that ..."

"... that I'm still just a boy and not a real partisan," he interrupted me. I gave him a kiss on his forehead and a warm embrace, like a father hugging his youngster when he has surprised him by an act of courage that deserves a pile of praise.

On the way back Hershele told us, without a trace of boasting, how he came by his booty. Directly after he had slipped away from us, he sprinted across to one place, and there he found a group of children playing. He joined them, presenting himself as a relative of the bridegroom, who had come with his parents for the wedding from a distant town. As he talked with them, he learned that two German army officers, friends of the village head, had likewise come for the wedding, and they were staying at this head man's house as his guests. For a good while Hershele played with the children, and then he moved out of sight, making sure no one noticed.

He made straight for the head man's house, and stole into the nearby barn on the farm grounds; and there he waited with longing and impatience for the two "distinguished guests" to "come home." He kept looking out through some cracks in the barn walls, listening intently to the slightest sound; and he didn't stop praying to the Almighty to help him — to join him in carrying out his plan.

By the time the two arrived at the head man's home it was no longer night but day. They crossed the grounds to the house, and couldn't find the door: They were too drunk. In fact, they could hardly move their feet, and almost went rolling along rather than walking. When they were finally inside the house, he heard them singing and singing, grunting and roaring, till at last their voices were stilled. Then Hershele knew that they had gone to bed and fallen asleep — dead to the world.

He waited a little, then went carefully out of the barn, walking on tiptoe, and stole his way into the village head's home. In one of the rooms he found them, not in bed but stretched out on the floor near their beds. When he saw the two automatic rifles, making them out in the moonlight, he trembled with excitement and fear, not knowing what to do with them. His first thought was to take one of the guns and shoot both men, just as other Germans had shot his family to death — every last one in the family. But he was afraid he might not know how to use the gun properly; so he quickly decided to take the two weapons and get out of there, away into the forest. And "by the way," for an added touch, he took along their fancy trousers that were lying near them on the floor — so that when they woke in the morning they would have to go looking for something to wear instead ...

We had never laughed so hard in our lives. The roars of our delight echoed long through the depths of the forest. We were certain that everyone in creation must be laughing with us at the two high officers whom this young Hershele, a small boy escaped from a death-pit, had left in the extra bedroom of the village head, their true and trusted friend, without their weapons and without their trousers.

❧ ❧ ❧

It was dusk when we left the camp. Rain mixed with snow had fallen heavily throughout the day, leaving our clothes sopping wet. Before we set out, however, the rain stopped completely and the strong winds died down, no longer wrenching off the dry, rotting branches from the trees and flinging them to the ground.

We walked a long time in the dark, down the forest paths. From time to time herds of wild boar or packs of yowling wolves passed by. By lighting matches repeatedly we drove them off.

This time I kept Hershele near me, never taking my eyes off him. Occasionally I grasped his hand in mine. We walked in silence, or spoke in light whispers, as though afraid of every utterance. When we came to the edge of the forest we saw that the heavy blanket of cloud had disappeared completely — melted, or swallowed up into the innards of the black sky above. We didn't expect any moon to appear. We didn't need it. We preferred that it shouldn't accompany us on our way to the railroad track, so that it wouldn't expose us to the enemy, who might possibly be waiting in ambush for us somewhere or other.

We made our way on foot, getting tired out from the endless walking. It was a late hour of the night when we reached our destination. The steel rails of the railroad track glinted before our eyes like sharpened knives. "Here goes," I thought: "We'll put the mine snugly under those rails and stroll back. We'll sit down somewhere, a safe distance away, and wait for the train. And when it comes we'll pull the cord, and we'll watch the railroad cars, with all their equipment, and maybe with enemy soldiers, go rolling down the sharp decline."

Before we could finish our work a heavy rain of bullets came pouring out at us. We returned the fire sharply, to defend ourselves. There was no sense in starting a serious battle with whatever unseen enemy we were facing. We were completely exposed on flat, naked ground — an easy target for them. So we exerted effort to get out of their target range; but the bullets they kept sending us didn't make the task easy. They pursued us; and the roundish moon that appeared in the clear sky gave the laugh of a traitor as it helped the Germans aim their fire at us.

And then we had trouble with Hershele again.

While the bullets went flying back and forth, he disappeared again before my eyes. He slipped out from under my hand. By the time I became aware of it, it was too late. I turned my head, looking for him all around; and I saw him lying on the ground near the rails behind a rock, firing his rifle blithely. We had given him the gun before he set out with us, so that he should be, for the first time in his life, a real partisan like the rest of us ...

I was covered with a feeling of shame. There he was, all alone, keeping the enemy busy to give us, the grownups, a chance to retreat with more safety. ... I looked at him in anger: Why was he doing this? Who asked him to? Why did he go off again on his own and put himself into mortal danger, without asking the group leader a word? "I'm going to pull him out by his hair," I told myself, "out of range of the fire." And when I reached him I would lace it into him: "You don't stay alone in a battle. Even a rank beginner of a partisan should know this!" He was going to know my wrath. He would know I was in dead earnest.

The idea was fine, but how in the world was I going to get to him, with all those bullets flying and whistling over my head? Nevertheless I tried to move closer to him, inch by inch; but I couldn't make much progress. A hailstorm of bullets came down around me. So I called out from afar. I pleaded with him to stop his shooting and draw back like the rest of us, because there was no hope of overcoming the enemy, when they outnumbered us so heavily, and our equipment was no match for theirs.

I called and called, and Hershele didn't answer. Perhaps the whistling of the bullets drowned out my voice; and perhaps — in fact, I'm almost certain of it — he pretended not to hear me.

"What a stubborn kid," went the thought through my mind. The whole time that he had been with us in the camp, I had seen him collecting bullets from the adult partisans, like a beggar collecting pennies. He had filled all his pockets with them. And now ... now he found a fine opportunity to get rid of them ... to send them off toward Germans.

"*Hershele, Hershele!*" I bellowed to him, desperately wanting him to hear my call, "Get back. Get back, for Heaven's sake. Have pity on yourself. Have pity on me!"

He turned his head to me, but all I saw were two flashing, glistening eyes. I sensed that he wanted to tell me what a pity it was to waste another second over him; what a pity it was that the group leader had given the order to retreat instead of fighting the enemy like him …

I put my head down low in despair. I was at my wits' end, with no idea of what to do …

A mortar shell struck the rock that Hershele was using for cover. I clutched the earth and wailed into it like a wounded animal … And now the shooting stopped. It died away. All was finally still.

❧ ❧ ❧

Shattered, brokenhearted, I went back to the forest. When I came there, I found the rest of the group gathered. They too had seen Hershele's escapade, his bravery.

When morning came we went back to the spot where Hershele had waged his "private war" against the German enemy. His body was covered with blood, but his face was clear and shining, as though he had just washed it very well. His two hands were clasped around the rifle, that was longer than his body. I remembered his telling me about the hands of his dead mother clasped around him in the pit where they had been thrown together.

We took his body and carried it further into the forest. I asked my fellow-fighters to let me be by myself a while, and sat down on a log. As I looked now at Hershele's face, I saw for the first time that his eyes were open. They seemed to be smiling, expressing satisfaction and contentment. It seemed to me that he was trying to tell me that from the time he escaped from the pit he had never known such a happy series of moments.

A thought from the Talmud sprang into my mind: "There is a person who can win his world — his life in the eternity beyond our life — in one short while." This had been Hershele's hour of glory.

CHAPTER EIGHT
Around the Fire

W E WERE SPREAD OUT around the blazing bonfire when Grischa Michailovitch Petrov suddenly appeared and sent a roaring laugh rolling out of his wide-open mouth. He shot out a few words, but we couldn't understand a thing.

"Devil take it," they asked him, "talk clearly, Grischa." They looked at him in curiosity, wondering at his wild laughter.

Grischa blinked his eyes and didn't stop laughing.

"Do you want to see him?" he asked at last. "Get off your rears and go down there, below. Do you hear me? I caught a really fine 'fish' today: first class. Now they're letting him eat like a pig. Let the worms go and eat him! Tomorrow I'll finish him off; do you hear?"

He sat down beside us and began telling his story in orderly fashion:

"It was so bitterly cold. I was lying in the snow, all of me, and I thought poor Grischa was going to die. The frost was nipping at my nose and my fingertips. And the night — O mama, pure gold. I wish we had nights like that all year round: pitch black it was, like in a deep cave, like in a tomb. But yet, how long can man lie in the snow like that, and then come back to the camp with nothing to show for it? When hour after hour went by I said to myself, 'Still and all, there's no reason why I should freeze to death. That isn't a good idea at all. What kind of a death is this? Let me get up and walk around a little.' That's what I thought ...

"And then, after I'd given up all hope about him, there he was. I felt an electric current going through my body, making me warm. Dressed in a long, thick fur-lined coat, this character came right up to the place where I was lying camouflaged. I saw he was almost frozen. I heard him muttering, *'Dunervetter! Kalt, kalt!'* (Thunderation, it's cold, cold!) Do you hear what I'm saying? On his feet he was wearing heavy wooden shoes, clogs, kind of little rowboats; and it was heavy going for him through the snow; it was hard for him to move fast.

"I held my breath. I swallowed the spit that came on my tongue. And I thought, 'You dog! You kept me in suspense. You took a long time coming here, and I almost froze on account of you ... Now you won't slip out of my hands.'

"On my belly I crawled like a turtle, till I found myself before the railroad tracks. I saw him inspecting the area, looking here, looking there, turning around — with his back to me. *Hah!* Look, fellows: Do you see my long hands: I swear to you that at that moment when he was standing there before me, they got longer. I got these two hands around him, and he just collapsed. I thought my belly would explode from all the laughter I was keeping bottled up in me. The two partisans who were with me shot forward now as though from under the ground, and they helped me tie this character up. We dragged him over to the sleigh that was waiting for us between the trees, and *zing* — straight to the camp with him."

Grischa took a minute to dry his wet lips.

"Do you hear? The squad leader says we brought a valuable piece of loot, a war prize that's worth a lot. He's gotten a good many right proper smacks across the face by now, to help loosen up his tongue; and he's talked: said he took the trouble to come especially to the railroad tracks, to see for himself how the partisans manage to get so many of their trains derailed and flying off the tracks. He didn't want to depend on reports, so he came in person, with all his honor and dignity, to look into the matter. *Nu,* so I derailed him also and brought him to us. Over there, at staff headquarters, they're going to explain everything to him — just how we do it."

Grischa was exultant with joy. He was already wearing the German high officer's clothing: a resplendent military uniform. The buttons twinkled like stars in the night. Grischa was decorated now with swastikas on the right and left sides ... He took out a small revolver that he had "only borrowed" from the captured man on the way back to the camp.

Before Grischa made ready to leave us, his good friend Ivan Ivanovitch raised his right shoulder high in a shrug of disdain and gave him a scornful look, to throw a "hint" to the people gathered around the big fire that they didn't have to believe everything he had told them: Some of his story could be doubted. But Grischa noticed this gesture of Ivan's, and he felt hurt. He left this group and went away to another bonfire, to tell his story over again to the partisans gathered there.

Meanwhile Ivan Ivanovitch remembered something that he had been about to do before Grischa appeared at the fire. He took off his winter vest, then removed his shirt, and spread it so close to the fire that it was almost completely scorched. At first what Ivan was doing shocked the men sitting around the blaze; but afterward he showed us that his shirt had undergone a thorough "cleaning," and it was now free of all the little crawling creatures that had made their home in it, to plague him.

One by one we began to follow his example. Five or six shirts were spread over the fire like pennants, and thus were "purged of their wildlife" as they turned yellow and blackened. Here and there, flying cinders made holes in them. A fine stink arose from the whole operation, but it was certainly worthwhile.

One sleeve of Ivan Ivanovitch's shirt became so scorched and riddled with holes that it looked like a coarse sieve. He let out a string of rich, fruity curses, one sharper than the other; and then he threw the whole thing into the fire, where it went up in flames. "The devil take it," he ranted, as his teeth chattered in the cold. "Tomorrow I'll catch a German and finish him off, and I'll strip off his clothing from him together with his skin!"

We moved closer to the fire, and everyone set to work on whatever needed mending in his clothes. Grischa had come back to us, and now he and Sascha of Smolensk took hold of a pair of trousers that had been torn by a bullet, whereupon it shed cotton waste like gobs of snow.

In the lapel of my military coat a piece of cloth was missing. It had been caught in a wagon wheel and torn away. I found an old jacket and cut it up; and with a piece of it I made my military coat "whole" again. Of course neither the cloth nor its color matched the coat, but when I finished the wearying task I took great satisfaction in my "tailoring ability." The finest tailor, I thought, couldn't have done the job better.

We had no wish to go into our tents for the night. On the

contrary, from time to time we added logs to the fire, and the blaze grew bigger and stronger, as though the flames intended to catch onto the whole forest. Pavel and Anton fell fast asleep, with their faces lying next to the hot ashes. Their trousers became so scorched that the odor irritated our nostrils.

"Fellows," we suddenly heard the voice of Ivan Ivanovitch, "I feel like eating a good meal now. If anyone wants to join me, I'll be glad to give him bread and meat. *Nu*, tell me fast, before it's too late."

No sooner said then done. Out of his knapsack he took a loaf of bread and put it over the fire. From somewhere or other he pulled out a chunk of hog meat and stuck the bayonet of his rifle into it, so that he could plunge it among the flaming logs. He didn't have enough patience to wait till the meat was completely roasted, but kept taking bites from it again and again, till there was nothing left on the sizzling bayonet.

Ivan's face turned red, shining as though it was smeared with some special ointment. Having finished his little feast, in which no one had volunteered to share, he brought himself a bottle of liquor, evidently from his tent, or from some hiding-place in the camp. He struck the bottom of the bottle with his palm, and the cork flew off into the distance. Then he lifted his head and put it well back, put the bottle to his lips, and emptied it without a pause and without a fit of coughing. As the hog fat was still dribbling from his mouth, he wiped it away with his sleeve and with his palm, that was as thick and broad as a shovel. Ivan looked like a man just stepping out of a hot bath, and in spite of all his efforts he was unable to wipe himself dry.

Meanwhile the liquor was having its effect: It put Ivan to sleep near the fire. In a few seconds he began snoring hoarsely, croaking like a frog in muddy water.

"That's what they're like," I sat there musing, "Ivan and his kind. They're almost all like that. They put their worries aside and live for the moment, here and now. They battle and fight when they have to, and they take good care of their physical selves: They eat and drink. And I — the only Jew in our squad, a solitary one of a kind among hundreds of Russians, Ukrainians, Byelorussians, Uzbekians, Georgians, and all those other nationalities ... I'm a Jew, different from them all. I'm not less devoted than any of them to our common, single purpose of striking at the Germans and battling them — I with my valuable machine gun. Why, I haven't missed out on one serious battle that we've had. Like them I go lying down near the railroad tracks; I go out on missions of sabotage ... Just a little while ago our squad leader gave my name to the partisan chief commanders beyond the front, as one who deserved a decoration for valor ... So what will their medal give me? Will it protect me? Will they treat me any better? ... A few days ago, when that Siberian character got stone drunk, he went running like a wild animal from one tent to another, looking for me, as his voice went booming over the whole camp: "Where's our Jew? Where's our Jew? Give him to me and I'll kill him. I'll kill him!" Finally he found me in one of the tents, and I had to wrestle with him for Heaven knows how long — till he managed to drag me out — and in sight of everyone he stuck his bayonet into me — just like that, for no reason. I had done nothing wrong, nothing bad to him or anyone else. He was just dead drunk, and I'm a Jew: some kind of strange, weird creature that ought to be killed ..."

❈ ❈ ❈

The bonfire died down, and finally went out altogether, leaving a mound of blue-grey ashes. By my watch it was three o'clock in the morning. I went into my tent and lay down near my friend Mischa. Through the cracks in the tent walls I stared at the dark density of the forest; and in those passing moments it looked to me like a black endless tomb.

But the night was clear. A silver sprinkling of stars was scattered over the clusters of trees, twinkling like electric lights hung on the tallest branches. A bright, shining orb framed in a wan halo, the moon skipped along its way smiling, seemingly winking to someone. From time to time it wrapped itself in a filmy cloud, as in a scarf you might put around your neck against the cold. Then it revealed itself again and continued its calm, steady, tranquil course across the sky, as befit a ruler in the sovereign domain of the night.

CHAPTER NINE
Before Battle

E LAY ON THE MUDDY GROUND, waiting for the order to set out. The cold of the last of the winter penetrated our bodies, and the sensation was not pleasant. Strong winds whipped us across the face and struck the tender branches of the young birch trees, bending their heads and forcing them down, till they had no strength left to spring back and straighten up.

The members of the staff of command sat not far away from us. The officers began their final briefing, and their meeting dragged on endlessly. We saw them bending their heads over the maps spread out before them on the ground or held on their knees, as they checked the compasses strapped to their wrists (which looked like large watches), gazed up at the stars, and conferred in low voices.

This time our pockets were filled with bullets. To the belts that held our torn overcoats wrapped around us we attached the hand grenades we had received, so that we could put them swiftly into action if and when they were needed. Equipped with this extra ammunition, each of us was now carrying a good few extra pounds of weight. In any case, we sensed that there was a serious enough battle ahead of us this time — something unusual; perhaps (and some said it aloud) we would even have to wage a face-to-face encounter with the enemy. We could judge how serious and important this mission was by the fact that for the first time we were taking into battle our "child of old age," as we called our little cannon. We had put it together with our own hands, out of parts and pieces that our men had dragged out of a German ammunition warehouse, into which they had forced their way. More than once the men had come back from there with live booty also: a few Germans who had been set there to guard the warehouse.

One of these was Karl Schlesinger, an older man who had served as a gunner in a German armored division. When we found him there during our foray into the ammunition warehouse, he actually volunteered of his own accord to join us and come with us into the forest; and he helped us carry the last, heavier parts that we needed to finish putting our little cannon together. And in this way he saved his life.

Karl continued to serve us well, even taking part in some of our missions. He joined us in ambushes, from which we fell upon German soldiers and took their lives.

Karl stood now beside the cannon, looking it over and inspecting it carefully. With his soiled, grimy hands he wiped his moist forehead, muttering to himself. Perhaps, like us, he was grumbling that he had to wait so long before we could set out. We knew him by now: He didn't like to stay idle, to wait with nothing to do. We had learned that battle refreshed him, brought him alive. He loved a situation of action, direct conflict with enemy. Without that, he found waiting around with us a waste of time, without any purpose.

From time to time Karl passed his fingers over his parched lips. I reckoned that if he were given a little barrel of beer, his mood would have improved considerably.

The meeting of the commanding officers came to an end. One result of their decisions was that the arrangement of the men was changed. I was taken out of my group and given a position closer to the cannon. I knew this wasn't done just to confound me and get me angry. Yet when I stretched out on the ground near Karl Schlesinger the German, I felt sick with misgivings. I wanted to put down my machine gun, leave it there, and just get away. "But," I told myself, 'hold on. Don't exaggerate your feelings. This Karl is going with us into a big battle with the Germans, his own people. He'll certainly be killing them, just as we'll be doing. He'll teach them a lesson. He'll get rid of some Hitler fascists. Then what am I objecting to about him? I have to see him as a man helping us strike at our enemy ..."

Fine. Well and good. But almost all the Germans who fell into our hands declared to high heaven and swore by their life that all their years they had been devout communists and pacifists, and they had been taken into the army against their will, and so on and on. And therefore, they always concluded, they begged us to forgive them and let them live. But who could believe them all?

Wasn't there reason, then, to ask if Karl could be trusted in the critical battle we were facing — the first battle into which we were taking our cannon? Could we depend on him?

Karl kept prancing around the cannon constantly. He attended to it and puttered with it as though it was his private toy. I forced myself to forget who he was, and thought only of the victory the cannon would bring us, since it was to be manned by a real professional, a cannoneer from an armored division of the German forces, who was now fighting in the partisan ranks ...

"When are we going to stop lying here in this mud and get up, so that we can start moving on to our destination? When?"

It was a strange thing: We always seemed to want to achieve two different purposes that simply didn't go together, or couldn't be reached together. On the one hand we longed to kill as many Germans as possible, the more the better. But we also had a longing to remain alive — and the chances of achieving that goal were not too bright.

※　※　※

I felt an urge now to go back to my tent, though I knew I would find nothing there but the pallet of straw that I used for a bed. For a number of weeks I had been there alone. Mischa had gone off on a long trip, and he reached the camp only a few hours before we all gathered to set out on this present campaign. In my weeks of solitude, on account of my wounded foot I had hardly stepped outside the tent. I would go out only to get myself some food, and then would head back at once, hopping on my crutch. And there in the tent I stayed quite alone. No one came in to visit, and I actually didn't want to see anyone. I lay there cut off from everyone and everything, peering through the slits in the tent, seeing raving visions and waking dreams; or else I would "welcome" dear close relatives who were no longer alive, when they "came to visit me."

Then the news had reached my ears that we were planning some kind of battle action against the enemy. I threw my crutch aside, telling it to go to the devil for all I cared; and I went to my commanding officer to protest against the decision to leave me behind in the camp with all the other sick and wounded men, and to give my machine gun to another partisan who knew how to use it. I raised a storm, arguing that no one had the right to meddle in anything concerning my health; no one should decide for me about my chances to live or die. My superior officer had no choice but to let me have my way. He even shook my hand at last, and sent me along with the whole group going out to the battle.

All was fine as we made ready. And then the long wait before we could finally start out began to get on everyone's nerves — mine as well. I couldn't bear just lying on the ground near Karl Schlesinger. The situation dampened my good mood and vexed my heart. It might have been for this reason that I wanted to get away from there and go back to my tent, to stretch out on my bed of straw and stay there.

⚘ ⚘ ⚘

Every one of us received a shot of liquor, to "get us into shape." Those who knew their way about (including me) managed to get two.

In the midst of the thick darkness I noticed someone dragging his heavy body along. I couldn't see his face, but only the bundles slung from his shoulder. When he came close enough for us to recognize him, we almost exploded with laughter. I was the only one who dared say something to him:

"Ivan Ivanovitch, you look as if you're getting ready for a trip to the North Pole."

For exactly one second there was no reaction from him. Then he hurled one word at me: "*Idiot!*" The expletive rang in the air like an empty bottle, fallen from someone's hand, that had smashed to bits.

And with that Ivan disappeared from our sight. Directly afterward, however, I was told that some of the fellows found him concealed in a thicket, eating his food to his heart's content, refusing to lift his eyes and answer when they spoke to him. "Well," I reflected, "he also knows how to cut himself off from the world around him to be all alone, by himself — to fill his stomach ..."

Very few in our group, I pondered, knew as well as Ivan the business of really eating. Hardly anyone else had his ability to take in food; and the same was true about liquor. What wonder was it then if he filled his knapsacks with "provisions for the way," when no one knew how long we would have to be away from the camp?

As for me, the truth was that on that day I drank more than I should have. I got my first dram when shots of liquor were distributed to all, one to a man. The second I "managed to get," like the others who had the knack of success. But I didn't stop there. In honor of our setting out from the camp, when my friend Mischa returned from somewhere far off we drank together. This time it was a truly different vodka — the genuine kind, brought from Moscow.

One way or another, we kept no count of the number of drams that went down the gullet ...

My reflections took me back to my tent. I remembered that at the beginning of the evening, when I was lying there on my pallet of straw, a beam of silver light, a courier of the moon, had leaped directly onto me: on my coat and the straw. It seemed to be looking for a place to hide. I would have liked to go back to the tent now, just to see if that beam of silver light was still playing around there all by itself; if it was still hidden inside the straw. If I found it there, I would cover it with twigs, leaves, anything I could use, so that it would stay there safely till we came back from the armed conflict ...

"Yes," went my thoughts. "But who says that we'll always be able to come back? Which one of us is certain that instead of returning to the camp, he won't be taken straight to the partisan burial ground — if others manage to get his body off the battlefield?"

I finally jeered at myself with scorn at my childish thoughts about the beam of light and my desire to save it, so that its warm glow could comfort my broken, grief-stricken, wretched spirit.

❧ ❧ ❧

I dipped my hand in a pool of water and passed it over my perspiring face. The sky was beginning to clear. A new day opened its eye and peered across at us from atop the hills that surrounded our forest.

Mischa stood near me, completely silent. He looked somber, in a glum, downcast mood. Till this moment I hadn't had a chance to ask him the reason for this mood, in which he had been stewing since his return. But partisans who had been with him in the proximity of General Platon, the commander of the entire partisan army in our region, told me that when they were there, word reached him that his fiancée had been taken by the Germans to a labor camp whose location no one knew, and his younger brother had died of starvation.

I wanted to wrench him away from his thoughts: "Look, Mischa: Just see how beautiful the woods are now, in these minutes. The night has retreated, and the gates open to let a new day in. Look at all that splendor of colors! It's new, fresh life coming into the world — isn't it?"

Mischa measured me up and down with a sullen look, and kept his silence.

"What's happened to you, Mischa? Is it all on account of that harmonica of yours that you left on your bed in the tent? Do you really miss it that much?"

"I don't know what to say to you, Philip. Till now I didn't want to tell you what's happened to me in my private life. I kept it to myself. But maybe by now you've heard about it. Among us everyone seems to know everything about everybody. But do you know? — when you mentioned the harmonica, you really did hit the nail on the head. Right now I need it badly. I would really like to have it with me. There are such terrible moods that a person gets into, when only a little music can soothe him and ease the ache, and help him forget his troubles a little. I really wish very much that the harmonica could come with me into the fighting that's ahead of us. I'd just keep playing the whole time, till the battle started. If I were carrying it with me and an enemy bullet struck me, it would probably damage the harmonica also. A fragment of a single chord would sound, and then it would just break and die away together with me, your friend. Death with a melody. A sort of funeral with music ..."

❀ ❀ ❀

For a long time we walked quietly, side by side, without a word. The dawn came up in stillness also, in a muted tranquility. Every few minutes Mischa gripped me in his arm and helped me walk. I had thought that my wounded leg had healed, or at least healed enough. But now it was giving me murderous pains. After the first twenty kilometers of our walk it swelled up, and every step I took after that was agony. Mischa didn't leave my side; and when our glances crossed and I saw his somber, glowering face, my agonizing pains grew worse.

We finally reached the place from which, according to the plan, we were to launch our attack against the German garrison that was stationed there.

We spread out on the ground and waited for the signal to let loose. Resting my head on my machine gun, I turned to look at Mischa. I wanted to whisper something to him, to make him share my sense of wonder at the beauty of that sunrise in the east, the wealth of golden rays that bathed the greening fields with their richness, as they were caught and held on the leaves of the trees like flashing spears. But at the very moment Karl Schlesinger appeared with the cannon and began sending his first shells over toward the enemy positions.

What happened after that was totally unexpected. According to the plan, immediately after the first cannon shells were fired at the enemy garrison, we were supposed to storm their positions. But that simply didn't happen. In the very first few minutes after the initial shelling, fierce fighting broke out, which we hadn't expected at all. We emptied all our pockets of the bullets we had brought. We hurled our grenades across, at a suitable distance from the German positions.

And they didn't accomplish their purpose. It became clear to us, furthermore, that their strength was far greater than what we had thought. The military equipment and weapons they used were of greater variety and higher quality than we had imagined, and seemed to be unlimited in quantity.

That fierce battle cost us the lives of several partisans, and a great many were wounded. But our disastrous failure wasn't only in the figures of our heavy losses. We were frankly puzzled — and many of us thought it mighty strange, even fearful — that not one of the cannon shells, on which we had pinned so much hope, struck the German positions. Not one of the structures in which they were entrenched was even damaged. They all just failed to reach their targets — as if Karl Schlesinger had never sent them there, but directly into the forest and the trees ...

Perhaps the matter was considered afterward at the staff headquarters. Perhaps Karl Schlesinger was asked to explain what had happened. Evidently, though, he wasn't found guilty of anything, because I saw him again the next day, and the day after that, walking around in the camp. There he was, eating, singing, puttering around the cannon. In the judgment of the staff of command — I assumed this was what they decided — the man who had been put in charge of the cannon had acted honestly and decently; he had supposedly been trustworthy...

CHAPTER TEN

Eyes

THE RAINS FELL WITHOUT A STOP. The forest was fairly flooded by the rainfall, and muddy ponds and pools of dirty water formed everywhere. The croaking of the frogs was now fairly deafening.

And our mood matched the weather: somber, gloomy, depressing to the point of suffocation.

Facing my tent, one bird chose a perch on the branch of a pine tree, and it wouldn't budge from there. It shed its feathers, till it resembled a chicken sitting on its eggs. The rain poured down on it and the branch together; and during the whole time not the slightest chirp came from its mouth. When I had a look at it from the tent, I saw that its beak was hidden among its feathers as though put into a sheath; and it seemed to me that the creature was trying to tell me something: "You're free to come out of your dwelling and capture me. As of now I surrender to you. Do what you want with me."

A few times during the day I threw it pieces of bread and other food, but it never took the trouble to come down from the branch and taste some bit of what I offered. It rolled its eyes a bit, and that was all. "A stubborn bird," I mused; "apathetic ... and maybe it's sunk in the same bleak mood as us."

The rains began getting into the tent. The pallet of straw on which I lay became soaked, and my clothing too was soon drenched enough — with the result that a desire awoke in me to run away. But where? Where?

The soil around the tent became one big pool, so that we seemed to be living now in a swamp, on an island, with no way to get to it or to leave it. There were some who thought that if the rain continued unchanged for another few days, we would be facing the danger of a serious flood, with no means of saving ourselves from drowning.

Meanwhile news reached us from the battlefronts, and they brought us only more sorrow. We heard that the Germans had reached far-off Stalingrad by now; that they had captured large stretches of Soviet soil, which contained hundreds of thousands of soldiers of the Red Army.

And here were we, on the soil of West Byelorussia, surrounded by Germans on every side. If they wanted to move on the forests, they could finish us off soon enough. With our poor, rusty weapons we could hold out against them for no more than a number of hours, perhaps a day or two; and then we would be torn to pieces and killed out. Many of us would be captured and imprisoned; others would surrender, in order to stay alive ... And what then?

True, we were carrying out all kinds of sabotage and guerrilla activities. We were provoking them, vexing them, causing them trouble. We blew up bridges, destroyed stores of their ammunition, derailed their trains, gave them headaches and distress, especially in the nights. After all, this was why we had settled down in the forests — to fight and take revenge from this cruel invader and conqueror. Yet how long could we go on? How long could we last?

Every day we asked ourselves questions of this kind. And since we had no answers, we went on with our actions against the enemy, hitting them as hard as we could.

One day, in broad daylight, we attacked a German garrison. I lay in an uncomfortable, even dangerous, position. In a stone structure, facing me at an open window, stood a German machine gunner, sending bullets toward me. I hid my head behind a big rock and returned his fire. From time to time I tried to get a clear glimpse of this German who was giving me his lethal attention. I wanted to see his face. Only his eyes appeared in the window. The rest of him was hidden behind the thick wall. But I realized that his eyes were blazing; a fanatic fire was burning in them.

"He wants my scalp," I muttered to myself; and like a mole I tried to bury myself in the earth, to shrink into nothing. So right then a bullet struck the rock behind which I was lying. It quivered backwards, and without my knowing how it happened, this time my right foot was injured.

After we returned from this combat to the camp, the partisan doctor found scattered fragments in my foot, and he assured me that the wounds would soon heal. His promise, however, didn't come true: The wounds developed pus, and my pains grew worse. The doctor couldn't find any way to help me. When a black mood took hold of me and I became sunk in grief, I was sure that at any moment now my end was coming — especially when I saw how the rag that served as the bandage was sunk in mud, in filth that could only worsen the infections ...

The cold nights still left the water frozen, but in the daytime everything melted, and the little ponds and puddles expanded. Had we been able to move about, through our devoted contact men we could have gotten from the town more effective medicines and better bandages; but under the prevailing weather conditions, that seemed a very unlikely possibility. Could my foot hold up till the roads became passable? Would the doctor have to amputate it, as he was forced to amputate, with a plain hand-saw, the wounded hand of Kulya, a fellow-partisan?

Day and night the sky was overcast, covered by thick dark-grey clouds. In the dark hours of rest, sleep would not come to me, and I longed for a sliver of moon, a patch of blue sky; but I was left with nothing but my longing ...

From the first day I came into the forest, I loved to follow the light of the moon that would steal into my tent through a narrow opening and go capering over my bed. I felt good with that light. It brought some cheer to my heart. Yet somehow the days of winter's ending were so dismally grey. Days and nights meshed together. Like blankets of dirty absorbent cotton the black clouds weighed down on the clusters of trees, emptying them of all their greenery.

❁ ❁ ❁

I was sick and tired of lying idle on my bed. If they only allowed me, I would go with the others to the railroad track, hobbling along on my crutch, and I'd take part in getting a train derailed, sending it speeding off the gleaming tracks into disaster. There at least life would be interesting. A mission of revenge against those bloody murderers would deaden the pains, help me forget my torment.

The smell of roast meat penetrated the tent and bothered my nostrils. I peeked outside. Ivan Ivanovitch was sitting, his legs spread wide, before a fire that he had made with two gnarled pieces of timber, and he was roasting a piece of hog meat. Straight from the fire went the roasting flesh to his mouth. With every bite he almost choked, and white saliva dribbled from his lips, probably because of the deep pleasure he had from the food and from the fact that no one disturbed him at his repast. His eyes were laughing, and so was his nose. His fleshy face, I saw, was glistening as if smeared with ointment. I felt an urge to call him, but I knew that with Ivan it was not wise to do anything to stir him up while he was eating. I might deeply regret it afterward.

In our early days in the forest, when we were still a fairly small group of men that had only just organized into a combat unit, the Germans had discovered us, and they pounced to attack us. We decided to give them battle. When the fighting was at its height, instead of snatching a rifle and doing his share, Ivan was seen running pell-mell with a side of beef on his shoulder. A few minutes later a bullet struck him in the back, and he fell to the ground — clutching the meat firmly. He wouldn't let that meat out of his hands. After the foray was over, for this lovely act of his he was sentenced to incarceration; and the result was that since then he became accustomed to having his rifle with him at all times, even when he was sitting idly around the fire or when he was roasting some of the meat that he loved so much.

From a nearby tent my ears caught the sound of melodies being played on a harmonica that the men must have lifted from someone during an operation in some village. I longed for Mischa, but he was away somewhere at the time. His playing was altogether different. The melodies that sailed out from his harmonica by the artistry of his mouth and fingers, captured the heart. They were poignant. And the thought came to me that perhaps, if he were in the camp now, holding his instrument and playing it, I would feel my pains easing off. Perhaps he would make me forget the pains altogether.

I put my head out of the tent, and caught sight of a bonfire burning low, its sparks dying out in the air among the tree branches. As I drew my head back into the tent, the bird that had been perching the whole time on the branch facing me, without a sign of movement, now fluttered its soggy wings. It evidently became frightened, or it lost its trust in me, for it disappeared among the thickets.

❀ ❀ ❀

The neighing of horses approaching the camp, mingled with the voices of happy, cheerful partisans, made a mess of my reveries. It didn't take long for the news to reach me that this was a group of fighting men returning from a successful task mission. They woke up the squad's cook and told him to prepare a good, hearty meal. The fire that had gone out by itself only a short while before was brought to new life now. Thick logs were brought and set to blazing brightly; and pots of meat and potatoes were put over the fire to stew. They made ready for a real feast.

"Philip! *Phi-li-ip!*" I heard my name being called distinctly, and couldn't imagine who it was that needed me at a time like this. But the men sitting around the fire took up the call like an echo: "Phi-li-ip!"

A courier from the command staff, from headquarters, stood at the door of my tent. He was the partisan Grischa. "Come down to headquarters, Philip. Come on now, hurry."

I gripped my crutch, and with leaps and bounds I reached the staff headquarters, to find the partisan officers seated around the table, with "a very distinguished guest" among them: a German officer adorned with medals pinned to his military jacket. He was corpulent and had a round face filled out with layers of hard fat.

While the people at the table were busy consuming meat and whiskey, I learned details about this German's capture. A group of our partisans had set out to sabotage a German railroad train. Two of the men were dressed in German SS uniforms, and they went ahead, onto the railroad tracks, to see if the terrain was free of enemy soldiers. Suddenly an officer of the German Wehrmacht approached them, and he advised them to get out of the area swiftly, because "those partisan bandits" might be hiding somewhere close by. The two men nodded in agreement, and pretending to be slightly drunk, they took a few steps with him as though to escort him — after which they hoisted him onto the wagon that was waiting for them, and sped off with him straight to our camp, to the command staff of the brigade ...

Entertaining as the story was, my interest was in the German officer. They seated me now facing him, so that I could serve as interpreter when they questioned him. I looked into his eyes — and they agitated my heart. I couldn't bear the sight of those fierce pupils of a wolf. I felt that if he were let loose, he would pounce on us all and destroy us. There was no fear in his eyes, but only a fathomless satanic hate.

I paid no attention to the conversation going on around me. I took no part in the lusty eating and drinking there. My attention was held by the eyes of this captured officer. They were different from those of the other people seated there. The grey irises were like clouds of sand in a dust storm, or like the muddy surf in billowing ocean waves ...

I was certain I recognized those eyes from the ghetto of Slonim, from the massacre there — the mass murder. True, on that bitter day of infernal fury I had encountered many eyes like those I now saw opposite me — the eyes of beasts, of wolves and jackals. Yet with every passing moment the conviction grew stronger in me that my intuition about this man was right. I remembered the singular pair of eyes that put terror and dread into everyone who chanced to see them that day. People fled from those eyes if they had the slightest chance.

"Tell me, you stinking dog," I spoke to him when the commanding officers had finished their meal. "Tell me: How many have you killed by now in this war? Do you know the total?"

He kept silent. He pursed his lips, and his stare froze. His eyes darkened slightly in their sockets, and the darkness in them froze too.

"Philip," one of the commanding officers called out, "tell him you're a Jew. Give it to him across the mouth!"

Feeling nothing, hardly aware of what I was doing, I lifted my crutch in the air and saw it make contact with the hog-fat face of the German. I was surprised that the crutch didn't break in two.

"Do you hear?" I felt that I was now one big blaze, a torch that had been kindled. "I'm a Jew — a Jewish partisan! Do you understand me? Tell me: Did you finish your work in my town? Did you kill out all the thirty thousand Jews there? — till the last one? Nu, open your mouth. Speak up. Talk! Talk, you rotten dog, you piece of filth!"

He kept still. Not a word came from him.

The chief officer told me to ask him a few questions now about military matters; but again I was unable to get a sound out of him. His silence continued on and on, till our patience snapped. And then he uttered a few single bold, daring words; "You fight for Stalin, and I, I fight for Hitler, our great leader!"

He said it quietly, deliberately, and the statement deafened my ears. I felt as if he had slapped me across my face. I translated the words into Russian for the commanding officer, and I felt myself collapsing. A few partisans had been permitted to be present during this interrogation. One held a thick stick, another an iron bar, and so on. They wondered why we were playing around so long, so delicately, with this vile human animal.

Nikolai Nikolaievitch ordered me to take the captured man out of camp limits and do with him as I pleased. Two partisans accompanied me, and we took him to a spot that they chose, where they tied him to a tall pine tree. My hand in which I held it seemed glued now to my Finnish pocket-knife with the long blade. In the dusk that enveloped us, the razor-sharp blade gleamed. My hands shook, but my fingers turned to implacable stone.

The sky was darkly overcast; but from time to time, through the dirty grey blanket above us a whitish stain broke across, like a single eye, wan and bleary, thrusting a mass of cloud aside to make its way in the firmament. That single eye was the full moon beginning its night journey across the sky. Perhaps it wanted to witness what was happening at a particular spot in the forest, among the tangled trees. But it was too late. When it pushed the cloud blanket aside to peer, nothing happened; it saw nothing at all. Perhaps it was looking for a pair of eyes. Perhaps it wanted to see a Finnish pocket-knife that someone threw into the depths of the night. It didn't find them. The darkness covered everything.

✿   ✿   ✿

A high fever took hold of me, and again I had to remain in my tent, resting. In my raving delirium I saw eyes roaming in the air outside, pushing their way into the tent, along with a whole array of Finnish pocket-knives. I covered myself with my coat, pulling it over my head; but they — the eyes and the knives — got in under the coat, to surround me on all sides. I shut my eyes, and they opened of themselves. Some imaginary power seemed to force my lids wide open. I had the sensation that a dazzling light was glaring into my eyes ... that I would go blind.

I didn't know what was happening to me. I kept saying things (so they told me afterwards) that made no sense. My whole body was burning with heat, on fire, ablaze. For a long while I didn't know where I was or who I was at all ...

CHAPTER ELEVEN
The Delayed Pesach Seder

FORTUNE DID NOT FAVOR US. This time luck was not on our side, and we didn't succeed in the task that was assigned to us. We were ready to place the explosives under the railroad tracks, when the Germans, waiting in ambush for us on both sides of the line, opened their deadly rain of fire. There were five of us, and in self-defense we scattered, each one fleeing wherever his legs would take him.

My mood turned sour and rotten. Only the day before, I had met with a few friends in the unarmed Jewish family camp, and we had agreed that the next day, when evening fell, I would come over to them, and together we would have a proper *seder* on that first night of Pesach. And then I was sent off on this mission, in which we failed completely.

I don't know how I ever reached the mountain that I now began climbing. The enemy's bullets continued chasing me, trying to strike home. I had serious doubts if I could successfully escape them all. I strongly wanted to reach the mountaintop, but I feared that some of those bullets aimed at me would find their target as I was struggling upward.

With great effort I reached the middle of the mountain; but the bullets were still flying around me, over my head, and my feet refused to carry me any further. They were tired. With all the longing of my heart I looked at the mountaintop, still so far away from me. I crawled on and on, and it seemed to me that I wasn't getting any closer to my goal, that I would never reach that acme, that I couldn't escape death any more.

"Just a little onward," I murmured to myself, "a little onward." My eyes went to my feet. I begged them to do me a favor and continue carrying me, upward, upward, promising myself, my feet, that when I got there, to the top, I would rest. I would most certainly rest.

Now hand-grenades were being thrown in my direction, and they exploded not far from me. They struck the trees, their branches, passing me by. I was afraid that if I were wounded, I would roll down the mountainside straight into the hands of the people who were in deadly pursuit of me. I greatly preferred that they should find me lifeless. Then I would be spared a great deal of unbearable suffering.

But it was so strange: My eyes longed to see the mountaintop, and yet it loomed higher and higher. It became more and more remote from me. The harder I drove my legs to get me there, the more it seemed to hide from my eyes, to turn into something inaccessible.

Onward I dragged my weary body, falling and getting up, falling and getting up. Through my mind went the thought that very possibly I would fall one final time and not get up any more — and with that everything would be over ... finished ...

From the earliest days, there had always been something wrong with my boots. There was nothing peculiar or unusual about my feet; I had simply never had much luck with boots. A number of times I "requisitioned" a pair for myself in the course of an armed action in a hostile village. I picked up a pair that seemed right and took them back with me. But when I got back with them to the base and put them on, they never quite fit. Either they were too small, so that they pinched and pressed my feet, or there was room enough in them for my feet to waltz around ...

Now I suddenly felt stabbing pains in the sole of one foot. I turned my head around and saw that my left foot and its boot had parted company. Hopping about, I saw the boot standing upright on the ground, as if waiting for me ... Only one jump, I thought, and I'd have it. I could put it on. Yet I knew that such a jump, backward instead of forward, meant a leap into the jaws of the death that had been looking for me since Heaven knew when, that kept searching for me relentlessly ...

❋   ❋   ❋

At last! My thanks went out of my heart to Heaven, which alone knew how I had ever gotten to the top of the mountain. I stretched out on the ground, that was covered with a verdure of tall, soft grass; and there I absorbed the fresh, invigorating, reviving breezes of spring.

For some reason, this part of the forest was devoid of trees. Those that had grown there had evidently been cut down some time ago. Their stumps stuck out of the ground, like low primitive tombstones that had been set out in rows — row upon row — to the memory of men who died in the war, or perhaps in earlier wars.

I began calming down slowly, as I relived in my mind the events of the beginning of the night: We had approached carefully, in stealth, till we reached the railroad tracks. We noticed nothing suspicious at all. We began digging a hole in the ground between the tracks, so that we could put the pail with explosives into it. As a machine-gunner, I remained a little away from the others, in order to give them protection. And suddenly the onslaught came: a downpour of a hailstorm of bullets. The Germans had deliberately let us get close to them, and then they let us have it.

There were no other details that I remembered, except for the fact that I retaliated with massive outbursts of machine-gun fire. I emptied a whole magazine — until I suddenly realized that I was all alone in the onslaught — literally the only one left. I retreated with all possible speed. I fled ...

But why did I ever decide to climb this mountain, so that I would remain exposed the whole time, in full sight of the Germans? How did I ever get to this place? And what happened to the others? Where was Fedka now — my "number-two man" for the machine gun? What about Sachka? And what became of the two others who were with us? What kind of fate did they have? Were they still alive? Killed? Captured?

As I was resting on the mountaintop, I remembered another detail: At the beginning of my retreat, as I first began running, the shouts of the Germans had reached my ears: *Yudeh, yudeh!* I realized now that I must have been close enough for them to see me and recognize that I was Jewish. Even in the dark of night it could be "read on my face."

But I had fired on them. I had retreated and fired, retreated and fired. My machine gun spoke for me, to try to kill them, but mainly to protect me, to give me a chance to save myself and escape them, so that I shouldn't fall into their hands alive ...

☙ ☙ ☙

I was so very tired now. I felt thirsty, but there was nothing I could find that would help. So I wet my lips with the dew that covered the grass.

Finally the shooting came to an end, and my self-confidence began to return. I sneered at those German soldiers who had held back from plunging further into the forest, or had been afraid to climb up the mountain after me, to kill me or take me alive. I jeered at them for having given up on me so easily — a bunch of craven cowards!

When German soldiers entered the forest, they never left the fine, smooth road, the "proper highway." They would always be afraid to plunge into the thick, dense parts of the forest, where the trees grew close and tangled together. That was our good fortune. They would shell us, bomb us, throw grenades. They were never stingy with their bullets. But they avoided any head-on collision with the "wild animals of the forest," as they generally called us.

A round, full moon traveled serenely high above me. In my imagination it became a brightly lit vessel, adorned and decorated, sailing on a pleasure cruise across a calm and quiet sea in unruffled self-confidence. Looking at it as I did from the top of a mountain, the moon appeared to be closer than always, and it looked smiling and friendly. I felt much better.

All at once I woke from my reveries. I remembered that the first night of Pesach was passing on — the night when I wanted to be in the Jewish family camp, to join in the celebration of a Passover *seder*. The people there had probably had their *seder* and enjoyed it quite a while ago, without me. By now, I mused, they must have gone to sleep. They certainly wouldn't wait for me such a long time into the night. Perhaps they would understand that something must have happened to me.

I rose up briskly and began moving down the slope of the mountainside. The machine gun pressed hard on my shoulder, while my left foot, that I had wrapped in some rags I found, became entangled from time to time in the growth on the mountainside, till I finally fell and rolled down the slope. When I reached the bottom I took the rag off and threw it away, and headed for the Jewish family camp with one foot bare.

☙ ☙ ☙

I found them up and awake. Happy to see me, they welcomed me with their warm handshakes. At the very beginning of the evening they had learned that I'd gone off on a task mission. When they heard the sounds of shooting from the direction of the railroad tracks, they realized that something had happened to the group which included me, and they simply feared for my life. So I told them everything that had happened to me, from the start of night till the moment I reached them.

"This is all very well," I said, "but what are you doing here? Why haven't you gone to sleep?"

They smiled. "What? Didn't you want us to celebrate the *seder* together? Did you want us to go ahead without you — not to have you with us when we'd chant and talk of the Exodus from Egypt? — all the troubles that all the children and descendants of *Yaakov Avinu* (our Patriarch Jacob) suffered till their Redemption? Don't we need a redemption and a liberation of our own?"

"We certainly do," I answered emotionally. "You're so right. Come, let's sit down and start telling about the suffering and the miracles that our people experienced in those times long ago, and in our times. And as far as I'm concerned, I have to thank the Almighty for my miracles of this night itself. I never thought I'd ever be sitting down with you to a *seder*. I didn't even think you would see me again. My chances of escape were so tiny. How I got away from them, I'll never really know. It was a kind of miracle over miracles ..."

There were about thirty of us sitting around the fire now: mostly young adults, and among them a boy of ten. On the day of the slaughter in his *shtet'l*, his townlet, his parents had forced him to run away and save himself, while they themselves were taken to the pits that became the mass graves.

The red-tongued flames of the fire leaped upward and almost caressed our blazing-hot cheeks. I said the four *kashes* slowly — the age-old four questions of the Pesach *seder* — and the boy said them after me in a voice choked with emotions of his own:

"*Ma nishtanoh ha-ly-loh ha-zeh* (Why is this night different) *mi-kol ha-ley-los* (from all the other nights)? *Sheb'chol ha-ley-los onu ochlin* (On all other nights we eat) *chometz umatzoh* (either leavened bread or unleavened *matzoh*); *ha-ly-loh ha-zeh* (this night) *ku-lo matzoh* (it's all only *matzoh*)." And so on ...

By heart we recited all that memory brought back from the Passover *Haggadah* (no one had a printed copy); and suddenly we all remained still. Our lips couldn't move any more. An oppressive silence took hold of us. We tried to fight free of it, and we couldn't. Anguish closed in on us and took us captive. It held us in its power and pressed down, pressed down, refusing to let us go free ...

❧ ❧ ❧

We held a *seder* night as best we could; but there was no celebration. We felt no joy. We couldn't. In each one's heart memories of home welled up. We told about our fathers and mothers. We relived memories of a world we had known a short while ago, a world of only yesterday, or perhaps the day before, when all of them where still alive ... all of them ...

We didn't have any *matzos*, nor any wine either; but the bitterness of *maror*, bitter herbs — of that we had more than enough.

We sat close together around the fire. Flaming sparks flew off around us, over our heads. They scorched our ragged clothing; they touched us; and yet they weren't able to warm any wretched, broken heart.

CHAPTER TWELVE
Yosef Rachmilevitch

YOU COULD ALMOST FEEL with your hands the intensity of the darkness in the underground room. A glass-paned window, its wooden base set into a hole dug into the ground near a tree stump, was camouflaged with leaves to be invisible from the outside.

Only after all the officers who had been invited to the session were seated around the table, was the kerosene lamp lit and set down in the middle between them. The people gathered there bent over the maps they had received, and they marked circles around sites and details that interested them. Then they lost themselves in reflections and ruminations.

Nikolai Nikolaievitch Bobakov, the squad commander, sat at the head of the table. The words he spoke now, to open the meeting, tore through the silence:

"The life of every heroic partisan is very valuable. Any one who dies is a tremendous loss to us. Therefore every plan of action brought up here has to be thought out well; it has to have maximum effectiveness. We reckon generally that one partisan behind the enemy lines is worth seven soldiers facing the German forces at the front. He's the equal of seven ...

"A small team of partisans, four or five men, has the ability to derail a train with tanks and troops speeding to the front. The men can just send it flying off to crash down a steep embankment.

"So figure for yourselves how important is every usual, ordinary sabotage action that we carry out. How many people's lives we save in the homeland, on the battlefronts, by plaguing the enemy behind the lines, by sabotaging and destroying some of their military strength in the terrain that they've captured, and by preventing their military shipments, as much as we can, from getting to the front."

He paused a moment, drew in smoke from his cigarette a few times, and then addressed the captains of the units:

"Large enemy re-enforcements are streaming now over the Baranovitch-Minsk railway line. The purpose of the troops is to smash and destroy our homeland, our 'Mother Russia.' Do we have the right to sit here, calm and comfortable, in the face of such a threat? Never! In no way! You and your men have to go to work night and day on those railway lines and make those trains rushing eastward go flying off the rails. If one team doesn't succeed at one spot, let another team come and do the job immediately at the same spot, or at a different place on the line.

"All right, friends, get to work: to concentrated, steady work! I wish you success!"

As the commander finished, the unit captains leaned over their maps again. The cigarette smoke moved from one end of the underground room to another — like a small cloud that had lost its way. The fog that filled the chamber grew thicker, more sticky and dense, till the people sitting at the table could hardly see one another.

❦ ❦ ❦

At the other end of the table, exactly opposite Nikolai Nikolaievitch, sat Yosef Rachmilevitch, a Jew of middle age who had appeared as a member of the squad only a few days ago. No one knew where he had come from, what he was doing among us, or what his exact position was among the fighting men.

He waited impatiently for the commander to finish talking, and then he asked permission to speak:

"It's not hard at all to reach the railway line that you mentioned. I can take on the job myself, on my responsibility. I'll need, altogether, some four or five partisans who don't know what fear means. I'll plan the action down to the last detail. Right now I already have all the details clear in my mind. We'll get a train hurtling off the tracks, and I'll make sure it's a train headed for the front. I know the layout of the spot I have in mind as well as I know my own hand —

and this is no secret to Nikolai Nikolaievitch. I'll pick the highest spot on the route, and from there the train will go down the slope, full speed ahead into hell. The truth is that the approach to the spot I have in mind is dangerous; but it's good and right for our purpose. Furthermore, the Germans won't be waiting in hiding for us there. So we can succeed completely, in full."

The officers picked up their heads. They exchanged glances, signaling to one another their amazement, and their doubts. Some of them even had trouble hiding the smiles that spread on their faces, hinting of their scorn at Yosef Rachmilevitch's boastful "big talk."

Yosef, though, paid them no attention. He blew out thick wafts of smoke from the cigarette he held in his mouth, as he tugged continually with two fingers at the ends of his long mustache.

Even Nikolai Nikolaievitch wasn't enthusiastic about Yosef's plan. It was his opinion, he said, that if such an important, critical operation was to succeed, and particularly in a location where no partisan had ever yet dared set foot, at least a whole troop of partisans should be sent into action, including a security force numbering a few dozen men. "So," he continued, "it's quite possible that the assumption that a group of four or five men can carry out the required action on this railroad line isn't sound enough. Maybe it wasn't thought out and judged with enough care. We therefore have to think well, consider and weigh the problem, till we find the right solution: the proper way to strike at the enemy at this railway line — because from a military viewpoint it's a vital, crucial target."

In Yosef's eyes, however, a flame of fury was burning, though not one of the people seated in that underground room noticed it. A powerful wish flamed in him to take revenge of the Germans, the people that had murdered his family with all the Jews in his hamlet. "Oh no," he was thinking. "It won't be difficult to carry this out." He was not going to give up his plan. No one was going to stop him. As he turned to Nikolai Nikolaievitch to speak again, his bass voice echoed in the chamber like a hammer striking soft wood:

"I ask of you to consider again the plan that I have proposed to you, but let me make it now more detailed and exact. I never disappointed you in all the time I served you as a contact, to keep you informed of what was going on in the region. I'm a native of the area. I was born there. I know every turn and corner; I know the people — all the different kinds and sorts. So please listen to me now:

"The best place to derail a train carrying ammunition or troops to the battlefront is located above the center of the hamlet where I lived all my life. The railroad track passes there beyond the houses, across the length of the mountain that surrounds the hamlet. At the foot of this mountain, right in the middle part of the hamlet, stands my house — the wreck of it that's left.

"By the forest paths I can get there with my band of men — specifically a small group — and we can do the job. From that spot, all the way up there, I'll send a train down to the bottom, with tanks and troops. I know the timetable, when all the different kinds of trains come there. I know when they're speeding to the front, and when they're coming back, going westward. I learned it all by paying attention and watching all time that I was in the area. I assure you, Nikolai Nikolaievitch, that the danger we'll be facing — and I'm not denying that it's risky — isn't all that great. But the mission is well worth while. It will pay us to take the risk ... and how!"

The atmosphere changed completely. Smiling, the squad commander came over to Yosef and shook his hand, and he wished him good luck. One by one the officers left the staff headquarters, to separate and return to their units.

❦   ❦   ❦

By twisting, winding paths, by all kinds of roundabout ways, Yosef led his men steadily. He himself knew how difficult was the task he had undertaken. It was far more arduous and formidable than the indications he had given the staff officers in describing the operation. But the burning desire for revenge against the Germans made the hardships and dangers seem small by comparison. He was filled with an absolute faith that he would succeed. And all along the way, he kept praying to his Maker that he shouldn't come to grief, that the whole thing shouldn't end in shameful failure. He prayed to be able to return to the base and report to Nikolai Nikolaievitch that he had fulfilled the mission he had undertaken: he had struck the enemy hard, where it hurt.

As they reached the edge of the forest, light and dawn began its appearance from afar. Mountain tops shone green; in the valley, grayish plowed fields became visible.

"Fall a little behind me," Yosef told his team, "and don't go further. We mustn't show ourselves during the day. I'm going to crawl ahead on my stomach, another few yards. I'll pick out a good spot for observation, and I'll have a look all around to see what's going on in the area."

After a moment he turned his head back and added, "Lie down on the ground and catch a little sleep — but not all of you at the same time."

As he made his unhurried examination all about, through his

binoculars he made out the stream that surrounded the hamlet — his native ground. He didn't take his eyes off it.

Everything looked just the same: the same hamlet, the same trickling shallow stream. Over there was the flour mill, there the church with its spire; and the row of houses going all around in a circle, where the non-Jews lived — all just as it had always been. Only the houses of the Jews, concentrated in a few roads and lanes, looked different now. Most of them had been demolished or dismantled. They were desolate wrecks, with not a soul to live in them. The old trees, with their branches reaching to the windows as if to hide them from human sight, were standing firm, just as before. In the past, though, life had been teeming there. Now not a human being could be glimpsed. Instead, weeds and thistles were flourishing. Where houses had been, now there were scattered piles of stone and rubble.

It was a clear day. The visibility was fine. Yosef could see now that many of the trees in the Jewish quarter were scorched and bare of any leaves. As he studied them from afar, high above them, they seemed to resemble human skeletons, from which some of the limbs had fallen away or had been cut off.

He wanted to pinpoint the spot where his house had stood, and with great difficulty he finally did it, though it was all blurred there, indistinct. As he adjusted the binoculars, he saw wild grass growing, thick, tall thistles thrusting up, and a few scorched trees that had been planted for shade. By the trees he identified the place.

He spotted again the water-driven mill, at the edge of the stream. The railway passed fairly near by. There it would be easy enough to approach and get close; but the spot wasn't suitable to carry out his mission. If a train was derailed on flat terrain, there wouldn't be much benefit out of the whole business.

The sun's rays thrust their way past the church roof. The railroad tracks of steel that passed nearby gleamed like sharpened knives. Neither was this spot suitable, and it was too dangerous. Non-Jews lived quite close together all around, and the great majority of them had no sympathy to spare for the partisans. They collaborated with the enemy. Should his small band of men be discovered, they would be lost. Where he planned to put his plan into operation, however, he believed it would be a different story. At the top of the high hill there were no houses. When darkness came, no people would remain, walking about and going anywhere. He only had to get there with his men, and under the tracks he could place the explosives they were carrying; and then the train would go rolling down helter-skelter. Heaven would help him … for sure …

His eyes scanned the entire area, all around, scrutinizing

everything he saw. He identified every detail, remembering everything. "And what's so surprising about that?" he asked himself. Of course he recognized everything. It was all so close to him in time ... only yesterday. The entire recent past came back, all the yesterdays, just as they had been:

❦ ❦ ❦

He had lived over fifty years of life in that hamlet which nestled in the valley. There he was born and raised. He was a Jewish farmer, with his own acreage of soil. It had taken him a long time to become the owner of ten hectares of plowable, fertile land.

With his six sons he worked it excellently. Into it he invested a great deal of sweat and hard labor. It was backbreaking work, but satisfying and rewarding. In the beautiful days of summer he loved to go walking, especially in the early morning hours, in the green fields where the produce was growing — to do some fixing and trimming here and there, lift up and remove a broken stalk, clean away harmful bugs, uproot wild grass and weeds, and look with wonder at Heaven's blessing, the bounty that came from nature in the Creator's world.

Not all the years had been blessed with good harvests and good incomes; but by and large he had never really lacked for anything. With his two hands and the help of his sons — good craftsmen — he had built his large wooden house, a handsome home, beautifully furnished. His sons had grown sturdy as lions. Every non-Jew in the vicinity was afraid of them — frightened of their glance. People in the hamlet were afraid to attack any Jew, knowing there would be others — these stalwart sons — to come to his defense and pay back double for any injuries he might suffer.

As Yosef's thoughts ran on, he forgot almost entirely the men he had left a short distance behind, stretched out on the ground. They rested, ate some of the food they had taken along, and caught some sleep.

Yosef sighed deeply now; and the sigh rolled down the hill, to become lost somewhere down the valley ... He began remembering again:

When Heaven gave you a blessed summer, you filled up your storehouses and granaries with so much wealth: rye, barley, even high-grade wheat, spelt, and oats. The fields became full of all kinds of produce, each in its season. You watched over them and protected them, so that no harm should come to them. Then, in the big city nearby, you sold what the fields had produced, and thank Heaven, you had a fine income.

Maybe all in all he had never managed to save a great deal; but there had always been enough for his needs, and a bit more besides. When the children were small, he had sent them to study in the *cheder*, the little schoolhouse for small boys, like all Jewish children through the ages. Then they went on to the *talmud Torah*, the elementary school for holy Jewish studies. They didn't stay there studying too long, to become any kind of learned scholars — because he needed extra hands in the field. Yet they had learned to know well that there is One who created the world, and He watches over the human beings who live in it; and to Him they always prayed together in the single *shul*, the modest synagogue in the hamlet.

Nor was that all. When the *yamim noraim* approached on the calendar — Rosh Hashanah and Yom Kippur, the holy days of awe — he went with his family to stay at his sister's home in the nearby city; and there he paid in advance for seats for the whole family in the large, handsome *shul*, where far more people came for the prayers than ever in his hamlet with its tiny Jewish population. He made sure, too, that there was a proper, respectable place for his wife in the women's section, next to his wealthy sister, in the very first row, where the *chazzan* could be heard very clearly as he led the *tefillah*, the holy prayer services.

Yosef lifted his head to look up at the blue expanse, and his lips whispered a prayer now: "Let me not seem to be boasting, Heaven forbid, about anything I've ever done. I've only been remembering things, reminiscing about a world that was smashed out of existence. It's just that I was never miserly when I lived there in the hamlet. I never tried to save money when I bid for an *aliya*, to be called up to the Torah. I bid against the richest people in the city, when I was in that large, handsome *shul* for the holy days of awe. I didn't do that to gain prestige for myself but to give honor to the Torah, and to show the sovereign Divine Master of the world I was grateful for all the bounty, the blessing, the good fortune that He bestowed on me. And there were the donations that I distributed with a generous hand in the days when I remained in the large city, between Rosh Hashanah and Yom Kippur. And I never felt afterward that I missed the money I had given away: never …

"*Ai*, we used to have *yamim noraim*, those days of awe … *yamim tovim*, the good days of the Festivals …"

Rivers of sweat trickled from Yosef's forehead, as the memories of the past held him firmly in their grip. He couldn't find any way to get free of them — perhaps because he didn't want to.

That whole world of his, that whole existence — destroyed, gone from his life: His devoted wife Sheind'l; his children Moshe, Lyubka,

Ber'l, Gershon, Hershel, Sioma, Sara, Gitt'l — not one of them escaped alive; not one!

His heart contracted within him. He lay on the ground unmoving, as though unconscious. A short distance away sat the others. They had awakened from their naps by now, and they took to eating again, drawing chunks of bread out of their knapsacks and pockets.

The hour of noon approached. A clear sun made its way imperceptibly across the blue, cloudless sky. It carried joy in its blazing light, in the rays it poured into the whole of existence: to the fields that were turning green, to the fruit trees that were blossoming, to the leafy trees in the forest whose fragrance floated out to fill the air.

The sunshine was filled with gladness, but none of it reached him. His eyes didn't leave his hamlet. He didn't stop gazing at it from the wooded hill where he was sitting. He sought his yesterday there; he looked for the past he knew so well; and he found it had been trampled out of existence, pulled up by the roots.

❧   ❧   ❧

"We're hearing echoes of heavy treads — some kind of movement somewhere around here," one of the men had crawled over to him to report. "Maybe they've discovered us here?"

"And you look as white as chalk already," retorted Yosef, looking the partisan up and down with an angry glance. "How fast you become terrified."

After a minute, speaking more gently, he asked the man to come closer: "Look down into the valley: here, straight across. Do you see it? That's the hamlet where I was born. That's where I lived till the war," he said as he pointed with a finger. "Have a good look. Take my binoculars and examine it carefully. Do you see that group of old trees down there — all scorched? It's all that's left of my ruined house. Do you hear? Now take a look over to the left. Soldiers are moving around there right now. They're still looking for me. They think I may still be hiding in a bunker, some secret place underground that I dug for myself in advance. Bunch of idiots! They think I'd stay there and wait for them to come and finish me off ... Hold still a minute. Just listen. We can hear their voices, all the way here. It's because the air is so clear and still. They're singing. They're looking for me, and they're singing as they go. That's how they are. They kill and they sing. They liven up their work of murdering with their sweet old songs!"

"And we're going down there? — right to the place where they are?'' The young partisans's lips were trembling and his teeth were chattering. His whole body shook. ''Maybe ... maybe we shouldn't ...''

Yosef gave him a scornful look. ''Get the men up on their feet. You've all rested more than enough. You've slept and you've eaten. And look: We won't be going down there before the sun sets; so don't go getting frightened so long beforehand.''

Ashamed, the young partisan crawled back to the group, while Yosef went on scrutinizing the valley and the hamlet, in which the German soldiers went milling about, foraging and searching, as they kept singing and singing.

The more he caught sight of them in his binoculars, the stronger burned his desire for revenge. He was most infuriated by their wild laughter that carried to his ears through the clarity of the day.

An incident of the past came back to his mind: One day he had gone from the hamlet to the nearby large city, where his sister lived. He stole into the sealed ghetto to bring his sister food supplies, so that she and her family could stay alive. Having finished his business in the ghetto, he broke through the fence and began getting away, when two German soldiers seized him and brought him to the Gestapo headquarters. He was thrown into a prison cell, where they beat him up severely, laughed at him, punched and beat him again, and sang lustily.

A few days after his arrest, perhaps a week afterward, they broke into his cell, shouting, ''You dirty, filthy Jew! You longed to escape from the ghetto? All the Jews were *kaput*, finished, done for — and you wanted to escape? — run away from the death you deserved?'' They laughed fiendishly as they struck and punched and beat him — till he lost consciousness ...

When he woke, he felt a strange emptiness in his mouth. His teeth were strewn on the floor; his face was befouled and grimy with blood.

That day, or perhaps the next, they took him out of the prison cell. He had no idea where he was being taken. Perhaps they intended to bring him to the market square, that was full of farmers from the whole neighborhood, so that they could show them the last Jew left in the city, before they shot him in the sight of them all. It was also possible that they were taking him to the local military commander for an ''investigation,'' and there he would be tortured to death.

As he was taken through the streets, the ghetto, which evidently had been burning a long while, was still going up in flames. Dead bodies were lying about on the sidewalks, scattered among piles of household appliances, utensils and broken furniture. As his captors led him along, they passed by a house that was still standing intact. In the window he saw an old man with a silvery beard leaning on the sill; but he realized the man was no longer alive. The German soldiers who were taking him stopped there, however — it was a little scene he would never forget — and for the sake of "a little fun" they put a few bullets into the dead man in the window, while they laughed uproariously.

In the devastated ghetto there was a great deal of activity. Many non-Jews from the neighboring villages were milling and moving around. He saw a large number of farmers from his hamlet too, but they turned a blind eye to him; they were too busy to notice him. The time had come to gather loot. They had all arrived to take chunks and pieces of inheritance which the Jews had left for them — inheritance that was obviously rightfully theirs alone now. They kept dragging about large sacks, which they filled up in the Jewish houses. Of course, it was not too easy for them to move about. They had to stride and jump over dead bodies. And the sacks were quite heavy to carry and drag. The stench of death and burning, however, didn't trouble them. The heavy, laden sacks gave them such a good, lovely feeling, filling them with so much satisfaction, that they were able to overcome any feeling of nausea or suffocation.

And suddenly Yosef saw that he was standing before his sister's house. An idea flashed into his mind. Without stopping to think, he hurled himself over the sill of a window, through which thick smoke was still pouring out. Caught by surprise, the soldiers who were guarding him were momentarily bewildered. Then they began shooting everywhere: into the house and all around it. That done, they set off in pursuit of him, shouting "Yudeh, Yudeh!" ... But he outwitted them and slipped out of their hands. He saved himself from death and triumphed over it ...

❧   ❧   ❧

"All right, fellows," he called to his men, "let's go. The time has come to go down into the valley. Come on."

Evening descended to meet them on the way, as its growing darkness covered them. They came to one of the villages near Yosef's hamlet, and entered the first cottage they reached. An old farmer named Vassily was there. When he saw Yosef standing before him, he crossed himself twice (evidently hoping to invoke divine aid with the sign of the cross) and almost fainted.

"Yosef, you're alive? But they said you were killed for sure!"

"Yes, old Vassily, they killed me; and yet I'm alive, you see. I'm alive, and I'm going to take revenge." In his voice was a grim determination.

After a pause in old Vassily's house, a young girl's voice was suddenly heard crying out, "Germans! Germans!"

A shower of bullets rained down on the poor old cottage, and the window panes were smashed to pieces. There was no time to make plans. A decision had to be made with lightning speed. Under the cover of outbursts of fire from their own automatic weapons, the six partisans leaped through a side window, spread out, and took up defensive positions. Yosef caught a bullet in his left thigh. He felt a searing pain, but paid it no attention. Instead, an idea came to him: He would outwit the attackers.

Crawling backward, he reached the wall of the cottage, and then he called out in Russian, in a ringing voice that carried far: "First division, to the left. Second division to the right. Main squad, in the center. *Attack! Fire! FIRE!!!*" And he let out ear-splitting war cries that shattered the night... As he kept up the din, the six partisans sent a barrage of concentrated fire against the Germans. They used up almost all the bullets in their pockets. It was a dangerous gamble — but the stratagem worked. When the partisans stopped shooting, they were answered with perfect quiet. The Germans had become frightened and they retreated fast, to flee the village in confusion.

"All right, fellows," said Yosef with a smile. "That was only an introduction to the job we have ahead of us: a little baptism of fire. But it was a good introduction ... I reckoned it was likely we would have a run-in like this with the Germans; but I didn't expect that the result would be so spectacular. We drove them off, and not one of us was hurt ...

"Now," Yosef dropped into silence for a second or so, to put his hands on the shoulders of the two partisans who were nearest to him, "now comes the main part. We have to derail a railroad train as it goes rushing to the front at top speed. This we must absolutely do. This is why we've come here. Now, I know exactly when it will cross the point I've chosen to get to. The way to get there is hard. It's going to tire us out, because it's a roundabout route — but it's less dangerous than going there straight. We'll rest a little on the way where we can, and we'll keep going till we get there."

It was wearisome toil and drudgery to go by the twisting paths they took. Most of the way they had to practically crawl, to avoid exposing themselves to view, not to let anyone catch sight of them moving. So they went, till at last they reached their destination. Two of them took Yosef in their arms and crossed the dangerous road with him. No, thank Heaven; there was no ambush, no trap prepared for them. They saw no sign of any guards whatever, and they wondered about it.

By Yosef's calculations they had yet a nice bit of time before the train came speeding on. So he gave a quick look at his trousers, where they had clung to his skin, all befouled with blood. He felt the pain of his bullet wound growing stronger in his thigh, and he thought he might have time to examine the wound and see just what damage the bullet had done. Right then, however, came the very time for which he had waited and hoped so long.

The steel tracks began humming and vibrating; somewhere far off they were groaning and screaming — under the immense burden of the approaching train. The tracks quivered and thrummed as if they were being splintered and cut.

Into the hole that they had dug between the tracks the team put the explosives they had brought, and covered them well, leaving no sign whatever of what they had done. And now there was nothing left for them to do but wait in anticipation for what was to happen. The team stole its way back to a nearby thicket, as Yosef held tightly in his fist the end of the long cord connected to the powerful mass of potential destruction that they had put nicely in position. At the right moment the cord would do its work instantly ...

The eyes of every one of the group bulged and protruded, as if wanting to push past the lids that were narrowed down. The men never took their gaze off the steel tracks that gleamed in the night's darkness. It was evident that Yosef too was under tension, all keyed up as he watched steadily. Again and again his lips whispered a prayer to the Almighty in heaven that the mission should end now in success.

Seconds passed ... and more seconds. The headlamps of the engine shone dazzlingly through the dark, as the train rushed onward, seeming almost to want to burst through the thicket and run the men over.

And then it came.

A giant thundering, deafening crash broke through the entire surroundings — a crash that split into a chain of smaller crashes, seemingly wanting to shatter the night itself to bits ... Fire, sulphur came reeking in the wind. Human bodies went flying about. Railroad cars laden with ammunition exploded in the air with incredible noise, to send one piece of them after another rolling down into the valley, down to the site of the hamlet, where they set everything aflame.

An infernal blaze spread over the whole area, thrusting aside the dark, reddening the sky, lighting up roadways and pathways. But it did not cast any light on the place where Yosef and his men were hiding. They made ready to return to the camp, yet they were reluctant to take their eyes away from the destruction they had wreaked on the train that had been speeding along with such pride and confidence to the battlefront ...

Yosef's incandescent eyes watched the spread of the fire in the valley. As he surveyed the hamlet, he prayed in his heart that the blaze should reach it in full, to raze and devastate everything that still existed there. Let everything in that hamlet be uprooted, he prayed; let it be destroyed at the roots, just as his family — his wife and children — had been destroyed by the roots, with all the Jews of the hamlet.

CHAPTER THIRTEEN
Between Life and Death

"THE JEWS ARE TO BLAME!"

"It's on account of them that we're being hunted down."

"They told them where the central headquarters was located."
"They led the Germans to the partisan camps."

With lightning speed the rumors spread through the whole forest, flying from one unit to another, from one squad to the next one. It all sounded so ludicrous, so stupidly vicious. No one even knew how harmful rumors of this kind ever came into being, or what foundation there was for them. In general, those who spread them around were known Jew-haters; and there was no lack of them among the partisans. But they had never had any real effect on our lives.

Now, at first, people drew away from them; they wouldn't believe the slander. Yet after a few days the atmosphere changed in the forest, among the partisan units. A campaign started to confiscate the weapons of the Jewish fighters who belonged to the various units as full, active members. In fact, some of these fighters had been among the founders of their units. If any Jewish partisan objected or resisted, refusing to give up his fighting equipment, it was taken from him by force, and he was ordered to leave the forest. Some became adamant, stubbornly refusing to yield. They were shot to death.

With my own eyes I saw two partisans from one of the units of our squad stop an armed Jewish fighter for "investigation." They wanted to confiscate his weapons, but he refused to hand them over. The two dragged the young man off into a thicket, and in a little while I saw them come out alone: Just the two of them. I hadn't heard any gunshot, I hadn't heard any outcry. I have no idea of what they did to him — but I never saw that Jewish partisan again. Very likely, the thought came to me at once, they had used a gun with a silencer.

What was going to happen with me? How would *my* fate be decided? Of that I had no idea either. Yet I allowed myself no illusions to wallow in. And indeed not a whole day went by before my freedom went. By orders of the command staff, Sverdlov, a Siberian without a trace of terror in him, was put in charge of me. I was forbidden to move from the spot where he put me, under his watchful care. So I reckoned it would not be long before my body would also be lying in some thicket. In general, dead bodies lay there strewn about — Germans, spies or traitors who had been liquidated on orders of the command staff. And now that the nasty, miserable slanders against the Jews had broken out like a plague, Jewish corpses began accumulating there: the remains of victims who hadn't been guilty of any crimes.

Well, for the time being I had the status of a person under arrest. Orders about me were expected to arrive from the command staff, but for some reason nothing came. I was a machine-gunner, a first-rate sharpshooter, a soldier who had served in the regular Polish army. In our group I was the only one who could handle the machine gun well. Perhaps this was keeping the command staff from making a hasty decision about me. It might even be the factor that would sway them in determining my fate. Yet who could know? Who could know what considerations against leaving me alive they might take into account?

Sverdlov took me away into a corner. By force he took my military coat off me, then my jacket, which was very much to his liking. There on the spot he put them on, making them his own. But that wasn't enough for him. He took the boot off my right foot, and found that it fit his foot exactly. His own right boot was torn, so he threw it away into a puddle of water and decided to wear mine. And that was that.

I obeyed all his orders with a cold calm, with indifference. I had a longing in my heart to have it all over and done with as fast as possible, without any interference on my part and without any delays.

My stalwart watchman's next step was to make an "investigation" of my pockets. He took from me the chunk of bread that I had been saving since the first day of the massive, German hunting-operation against us. I had been using it to keep myself nourished somewhat, by taking a bite out of it now and then. He took my watch off my wrist, then lifted my large packet of quality tobacco — lock, stock and barrel. Everything was his now. And I wasn't angry at him at all. When a man's end is waiting for him somewhere out there in the thickets, when he doesn't know if he is going to live one more day, why does he really need tobacco? Of what use is a watch to him? How can it matter to him what time it is? And why should he need bread? What difference will it make if he dies hungry?

And yet I felt a little otherwise about that tobacco. I would have liked very much to roll myself a cigarette and smoke. The thought even occurred to me to beg Sverdlov to let me have a little tobacco out of the packet, because it would take yet a while till ... so perhaps he could give me at least enough for two or three cigarettes ... But no — no, I didn't do it. I didn't ask him for anything. I decided to forget it. I didn't want any favors from him.

Night fell. A sliver of moon appeared in the dark-blue sky that was sprinkled with stars like silver dust. Only a little while later, though, heavy clouds massed up from somewhere, to block the starry sky and darken the whole forest as well as the sharp, fierce eyes of Sverdlov as he sat beside me. No rain fell, however. On the contrary, the clouds were soon gone, and the sky became clear again. The moon reappeared, to go sailing calmly across the firmament. My glance caught Sverdlov's eyes again: they were aflame with a hatred for me, the Jewish machine-gunner who was now a prisoner in his hands, as my life hung in the balance.

Late in the night Sverdlov fell asleep. His head leaned over to the side, till his hat fell off. His long, straggly unkempt hair became entangled in the blackberry bushes; and I was certain that when he woke up he would not be able to get those unlovely locks of hair disentangled so easily.

He kept snoring away, the sounds mingling with the wailing of the wolves and the wild boars that ran about in packs somewhere close by. As he slept, Sverdlov stretched out on the grass, and he managed to get the open end of his rifle pointing straight into his wide-open mouth. He seemed to be breathing "musically" into the narrow cylinder as if into an oboe made of steel.

Now I felt myself more free ... and various thoughts came into my mind. I examined the situation. The phosphorescent numbers on my wrist watch glowed from Sverdlov's outstretched arm. A long knife was attached to his belt, which, as I saw, I could easily take from him. And a strange wave of heat coursed through my whole body, pressing on my temples.

"Go ahead, do it," whispered the thought in my mind. "Get out of here. Don't hesitate!"

"Have courage. Get that knife of his away from him, and snatch the machine gun back. It's yours! Are you a partisan or aren't you!"

"It will take you just a split second, and you can escape with your life. Do you understand?"

But I was too full of lethargy to do anything whatever. A tremor went through me. I wiped the sweat from my forehead, as my heart asked: Where would I escape to? Where would I go wandering with the life I would save from Sverdlov's clutches? What in the world would I do with it? The kind of life I could have would only bring me bitter trouble ... Then why did I need it? What for?

I drew back my hand as my fingers were already touching Sverdlov's knife. I felt revolted by it; it was repulsive to me ... it reminded me of my dread, and I felt nausea ... "Another short while, and the sentence will arrive from the command staff. It's just a matter of hours ... and then it will all be over: perhaps right here, where I'm sitting; or they may take me away into the thickets ... as usual ... as usual ..."

Leaning against a thick tree, I watched the night drawing away. Fragments of it thrust their way into a place where, like me, it would soon end its short life: into the midst of the thickets, the tangled clusters of growth in the forest. At first the sky was clear, but it became overcast quickly, as full, billowy clouds covered the whole expanse. The clouds met, exploded in flashes of lightning, and became emptied of the rainwater that they had gathered within them. I pushed half of my body into a mound of tangled leaves. The rain now flooded the forest, drenching the multitude of trees and penetrating the tangle of leaves in which I tried to find shelter. I had the sensation of taking a shower under an open faucet.

A large pine cone detached itself from the tree and landed full square on Sverdlov's nose, making him wake with a start. He seized his rifle and yelled, "Philip!" When he realized that I was sitting right there, next to him, he calmed down and returned to his deep slumber.

I could find no shelter from the strong rain, and I became thoroughly drenched. There was nothing I could use to cover myself, since Sverdlov had taken off my coat and jacket from my unresisting body. I had nothing but my shirt left on my torso. Waves of cold went through me; I shivered, while my wet skin burned and itched like sulphur.

"How long am I going to be left in this tortuous suspense? When will my verdict come from the command staff? What in the world is holding it up? And why does my fate have to be so confoundedly bitter?"

Sverdlov went on sleeping. Not a trace was left of the night that had gone, and I had time enough on my hands now to ask myself all kinds of questions: Who would be given the task of carrying out the sentence against me? Sverdlov himself? Ivan Ivanovitch? Or, perhaps, out of some vicious streak, they would impose the task particularly on my good friend Mischa ...

No! I was certain Mischa would refuse to carry out the order. He would never agree to it. Sverdlov, Ivan, Grischa the Siberian — any one of them would be happy if it fell to his lot to be my executioner. Ivan, for example, did such jobs regularly, and very effectively. His gun was always loaded. His fingers tended to rest on the trigger. He needed only a signal, and he carried out the order. His work was swift, neat and accurate. He didn't miss. He did a nice, perfect job: one shot, and it was over. He was a true professional!

Like Grischa and Sverdlov, Ivan, too, was a Siberian. He would probably do his best to forget the first day of the massive German hunt against the partisans, although it wasn't many months ago but only very recently that the manhunt had begun. On that day we were lying together in one pit, and if not for my machine gun, our entire fighting division would never have gotten free of the enemy that attacked us without mercy. Of Ivan, of Sverdlov, others among us, not a trace of life would have been left but for me; or else we would all have fallen captive to the Germans.

As the fighting against our attackers continued, we finished a bottle of liquor among us, "to mark the brotherhood between us," as Ivan proclaimed in the sight of everyone, and "to mark the great bravery that Philip demonstrated," as he put it, "in those critical moments of danger." But Ivan didn't stop there. He went on to give his word on oath that if he came out of the siege alive and well, he and I would remain friends forever ...

In the bleak, grim hours we experienced that day, bullets were collected for me from every one of the partisans — not for me personally, but for the machine gun, so that it could defend us, all of us — so that I would have ammunition to use against our vicious enemy. They all gave, gladly enough, shares of their stocks of bullets, that each one of us needed so badly for himself. They knew, though, and they knew it well, that the machine gun gave us far better chances to survive the powerful enemy attack: either by breaking the siege or by letting us retreat to safety.

So they relied on me then. They all had faith in me. And we succeeded: We broke away from the enemy and retreated under cover of the barrage of fire from the machine gun that I kept steady in my hands ...

On that first day of the siege no one, not one solitary partisan, had the nerve to start a vile accusation like that against the Jews in the forest, to dare whisper that it was they who brought the Germans — forty-five thousand of them — to mount this siege against the partisans, including themselves; and if that wasn't enough, the rumors went further: It was they, the Jews in the forest, who had even led the enemy straight to our secret staff headquarters ...

Such ugly, filthy slanders could never have sprung up on the first day of the siege. Yet after a number of days they reared their poisonous heads: after our situation grew worse and we couldn't withstand the brutal push of the enemy, after they broke our resistance and struck us hard. Then, wounded, beaten down, the gentile partisans looked in their desperation for someone on whom they could hang the blame, someone they could condemn for their bitter defeat. And in the Jews among them they found their scapegoat. So of course the Jews had to be stripped of their weapons and eliminated, just as all traitors were eliminated. Of course!

All reason disappeared from their minds. Against the rapid spread of the foul accusation, no protest was of any use. With the sanction and approval of the command staff, those who pushed and promoted the rumors rode triumphantly over every obstacle and resistance. And after a day or two, the feedback became audible: You could hear people saying, "Who knows? Maybe there is some truth in it. When they're all telling the same story, there must be some kernel of truth in it."

"So today, Yechiel, they'll get rid of you also ... in a little while ... in an hour, perhaps two hours. The end has to come." The trees seemed to bring the message to me. The whispering leaves revealed to me what I could expect, what was bound to happen. "There is no escape. This is how it is. Sverdlov even prattled about my finish in his sleep, muttering that he would be the one to do it ...."

❀ ❀ ❀

They changed my place of detention. They moved me closer to the site where my division was camped. But they still kept me isolated, at a good distance away from everyone. I saw several of our group cooking food for themselves in a pot; the smell reached my nostrils, arousing the hunger in my stomach that I had felt sharply enough without their help. But a moment later, there was Sverdlov, evidently to make sure that I hadn't disappeared from the spot where he had deposited me. I looked at him, and all I saw was the angel of death, with no time to spare: Time was pressing hard on him, as he waited for the condemned man to breathe his last and be done with it.

On one of his visits he even stopped a moment near me and let me have the benefit of a few words: "You know, Philip? I really feel so sorry about you. You're a damned good machine-gunner. But what can we do? They're going to eliminate you in any case." And he gnashed his teeth like a hungry wild animal waiting impatiently to tear into its victim.

As he stood there before me, he repeated all the stupid, nasty accusations that had been leveled against us — that we Jews had brought the Germans into the forest. Without knowing why I bothered, I begged him not to believe these fantasies, because cruel people had only dreamed them up out of their evil hearts. To prove that they were lies, I pointed out, first of all, that the Germans directed their attack specifically at the Jewish family camps, and a good many poor souls had been killed there in the early hours of the hunt.

Moreover (I continued trying to get through to Sverdlov's brain), was it possible to imagine that victims of the Germans, people who had escaped the ghettos and fled to the forest, would bring the Germans in to get rid of them along with the partisans? I swore to him by everything I held dear that there wasn't an ounce of sense or a bit of foundation for these accusations. It was pure vicious cruelty to spread these rumors against the Jews.

But Sverdlov only chortled with delight. He obviously enjoyed watching me storm and fume in frustration. It was a real pleasure to him. White foam appeared on his thick lips, and his sadistic eyes sparkled, as all of him shook with delirious laughter. It was hard for me to understand how such a malignant face could also laugh.

☙ ☙ ☙

The machine gun, that was no longer mine, stood on a path off to the side, nearer to the group of partisans who were sitting and eating their hearty meal. Still guarding me, Sverdlov smiled when he saw me gazing at the gun. He seemed to want to ask me, "What's that machine gun got to do with you? You've got no relationship to it any more."

My heart was storming. My relationship to my weapon — no one could rob me of that! In the days when I was still in the ghetto of Slonim, after the first massacre, when ten thousand Jews were slaughtered within eight hours, in the course of a single day, I was one of a group of young men who hid, each in his own place of concealment, and we saved ourselves. When we couldn't hide any more, we were taken to work in the ammunition warehouses that the Russians had left behind when they fled the small city in confusion, helter-skelter. It was backbreaking work we did, but there was great reward in it: Day after day we took various pieces of weaponry out of the warehouses. Children brought us meals from their homes; and before they left, in the empty dishes that we returned to them we would put small bits and pieces: metal screws, little parts, and so on. We knew very well that by this we were putting in danger our own lives, the lives of the children, and the lives of many in the ghetto. Yet we took the risk and exposed us all to the mortal danger. We were certain that life in the ghetto was really worth nothing any more. No matter what, our lives wouldn't last much longer. We were endangering lives that the Germans would cut down in any case.

In the late hours of the night, in basements from which no light was allowed to show outside, we made whole, complete weapons from the pieces we had smuggled out of the warehouses: guns, rifles, other arms. These we buried in the ground, and in one sort of way or another, at enormous risk to life, at various times they were smuggled out to nearby forests.

So there was the machine gun now, that I had managed to put together and hide — the machine gun I had dug up from its hiding-place and brought with me. No: I couldn't stop looking at it. And I suddenly wanted to shout: "You rotten devils! Why don't you ask how that weapon was put together? How it got here? If that gun could talk, it would tell you how every screw, every bit and piece was stolen out of the arms warehouse that was guarded and watched so heavily by the German soldiers. It would tell you how I carried the bigger pieces, concealed around my body, when I left work at the end of the day. And I wasn't the only one who did this. Fellow workers did the same thing — every one of us. Every moment we walked with those parts, every step we took, our lives were in mortal danger. If we gave any kind of suspicious or unusual glance, if we made any careless move, we might give the whole operation away and bring down disaster on our heads. And yet we didn't flinch. We took the risk. We put the whole Jewish community there into danger with us, and well we knew it. But the pulsing rebellion in our hearts drove us to do such things. We didn't want to go to the death pits, to the mass graves, all docile and quiet. We wanted to fight off the death that was being forced upon us."

❀ ❀ ❀

Only the day before, I had shined and polished my machine gun. It had glistened and shone with a sparkle. Now it stood far from me; and when I gazed at it, for some reason I saw it as a bird of steel with one alarming, frightening eye. For the umpteenth time I was reminded, once again, of the evening after that bitter, terrible day, when I reached the garden of our demolished house to get the gun out of the ground where I had buried it. There it was before my eyes, whole, in perfect condition, protected from rust by the coating of heavy oil that I had given it. In the very first instant I saw it there, just as I had left it, I had a peculiar sensation, as though it was lifting itself out of the soil and moving into my quivering hands, to whisper to me: "Take me with you. Let's go together into the forest. Don't you forgive them. Strike this enemy as hard as you can, for everything they've done to you, to your family, to all those Jewish people ..."

I didn't show the enemy any mercy. I fought the Germans no less than anyone else in the squad. With my machine gun I always had to be in the front lines, where the main fighting was going on — in every action, in every battle — to defend, to protect, to kill ...

And now? Now Sverdlov told me the machine gun didn't belong to me any more. It would be given over to someone else. And I would be finished, eliminated, rubbed out ...

The skies cleared. An obliging warming sun made the blackberry bushes lift their heads again, after the rain had bent them down to the ground. I stretched out full length on the earth. The soil was still quite wet, but the kindly sun quickly dried my cotton trousers as well as my torn shirt. During the whole night I hadn't slept a bit, and I wanted to doze a little now. If an order about me came from the command staff, I reflected, it would be better if they shot me while I was asleep. I would be spared agony and suffering before the end came ...

Yet no matter how I tried to doze off, I couldn't do it. I shut my eyes, and they opened of themselves. Events of the first days kept coming back alive before my eyes — things that happened early, when the infernal lies and slanders against the Jews started spreading. A Jewish lawyer from Lemberg had fallen in the very first day of the German attack, struck down by one of their bullets when the enemy began hunting us down. His wife Anya became one of the first victims of the new, malicious attitude toward the Jews by our fellow-partisans.

During the day I served at my assigned position. Together with other partisans we did all we could to halt the advance of the enemy after they had forged their way into the forest. Toward evening we met with the members of the command staff, to report on the activities of our division in the day that had just ended; and I saw Anya being brought to their headquarters for interrogation. The woman who commanded the partisan women's division accused her of not carrying out the order given her, to clean up the area around her tent. Over this trivial, picayune matter an argument had broken out between Anya and the woman officer, whereupon the officer had put Anya under arrest, taken her weapon from her, and brought her to the command quarters.

Anya admitted her guilt in the matter and apologized for her behavior. The death of her husband that day in the battle against the Germans, she explained, had broken her, and she had simply collapsed. Such a thing, she assured them, would never happen again.

Well, the deliberations at the command headquarters took only a few minutes. Two partisans took Anya out of the tent and turned off into a side path with her. A short while later we heard a gunshot together with Anya's scream of terror. We were sitting only a few yards or meters away from the place where it happened; and we went on with our report of the events of the day, telling what our division had done in our sector of the fighting. The people there debated about the steps to be taken in preparation for the next day; but I took no further part in the conversation. I sat there as though paralyzed, as though my tongue had been taken from me.

Now I saw Anya's image materializing before me, as though risen from the grave. She came to stand before me, to half implore, half demand, "If you remain alive, if you survive all this, tell about me! Tell everything! Remember. Remember!"

But I myself was going to be sentenced to death. What did they still have to do to finish me off? — just to take me into some secluded corner, behind a tree or among the thickets, and give me one bullet in the head or the chest — only one bullet ...

Some members of the bunch sitting around the fire were having a hearty meal now with the chunks of meat that they drew out of the pot boiling over the flames. And my innards were writhing and churning with hunger. I wanted to stop the "music" in my stomach somehow. How would they react, I wondered, if I went over to them and asked for a piece of bread? — just a piece of bread? But I was angry with myself for having brought the thought to mind. I was ashamed of myself. No! I wouldn't budge from my place! I felt a wish to curse my aches and pains — all my suffering — and even the sun that was casting its glorious radiance over everything, as it slowly warmed my frozen bones ... But this I didn't do either. Not one indecent or improper word slid past my lips, as my heart continued to throb and writhe with pain. I couldn't understand how my heart wasn't altogether paralyzed by the pressure and stress, by the agonizing constraint that held me bound.

❈ ❈ ❈

I hardly noticed at all how the day went by and evening came. The sky overhead was starry, and a smiling moon traipsed steadily along, quite certainly in a mood of serenity. Well, hadn't the time come for that moon to bid me farewell and be gone from me? Did it want to be a witness to what was going to happen to me?

"In the next few hours we're all going to get out of here, Philip. We're moving on to other woods. So you don't have too much time left till ... Oh, I forget to tell you: They're going to give your machine gun to Little Kulya. You've got nothing to worry about. It'll be in good, reliable hands. That little fellow knows how to fire the thing. He's a real sharpshooter."

I listened to Sverdlov, and I didn't give any reaction. Yet neither did I feel how my body, leaning against the trunk of a pine tree, began to sink down, as though, with a will of its own, it wanted to be absorbed into the ground. His words gave me the feeling that I was living my last moments, a brief while between life and death.

Suddenly a mood of utter fear befell me, and I didn't know where it came from. I was confounded by every little sound that reached me from close by. I remained seized by a terror of the partisans, my fellow-fighters, who were sitting there, not far from me. I was even frightened now of the Germans they held captive.

And then the thought came to me: I was likely to meet my end another way. They might not kill me themselves, but turn me loose to come to grief on my own, with no way to survive. They might order me to leave the forest, to get far away from it. They had done this to other Jewish partisans, and mainly to people in the Jewish family camps who had no weapons whatever, nothing that could help them defend themselves.

A chill went through my body. The torn shirt I was wearing billowed out like a balloon, blew itself up in the wind, and collapsed. There was nothing I could use to wrap around my bare, unshod right foot. I tore grass and blackberry bushes out of the ground, and with them I covered half my body.

I could only stare with envy at those who were sitting around the fire, warming themselves. I wanted to go close for a minute, at least to draw some warmth into my uncovered, unprotected foot that was now so dreadfully cold that it was giving me stabbing pains, as though with needles. I wouldn't exchange as much as a word with the men sitting there. I wouldn't look into their eyes, so they wouldn't think I was standing there to beg them to take pity on me. I would only dry and warm my wet body that was chilled through and through, along with the frozen bones inside me — and nothing more. But my last bit of pride held, and I remained where I was. I pushed my body in among the branches and leaves, so that the foliage should protect me.

A mood of poignant, haunting reflection flooded over me now, heavy as lead. For some reason I suddenly felt as though I had been thrust between two rocks that pressed in on me. "Well," I mused, "it seems the process of dying has already begun, before the order of the command staff has arrived.

"Dear Maker of mine, Almighty who redeems and saves ..." The words touched my lips lightly, and their echo spread over the forest, to be held in the darkened void of night.

"O Mother, *Mother* ..." I held out my two hands and tried to embrace the image I saw next to me, that seemed so real. I opened my eyes wide. The density of the dark became yet more concentrated. I searched for my mother, whom I had just now felt so palpably, so actually, taking my hand in hers. And she was gone ...

"Mother! *Mother!*"

In my imagination it seemed to me that my shouting was drowning out the strong rustling of the leaves as the wind agitated them back and forth, the neighing of the horses in the camp, and the wild laughter of the partisans spread out by the fire after their glut of a meal.

I managed to shake loose from my tormenting thoughts. I spoke to myself sternly: "All right, so death is already at the door; but I mustn't let it confuse me. Whatever happens, I have to face it without anger, without ranting and complaining. I have to accept it calmly, quietly."

And I calmed down. A mood of serenity enveloped me, that was so good, so very peaceful.

❦ ❦ ❦

A man's footsteps came closer. I passed my hands through the wet grass and washed my forehead a bit. Then I noticed that even those who were sitting at the fire had their ears focused, wanting to know what those approaching footsteps were all about. They put out the fire and stretched full length on the ground; and at that moment I put out my hand to take hold of my machine gun and get ready with it for whatever might happen — forgetting completely that it wasn't mine any more, that I no longer had anything to do with it ...

"Who is that?" I wanted to shout the words, but so strong were my emotions that I couldn't get a sound out of my throat. The words that rose to my lips died in silence. He bent over me, embraced me in a powerful grip, and burst out in a fit of weeping.

"*Philip!*"

Imagine: someone was speaking my name ... in the moments before my death ... Why? What for? I was thrown out from the entire squad, the whole bunch. I didn't belong anywhere among them any more. My life was declared worthless; they didn't want it any more ...

And yet I pulled him to me, because I bore him affection. He put around me the coat he had taken off, and he stuck some sort of food into my mouth; and I had no idea why I did nothing to stop him.

"Mischa!" I protested for no reason, pushing him suddenly away from me. "This isn't the time and place for any show of affection. A new season has come upon us: a time of pogrom! Remember: I'm a Jew — so get out of here. Make sure you don't see me. Go on, Mischa, get away from me. For your own good, leave me and disappear. I have pity on you. Do you know what they're going to say about you? — "He's a friend of a Jew, a traitor!" — because it was I and others like me, of my people — who brought the Germans into the forest to hunt and attack us all ... all the partisans ... And we even revealed to them where the staff headquarters was located ... So what business do you have with me? It's true that you weren't here with us. You were away on an assignment somewhere else, and I don't know what's been happening in other places. But here, right here in our forests, in the wide stretches of wooded land where we've been operating, these partisans are killing us out, getting rid of us. When they want to 'be good' to one of our people, they just take away his weapons and drive him out of the forest. If that isn't driving him into certain death at the hands of the Germans and their collaborators, tell me what it is ...

"Oh no, my dear Mischa: This is no time for any friendship with someone like me. I've got to share that fate of my brother Jews. Go on, get out of here. Leave me ..."

❧ ❧ ❧

I woke from my sleep, not knowing how many hours had passed since Mischa sat by my side. I remembered not a word of all the things we had talked about.

When he left me, did he really go to the command staff to plead for my life? I had begged him not to do that. I advised him to go to our tent and get some rest, because I saw how dead tired he was from his traveling. I told him to lie down and go to sleep, and whatever would happen to me — would simply happen. He would remember me, and that would be all.

An incident came back to mind now: something that had happened in the first days of this massive manhunt, before Mischa left us to go off on his mission. Mischa was then the leader of a group of five of us. With the two of us we had Sverdlov, Ivan Ivanovitch, and Grischa — three of the Siberians in our division. The Germans were bearing down from every side. They blocked all the roads. And as we were moving along, Mischa suddenly felt ill as he developed a high fever, and he was unable to move a single step forward. The other three left us without even a word of parting. They simply vanished; and there I was, alone with Mischa.

The danger was immense for both of us, but never for an instant did it enter my mind to leave him to himself, in his helpless condition, in order to save my own life. The Germans were swarming everywhere, combing the forest; our worst fear now was that they might take us alive before we had a chance to end our own existence ...

Without hesitation I put Mischa over my shoulder. Heavy as he was, I carried him — or rather dragged him — almost collapsing under the load, till I found a dense, tangled thicket. With my load I burrowed my way into it ...

The Germans didn't find us. They went around and about, but never into the thicket. And finally they withdrew from the whole area, to leave us in peace. I emptied my tobacco can and boiled in it some blackberries that I gathered, and garnetberries that I found nearby; and this I fed him, till his strength returned to him.

☙ ☙ ☙

It was Mischa who woke me from my slumber. I opened my eyes, unable to believe that I had really enjoyed a good, proper sleep. I saw him standing before me, one hand holding the reins of a saddled horse. In the stern voice of a commander he ordered me to get on the horse and come with him to the nearby path.

Without knowing why, I obeyed everything he told me. Tied to a pine tree stood his horse, also saddled. We cantered out to the road and galloped off together, in complete silence. In the soundless passage of time, a new day rose. And so we reached the command headquarters.

We were kept there for hours. I was asked a multitude of questions, one of them being if I would continue fighting the Germans with a passionate dedication as I had done till the massive manhunt. There were many questions that Mischa answered for me, because I could find no words in reply. I simply choked up with emotion. I flinched from looking them in the eyes — those people who were questioning me. I felt mortified, humiliated to find that I had to beg for my life ...

That very day, plans were made to sabotage the railroad line running from Brest-Litovsk and Moscow. The machine gun was returned to me; and Mischa made me a present of his jacket. Sverdlov, however, gave me back not a thing of all the items he had taken from me: not my coat, nor my boot, nor my wrist watch. He continued strutting around in my jacket as though it had always been his. Having no choice, I wrapped my bare foot in rags, which I tied with cord.

Mischa didn't leave my side for even a small minute. But I couldn't bear to look at him directly. I felt shamed, humiliated, knowing that I had been given my life back as a gift, like a poor man holding out his hand for a rubbed-out penny ... I knew Mischa had had a hand in it: they had consented to yield to his plea for me.

No, I couldn't feel happy at this present that I had been given. It nauseated me. But on the other hand, I did nothing to oppose it. I didn't throw it back to the people who had done me this favor. I just felt degraded, abased ...

CHAPTER FOURTEEN
The Massive Manhunt

NOT ONE OF US KNEW toward what destination we were heading. We had only one purpose: to get out of the vise, to break the siege that the Germans had mounted against us. We were tired of the endless pursuit by the relentless enemy. Yet we seemed unable to break free of their grip. We couldn't find a way to elude contact with them; and every encounter cost us losses. The paved roads and pathways that crisscrossed the forest were filled with armed enemy soldiers. There was no end in sight to this terrifying state of hell.

Groping our way along, we managed to cover a distance of a few dozen miles or kilometers. At times it seemed to us that we had succeeded in breaking through the stranglehold, that we were free of their pursuit at last. But it became clear to us immediately that it wasn't so at all: All the roads ahead of us were blocked, and we were forced to go back to our starting-point. And the ring of Germans around us tightened. Here and there, a solitary partisan, or at most two or three together, succeeded in getting across a road that the Germans held in their control. It was a different story, however, when larger groups of us went on the move. Then we had to go into armed conflict, to try to break out of the encirclement. And we couldn't do it.

Our movement forward took us into swamps, into wild, desolate stretches of the forest. We were unable to go into villages, because the Germans were there too. And when they knew that the majority of the local people there helped the partisans, the Germans set whole villages on fire, destroyed the farmers' cottages, and robbed them of the pitiful little that they had.

Days went by without a bite of food for us to eat. We pulled up blackberry plants and nourished ourselves with the small, tangy fruits. Neither could we find any water fit to drink. With our mouths we squeezed damp leaves that grew in abundance, and the drops of moisture we extracted wet our parched lips.

"How are we going to stay alive?" we asked one another. "When are we going to taste some decent food again? What's going to become of us?"

Before this mass-scale manhunt had ever started, around the base where we were camped we had hung up signs on the roads that went through the forest. In huge bold letters we had warned the Germans against entering our territory: "The forests are for us," proclaimed the signs, "and you have, temporarily, the cities and towns. Entry here is forbidden. Anyone coming in will be killed." Now they had turned the tables on us. The Germans were driving us out of the forest.

We moved aimlessly about like people under a curse. We wandered from one place to another, and found nowhere to stay. We would rest a bit, and move on in our planless journey to the unknown. Sometimes we wondered aloud, "Will we ever come back to these woods where we were active till this manhunt? When? When will we be able to? How long do we have to wallow in these swamps? Which of us is going to fall on the way, unable to continue? Who is going to stay alive?"

Mischa and I marched side by side the whole time, finding the silence congenial. Words simply seemed unnecessary to us. As for me, even the machine gun that I was carrying on my back night and day seemed unnecessary. It only seemed superfluous, something I could readily throw off from me. Moreover, from constantly carrying the heavy gun, the skin on my shoulder and back became rubbed away, till I developed open, running sores; and I had nothing with which to bandage them. From time to time my shirt clung to the abraded, pustulant skin, and the aches and pains became more than my already miserable, wretched spirit could bear.

Sverdlov always looked at me with a fury in his eyes. I tried to escape from his stares as from a demon, as I realized that he couldn't forgive me for still being alive; he couldn't forgive himself for having let me escape death; and here I was back in the fighting unit, together with him. He just couldn't get used to the idea and accept it.

Time and again the question rose in my mind: How does my poor, miserable existence bother him? Why is he so disturbed if I'm still living my pathetic, little life?

From the day he had taken my boot off my foot and put it on as his own, I had walked dozens of miles, with one foot wrapped in rags that kept falling off from time to time. I never asked him to give me back what he has taken as an outright robber. I never asked him to return my wrist watch, my jacket, or my winter coat — that I needed so badly. I didn't want to exchange a word with him — not a word. I realized right from the beginning that all he had taken from me was not enough for him: It was my life he wanted, the satisfaction of never seeing me again before his eyes, or anywhere near him.

"How long can this situation continue?" I wondered, "How much longer?" In my mind I could find no answer.

❧ ❧ ❧

On that long, endless journey, especially during the hours when we rested, by day or by night, in my mind I would go over, again and again, the events of the first few weeks of this general, widespread manhunt.

I remembered Ber'l, the partisan in the Jewish fighting unit who used to join us sometimes on our task missions, always showing unusual bravery and courage in his determination to strike the Germans hard. A locksmith by profession, in his free time he was always fixing rifles for our squad. He had a pair of "golden hands," that seemed able to repair anything.

And then, in the early days of the mass manhunt, Sverdlov found him hidden in a thicket. The brutish Siberian made an attempt to confiscate his rifle, whereupon Ber'l replied (so it was told afterwards) that Sverdlov could take anything else from him that he wanted, but he would not get the rifle out of his hands. With a few lusty shouts Sverdlov brought a few of his buddies to the scene, and the lot of them dragged Ber'l off to the staff headquarters. Hardly any trial took place; hardly any thoughtful consideration or judgment was given the matter. Sverdlov merely reported that he had found the Jew with his weapon drawn, ready to shoot, and when he demanded of the Jew to give it to him, the man had refused: Under no conditions would he give it up.

They passed sentence on Ber'l at once. The command staff remembered well the battle against the German garrison stationed at the little town of Kossov. They remembered Ber'l's act of courage, when he had moved forward alone to the central position of the Germans, and threw into it a number of hand grenades — and as a result, the partisans overwhelmed the enemy and captured the little town from the Germans who fled.

In those days Ber'l had been a hero, famed and praised among the partisans. His name was transmitted to Moscow, as deserving of an award of merit. In the order of the day, Nikolai Nikolaievitch Bobakov, the squad commander, had praised the brave action of Ber'l and his dedication to the goal of destroying the enemy.

Now, with the passage of time, the situation had changed. This widespread manhunt came upon us, and we suffered setbacks and defeats; so false, baseless charges were hurled against the Jews. The devotion and courage of the Jewish fighters were forgotten, and the brave action of Ber'l too was wiped from their memory ...

One partisan who was there at the time related afterward that before his sentence was pronounced, Ber'l burst out at the members of the command staff in the tent: "Comrades," he shouted, "I won't let this rifle out of my hands! It's my life — do you hear? I stole it in the ghetto from the murderers who shed Jewish blood, the blood of my relatives and kin. If it's what your hearts desire, you can do with me what the Germans did with the Jews in the ghetto. This is all I have to tell you in the last moments of my life. You can kill me first, and then you'll be able to take the rifle from me!"

Sverdlov and Grischa took him out of the headquarters' tent by force, as Little Kulya, the shepherd, went prancing before them. I saw Ber'l as they were hauling him off among the density of trees, and my world grew dark before my eyes. I prayed for a grave to open up beneath my feet and swallow me alive. I was ashamed to glance at Ber'l's dark, flashing eyes, to see his proud look, so alert and vital. I think he saw me, sitting on the stump of a tree, and he gave a little smile. Perhaps he meant to send me a message: "Well, yes: You had Mischa pleading for you. He spoke up for you and brought you back to life when you were as good as dead. You'll go on living in companionship with your fellow-fighter Sverdlov. You're lucky ..."

"It's a worthless life," I whispered, "a shabby, rotten life compared to the hero's death of Ber'l ... I received a present from them, a gift; and it's nothing to be proud of. It's a humiliating gift — so rottenly humiliating."

After a short while, there was Little Kulya, the seventeen-year-old shepherd, parading around in Ber'l's suit of clothing. He proudly showed everybody the wrist watch with fifteen diamonds that he had received in "payment" for "carrying out the order."

"But didn't Little Kulya's hand tremble at all?" asked a voice in my mind. "He's so young, and he's already been able to learn this bloody business from those brutal Siberians? And yet, maybe," I tried to delude myself, "maybe they didn't really take his life. Maybe they only stripped him of his clothes, took away the rifle, and drove him out of the forest. Maybe they just sent him off to become a prey to the Germans that are swarming now in the forest? Perhaps Ber'l is still living, hiding out somewhere?"

Little Kulya came prancing around me now, laughing his head off as I dragged myself slowly along, because my unshod foot, with no proper footgear to protect it, often became stuck in the mud. Kulya responded with raucous scornful laughter, by which he was trying to tell me that all my trouble, all my effort to keep up with the rest, was in vain. "Don't worry," he seemed to be telling me. "You'll be freed from this burden of yours; you can be sure of that; you won't keep on like this much longer ..."

I dammed up the anger inside me, consumed by shame. A pile of curses came to my lips, that I was ready to pour out on the head of this young brat; but as not a sound escaped from my mouth, they only choked me — unbearably.

※　※　※

Just as we began crossing the road leading from Brest-Litovsk to Moscow, a unit of German soldiers discovered us. A storm of bullets, hand grenades and mortar shells came raining down on us, and we scattered in a hurry. We went down flat on the ground and crawled, each one to his own fate, each one to keep his life or find his death. Gobs of sand, like boiling-hot chalk powder, filled my mouth. Glittering golden strands of shining sunlight blocked the enemy's positions from my eyes. Bullets beyond number kept crisscrossing the air around us. The barrel of my machine gun was hot from all the rounds of ammunition that I had fired toward the enemy. For me, however, the main thing was that the clouds of dust which kept rising over the ground prevented the Germans and their bullets from locating me. Over and over again they missed their mark.

I desperately wanted to reach the other side of the road, to escape to safety, to get out of contact with the enemy. Yet every movement of mine to crawl forward on my stomach only invited a new rain of bullets, whose sole purpose was to add my body to those that were already lying in the middle of the road, sundered, full of holes like a sieve. Going ahead of me, Fedka the medic reached the middle of the road, when a hand grenade thrown at him cut off his right hand. It flew in the air, and as it landed, it seemed to explode in my face, that was all covered now with gobs of mud and filth.

Thank Heaven, somehow I still reached the other side of the road safely. I examined my body carefully, and by another miracle I found it intact, without injury. The only trouble was that my woolen trousers looked as if mice had eaten their fill of the cloth. Whole pieces were missing. The bullets aimed at me had evidently changed direction slightly, taking with them whatever they took.

We did not know yet who and how many of us were missing, but we reckoned that the number would not be small. I lay on the grass, breathing heavily, and I pondered about those fateful few seconds when my life hung in the balance. "What is one second of time when a battle is going on?" I asked myself; and I answered at once: "In normal life it's one sixtieth of a minute. It comes and goes, whizzing by, slipping out of your hand. But one second on a battlefield, in mortal combat, is a mighty long time. You can lose your life in a fraction of a second. A bullet flies through the air and heads toward you for a landing: You don't even have enough time to give a proper groan before it's all over — in a tiny part of a second ..."

We came together on the other side of the road, and a roll call was taken. Apart from Fedka, many partisans were missing from other divisions as well as ours. There was yet no way of knowing with any certainty who among them had really been killed and who had only failed to find their way to us, and so had to go on groping separately. From our division, a few of the newer partisans were missing. Likewise, Big Anton, Semyon and Sverdlov didn't turn up in the roll call. As far as Sverdlov was concerned, I didn't know if I should feel sorry that he wasn't with us. Every fighting man gone was a serious loss to us; we needed every possible man at a time like this. On the other hand, it was consoling to think that his stares, full of noxious hate for me only because I was a Jew alive, would no longer stab through my heart.

As it turned out, though, nothing had happened to Sverdlov. Late at night we heard footsteps coming closer toward our group, till we set our weapons ready to fire. We were about to shoot, but as he drew closer, the gang identified him, and we relaxed. He threw down the heavy sack that he had been carrying, and the large wide-open eyes of a young lamb looked at us in alarm.

"Ivan Ivanovitch the second," laughed the gang, grateful to him for having brought it. Without delay a good roaring fire was started in a deep pit, concealed from sight from afar. The animal was soon slaughtered, and pots were set on the fire to cook the meat. While they waited for the "feast," Sverdlov related how he had noticed the young lamb wandering alone from one place to another, bleating pathetically. He began following it, till he seized it with his two hands and brought it to us.

I sat off to the side, so that the tongues of flame hid my face from Sverdlov. He didn't ask about me; he made no attempt to find me; and I was grateful to my Maker that he ignored me or perhaps forgot about me.

❧ ❧ ❧

My feet hurt from having walked such a long time. The pain tugged at my heart, but I groaned inwardly, so that no one sitting close to me would hear me. Slowly, slowly the fire died down. The last sparks were still flying in the darkened air, to become entangled in the void of the night. My tired eyes followed them on their final course, till they became nothing.

Out of the thick darkness, the last smile of Ber'l on his way to death suddenly came to me. I clutched my head with both hands. I wanted to get the oppressive thoughts away from me; and then not only Ber'l's smile was there before my eyes, but all that had happened to other Jewish partisans. I had never even known that those other men were in the forest at all, living and fighting as members of other units. I met them or came across them only during the infernal confusion that we lived through in the early days of the massive manhunt. A great many of them were no longer alive. They had been tortured and put to death, not by the Germans but by our own fellow-fighters in the forest, by orders of the partisan commanders, or merely with their knowledge, or without even that.

The night passed by, and I didn't have a wink of sleep. Bands of light shone their way at last into our hiding place, and found the partisans tired out and fast asleep. Only the birds were stirring awake. They flew out on their first sorties and returned at once, to settle on the tree branches, where they began chirping and trilling their prayer-song of the morning to the Creator who provides for all living creatures, the Creator who would prepare food for them as well.

Rest, relaxation, ease — all stayed out of my reach. Inside me a storm was raging. There was a scream, a shout in my whole being, and it took all my strength to keep it soundless. It seemed to me that if ever that screaming shout burst out of me, it would have enough demonic force to tear everything out by the roots.

I knew how wretched I was, how utterly downtrodden and miserable. Pain filled me now only because I couldn't find the strength to overcome all the torture and torment that had come to rack my soul.

CHAPTER FIFTEEN
In Those Days

AFTER LONG WANDERING from one location to another, we found a stretch of ground full of little pools and lakes, and we settled down. We felt a good bit safer there from a sudden onslaught by the enemy.

The first night we were settled there, Little Mischka and I (he was called Little Mischka to differentiate him from tall Mischa, my friend) went out to find potatoes, so that the lot of us would have something to eat. Where should we go? Where were potatoes to be found? That we weren't told.

The region was completely strange to us. We didn't recognize the nearby villages, nor the people who lived in them. We weren't even familiar with the roads. We received two large empty sacks, and we were supposed to fill them up with potatoes. That was all. So we took our weapons and set out.

The night was clear. The moon sailing along up there above us helped find smooth walking, and we could see how to find our way among overturned trees that were strewn over the ground.

For hours we walked through the night, further and further away from the place where we had camped; and no inhabited areas or planted fields could we find wherever we looked. Then the moment came when our ears picked up a blurred echo of trampling or walking. I stretched out full length and put my ear to the ground. Now the sound was unmistakable: Thin branches were being crushed under the feet of a man or of some animal. After a short interval we clearly heard footsteps approaching. I put a slight pressure on the trigger of my machine gun. Little Mischka stretched out next to me, and he likewise became ready to fire his rifle.

As though from underground, an unarmed man suddenly appeared before us. We seized hold of him and took him into the road with us. We wanted to know whom we were dealing with, as the moon illuminated the scene. Then, as it held fast to him, my hand shook violently and let go of him. We looked at each other, and I didn't need any basic information about him. Before me stood a human living skeleton. He was tall, but either from lack of food or from illness, or for Heaven knows what reason, his body was a wreck.

The man spoke a good Russian as we talked, but from time to time he threw in a few words in Yiddish, which Mischka (of course) didn't understand. I learned from him that he was a partisan, a member of a group that had operated in one of the sections of the woods where we had previously lived. When orders came through from the upper echelons to confiscate the weapons of the Jews in the forest, he had taken his rifle and fled. He went wandering and meandering, till he reached these woods, which he recognized and knew well: He had been born and raised close by.

As we talked, I asked him in Yiddish to tell me just where we were. We were standing, said he, directly above his hidden shelter, although the entrance to it was further off. "It's a sort of long, narrow gorge, that only a wild boar can get into, if it keeps burrowing." He went on to tell me that as a rule he didn't carry his rifle with him: He was afraid he might run into other partisans, and they would surely want to take it away from him; and when he refused, they would just finish him off. So he kept his rifle in the secret gorge, with a good supply of ammunition, ready for use when it might be necessary.

Little Mischka sensed that something wasn't "kosher" here, as our conversation flowed on. Here we were talking in Russian, yet somehow strange, peculiar words were mixed in, which he didn't understand. "Come on," he snapped at me suddenly. "Let's go back with him to the base and turn him over to our officers."

That was exactly what I didn't want to do. I explained to Mischka that we had been sent to get two sacks filled with potatoes, to feed the tired and hungry men. We had to look for potatoes, find them and bring them back with us, instead of bothering with a miserable creature like this — a weak, unarmed man who went wandering around in the forest.

Arguing back and forth, I finally convinced Mischka that I was right, and he gave way. Before the poor man left us, I managed to put some shredded tobacco into his hand without Mischka's noticing anything. Now there was not a sound around us, and I judged that my fellow-Jew had been able to get back to his hidden shelter.

Before the night ended, we returned to the base. The company wasn't sleeping, as their hunger had kept them waiting for us. We emptied our sacks, while two large pots were set on the fire to boil; and we stretched out on the ground to wait ...

As always, the men began poking pointed sticks into the pots, and many brought up potatoes that were still a long way off from having cooked enough. The men just didn't have the patience to wait. By the time the cooking was done, only a flat level of potatoes remained at the bottom of the pot.

❈   ❈   ❈

The next morning I was called to staff headquarters, to report to Grigory Pavlovitch, who was taking the place of Nikolai Nikolaievitch. He was alone in the tent. When I entered, he came toward me and shook my hand, with a wide smile on his face. After a short talk that lasted only a few minutes, he suggested that we go out for some air on the forest paths. He took me by the arm, and out we marched, taking our time as we went. There was no reason for us to hurry. When we were far enough from the base, Grigory Pavlovitch started directly, without preamble, on what he had on his mind:

"When you went off last night with Little Mischka to get potatoes, you met a Jew. About what did you talk with him, in your own private language? Who is he anyway? What's he all about? Where is he hiding? I think, Philip, that if you're a loyal partisan, you won't hide anything from me; you'll tell me everything."

We chose a good spot, and sat down. Aimlessly I picked off some blackberries at hand, and ate them. When I lifted my eyes, I saw that Grigory Pavlovitch was doing the same thing.

I felt his eyes probing me now like two searchlights, trying to penetrate right into me. I spoke slowly, not trembling, not shaking, not hesitating. I hid nothing from him. I knew he was out to get me and put a finish to my life. I knew there were tears at the corners of my eyes, and I made every effort to keep them from pouring out in a flood.

I talked. From my heart rolled all that pressed on it, all that oppressed and tortured me. Grigory's looks turned softer, grew calmer. At last I seized the moment and asked him point blank, "Tell me, Commanding Officer: Now that I've given you the whole story, what do you honestly think that unfortunate man I met could have asked me? What could he have wanted from me? The only thing he could want was some advice: how and when he might be able to come back, to take his place again among the partisans, in the ranks of the fighters, where he was till this infernal manhunt began. That's all he hopes for; that's all he looks forward to, to get back and hit out at the Germans, our common enemy. All right, there is something more, and I won't hide it from you: The poor man asked me what he could do so that he shouldn't die like a dog in his shelter."

We stopped talking. All around us there was an amazing silence, broken from time to time only by the rustling of the leaves as a light breeze went through the forest ...

"Now let me ask you, Grigory Pavlovitch: As a Soviet citizen, as a commanding officer of partisans behind the enemy lines (I knew I was talking with a boldness that was crazy under the conditions, but I went on), do you think that that young Jew has the right to live and fight, just as you have the right? Just as I have the right? Just as everybody else in this forest has the right? Answer me like a man, in plain words: Tell me if the person I met doesn't deserve the right, the chance, to strike out against the Germans, the people that murdered his people, including his family. Was he sentenced finally, absolutely, that he has to remain afraid of his fellow-partisans, his fellow-fighters, because if they find him they may kill him? And this only and solely because he's a Jew?"

❧   ❧   ❧

At the spot where we had our long, open-hearted conversation, I remained alone. Grigory Pavlovitch went without me, as I wasn't ready to go back yet. I was in no hurry. I was boiling because he wouldn't give me any clear answer to my argument. In my mind I went over every word I had said, and I couldn't find anything wrong that had come bursting out of my mouth, nor even any exaggeration when I had let go and described what the Jews in the forest were forced to suffer, what the Jews in general were forced to suffer, like wind blown playthings.

Then I thought: Perhaps all that bold, daring talk to Grigory Pavlovitch was *too* bold and daring. This argument of mine, that hatred against Jews had also infected former members of the Red Army, might cost me dear. Now they might really decide to get rid of me, and they would find an excuse and an opportunity. And yet I didn't feel sorry that I had opened my heart and spoken out like that to one of our chief commanding officers. Maybe, I mused, maybe our talk would lead to some changes … It could be …

A short distance from me, a small strip of sunshine went skipping about. It leaped onto one tree, and from there it jumped like a squirrel onto another. After a few minutes it vanished altogether from my sight. The daylight shrank and expired from our world, as night thrust its way in from somewhere, to cast its darkening mantle over the woods.

I meandered slowly back to the base, as I kept taking all kinds of side paths. In my mind I went over everything I had told Grigory Pavlovitch, to see if I had deviated anywhere from the truth. No! I couldn't find a single wrong word that I had told him.

The day came when we had to leave the woods where we had been staying. Our resistance against the Germans broke, as their siege against us became too much to bear.

That day, several fighting men in our unit, headed by Sverdlov, were given the assignment of getting on the track of Dr. Zucker. He had been our medical officer, till the massive manhunt made us lose sight of him; but we knew he was now in one of the areas where the German onslaught was particularly severe and our losses were heavy.

After long searches they found him. In the name of the command staff they informed him that he had to return to our squad, to accompany us when we moved into action to break out of the siege once and for all. And then (they added) he would have to stay with us when we traveled on to other woods, where we could hold out till the siege ended and we could return to our original site.

Dr. Zucker packed his supply of medicines and got his wife and children (who were there with him) ready for the journey. Sverdlov, however, was of a different "mind": The orders of the command staff, said he, were only about Dr. Zucker. He alone had the right to accompany the squad, as a medical officer.

One of the men who went with Sverdlov told me afterwards what happened next: Dr. Zucker gave a bitter smile. If he left his wife and children behind, they were sure to be killed. Yet this fact evidently meant nothing to Sverdlov. The Russian partisans needed only the medical man.

Dr. Zucker picked up his youngest child, swaddled in rags, and pressed the little boy close to his heart. "I'm not coming with you!" he roared at Sverdlov. "Without my wife and children I'm not going with you. The Germans in the ghetto made me the same kind of offer: I could serve them as a medical officer, and my life would be safe and sound — but without my wife and children. And I turned the offer down. *Do you hear?* I won't abandon these souls that I love. You can't make me do anything as cruel as that. I won't accept your wonderful offer of life, if it will cost me the lives of my wife and children!"

We were already well on our way, traveling east, when Sverdlov and his team caught up with us. We looked at the men in wonder: Where were Dr. Zucker and his family? What happened to them? These men kept silent. Not a word could we get out of them. By the next day, though, everybody knew the story: When Dr. Zucker remained unmovable in his refusal to join the squad alone, without his family, Sverdlov ordered all his men to return, except for himself and his buddy, Grischa the Siberian. Those two remained, and they settled the matter neatly — with a few bullets — that finished off Dr. Zucker, his wife, and his children.

🦋 🦋 🦋

We had managed to scatter and try to get some rest, when German planes discovered us. When they flew low, they must have caught sight of smoke rising from the fires we had lit to get some warmth, although we had done our best to keep them concealed.

The planes made a few circuits overhead and flew off; but after a little while they came back, to drop down on us fire bombs and other explosives. Then they gained the altitude and left us; and another group of planes came along to bomb us.

In a good many places in the forest, fires broke out. We ran like mad from one spot to another. We crawled on our bellies like poisoned animals looking for a soft place to lie down and expire ... Some time went by, and we thought this enemy action from the air was over, when another group of bombers appeared and flew low, and spattered us with bullets that went in every direction.

Yet most of our confusion and terror was really unnecessary. We didn't realize that in a forest, bombs from the air were almost useless. It became clear to us that we could easily avoid injuries, unless there was a direct strike. The tangled trees with their multitude of branches misled the pilots and confused them, and the same trees absorbed most of the shells and bullets.

Only in the evening did the German air attack die down and come to an end. At twilight they hurled down on us their last load, then moved off and didn't come back. All in all, they didn't achieve very much. They had only succeeded in bewildering us and frightening us to death ...

I remember thinking: For their newspapers, and for the local population in this part of the world, they would have something to tell — boastfully. They would write and proclaim in public how they had managed to destroy entire camps and bases of "those robbers of the forests — the Jewish and Communist bandits who call themselves partisans." Well, went the thought in my mind, it wouldn't help them much. It would take only a short while for the local population to find out that we were still around, alive and kicking. The Germans hadn't wiped us out. And the Germans themselves would soon feel our punch again, when we started hitting out against them once more, to land some body blows where they could be felt.

Nevertheless, we left the area that had been bombed. There were too few of us partisans to be able to wage any kind of assault, or even to defend ourselves properly against the forces that were likely to reach the area and attack us, now that the enemy's planes had discovered us. We kept going deeper into the swampy regions, to get as far away as possible from where we had been.

As we were walking through the dense, tangled woods, someone among us noticed a blinking light of some sort penetrating from a coppice somewhere. A few men were sent out to scout the area, but when they came back they had no clear information for us. They hadn't been able to get close enough to the spot, from which, also, smoke could be seen rising. Without a thought in his brain, Little Kulka blithely burst out jokingly, "Hey! Maybe it's a bunch of Jews?"

No one paid him any mind, but my own heart was storming with doubt. "Who knows? Maybe there is something in what he said? Maybe by chance Kulka is right?"

We continued on till we were about thirty or forty yards from the site, and then the commander ordered us to open fire. When there was no response of any kind to our spurt of bullets, we moved in carefully till we reached the crackling flames; and sure enough, around them we found about twenty unarmed Jews stretched out on the ground and warming themselves. Not one of them, I noticed, had been wounded by our outburst of bullets, and I did my best to hide my joy.

The partisans didn't know what to do with these people, but the first thing they did was to rob them blind and strip them of whatever they could. Ostensibly to learn who they were and what they were about, the men searched the pockets of every one of them. If there was an article of clothing that the men liked, the poor Jew who wore it had to take it off, and one of the partisans put it on. Sverdlov, Grischa the Siberian and Little Kulka were particularly outstanding in the cruelty they showed this little group of Jews that we had found. They literally robbed them of everything they could, and rubbed their hands with delight over this "lovely treat" that had come their way in their wanderings. It had really been so worthwhile, they felt.

They would certainly have turned this group of people into a bunch of battered corpses, if not for Grigory Pavlovitch, who had come along with the squad. He gave the men strict orders not to do the Jews any physical harm. With that, however, he ordered the group of Jews to leave this area within twenty-four hours, as he planned to have the partisans settle down here.

After all that happened, I plodded along with my division now like a stranger, who really had no connection with it. My eyes looked all around, stunned. The terrifying scene of the plunder and degradation of the little group of helpless Jews created a storm in me, and I could find no peace in my heart. I could take in nothing of all that was going on around me. Some of the men spoke to me, and I didn't answer.

I was taking myself to task, harshly calling myself to account. And I condemned myself as a weakling. I was infuriated that I hadn't obeyed the thought, when it came to mind, to throw that machine gun of mine to the devil, to break it in pieces, and go join the twenty-odd plundered, pitiful Jews — to go with them out of these woods, where, by Grigory Pavlovitch's order, the squad had to camp down. I should have shared with my fellow-Jews their bitter fate!

To my sorrow I stayed, and Sverdlov came looking for me, till he found me. He hurled arguments against me, speaking with a brutal arrogance, loud and vehement. When he calmed down a bit, he finally stopped cursing me. "So tell me," he said: "How did it happen that not one bullet from such a great machine-gunner, such a terrific sharpshooter, never hit their target — never wounded even one of those people warming themselves by the fire? How did it happen? Explain it to me, Philip," he roared.

I didn't answer him. I simply turned my head the other way. When he saw that he wouldn't get a word out of me, and he couldn't find anyone to support him in his tirade — because after all, it was not only my machine gun that missed the target; none of the bullets fired had injured anybody — he went off and let me alone. I thanked my Maker in heaven that that this man, at whose murderous eyes I had avoided even looking lately, had finally let go of me and had gone his own way. I thanked my Maker that I hadn't been forced to get into a conversation with him — because then he really could have raised embarrassing questions ...

For actually that vicious Sverdlov was right in shouting at me. There was a basis for his accusations. What should I say? I take heaven and earth to witness that when the order was given to fire, I sent off a small round of bullets that certainly couldn't injure anyone

... Sverdlov, the most despicable savage I have ever known, happened to be right this time. To my great joy, however, he didn't know exactly why: He couldn't know that soon after Little Kulka chortled out scornfully, "Maybe it's a bunch of Jews," and it could be anticipated that whatever happened, the order might be given to open up with our guns at the site where the fire had been detected, I had raised up the gunsight on my weapon just a trifle, and very properly, my bullets had gone right into the trees and branches, perhaps into a few birds perched on them ...

We kept moving on. My thoughts were fixed constantly now on the group of Jews that had been ordered out of these woods. I knew they wouldn't obey the order. I knew they would continue hiding, taking cover; and they would continue suffering from the partisans who, one day or another, would find them again.

My machine gun pressed down so heavily on my shoulder. It was only by chance that I remembered that I had to adjust the gunsight back to its correct position. At any moment, at any point as we walked, we might encounter Germans lying in wait for us; and I wanted to be ready to strike at them without missing the mark and hitting the trees ...

The short summer night came to an end. A new day rose, and I went on wondering and doubting if I had a right to remain alive. What was my life now? — a gift granted me by those who had taken the lives of other Jewish partisans ... I was convinced that I had criminally sinned, that I was continuing to sin, by evading my true fate and not joining other Jews in the forest: The thought held me fast that it was a crime to have decided to go on living, in the company of a vileness called Sverdlov, in the company of Little Kulka, Ivan Ivanovitch, and so many others like them.

CHAPTER SIXTEEN
In the Swamps of Pinsk

THE DAYS BLENDED INTO THE NIGHTS, and each night expired as a new dawn rose. And we dragged our tired bodies on and on with difficulty. Wild, unkempt beards covered our faces. Grime clung to our skins, till we couldn't shake it off. Day and night we were hungry. Lice bit at us, as they festered in our underclothing and outer clothing, and even in our hats. We became disgusted, fed up with life. A general wish prevailed to spit on everything and give it all up. There was only one thing that everyone longed for, that everyone powerfully wanted: a good strong drink of vodka, to burn out all the bitterness stored up in the heart and renew our miserable spirits a little.

Wandering in the swamps as we did, without a halt, we never noticed that not only had the summer passed by but the fall too had come to an end. Strong winds blew, as the weather grew colder from day to day. The last leaves became detached from the trees, to be carried through the air this way and that, till they landed on the ground and were trampled under our feet.

Thanks to the heavy mists and fogs, and our ignorance of the local topography, we often walked by mistake into the muddy swamps, and only with difficulty did we manage to extricate ourselves and get back on more solid land.

In the nights we slept stretched out on the damp, wet ground, and my trousers were torn, quite open to the wind. The penetrating cold got to my body, until my skin shivered and shrank with its goose pimples.

One day we discovered a little island that seemed a suitable place to strike camp and settle down. We examined it, and we stayed. A few days later our patrols were able to make contact with other groups of partisans that had come into the swamp area, in the wake of a mass manhunt that had covered enormous stretches of several forests. These partisan groups came along and joined us now; and together, we felt much safer.

One evening the commanding officer gathered our whole unit together around a large bonfire. Without wasting words he told us, "Tonight one of *our* planes is going to reach us. It's going to drop down a considerable amount of weapons and ammunition, and a little something else besides."

Our glances froze as we heard this. Wheels in our brains began turning and sharpening. Right then and there some among us began arguing that from the start we had been led here in our so-called traipsing and wandering — to this island — but we were simply not let in on the secret. But then, how was it that the Soviet pilot flying "our" plane would be able to spot our island only now, a few days after we had gotten here? Then we wondered: What did the commanding officer mean when he said that apart from arms and ammunition, the plane would send down with the parachute "a little something else besides"?

These were the questions we raised among ourselves; we didn't dare ask the commander for answers, when he gave us his message curtly and added no explanations. Only after he left us did every one speak up with his own guesses and conjectures about this surprising business. And then, impatiently, hardly even believing it, we waited for the unexpected event: the arrival of the Soviet plane in the sky overhead, after it would have made its way from somewhere on the other side of the front. We waited to see with our own eyes the flying vehicle from which we were going to get presents ...

Toward midnight we reached the spot that the commanding officer had chosen. We separated widely in the area, and never stopped looking up at the sky, across which a dark layer of cloud was now spread like a broad blanket. We lay on the earth without making a sound. Only from time to time was the stillness torn by the strong hum of German transport planes, as they flew eastward to the front. The beams of their colored lights shone from the planes steadily, piercing the dark veil of night, resembling some strange cluster of stars that the sky had emitted, so that they could continue soaring through the dark under their own power.

A long while ago we had learned to recognize the flight of the German planes. We identified them by the hum of their engines. They were heavy planes, laden with a large burden of arms and ammunition. But not for them were we waiting now, and it was not them we wanted, as we lay flat on the ground, tense and impatient.

A considerable amount of time went by, and there was no sign at all of any Soviet plane heading our way. Disappointment began gnawing at us. We realized that to get to us behind the enemy lines, the plane had to run the risk of flying over the battlefront, and its route was strewn with dangerous obstacles that couldn't be ignored. It could be shot down. It could be hit and damaged. How could anyone know what happened to this airplane that was supposed to reach us? If it was not shot down, it might have been forced to turn back in midflight. How could we know?

We stood up, ready to get together and go back to our new base. And suddenly we heard a throbbing in the sky different from the humming sounds we were used to hearing. With lightning speed we lit the torches and piles of straw that we had prepared beforehand. We moved the torches in the air in all directions, to make it easy for the pilot to identify our location.

It didn't take long for the plane's crew to spot us. The aircraft circled a few times overhead, and in each circuit it dipped low to parachute down some full, heavy sacks, which we collected and brought to one place. Then the metal eagle gathered altitude, and we reckoned it had finished its mission and would begin flying back. But it only circled overhead once more, and plunging down came a sort of bundle whose contents we couldn't puzzle out. The parachute opened at once, however, and a human head lifted out of it. As it came closer, we could identify the figure of a woman. While still in the air she exclaimed happily, "Hello, comrades; hello! Give me the password, please. Come on, talk!"

We had been given the password before we left the base; and in a great single shout, we sent it flying through the air toward the figure descending gracefully. A few yards from the ground, however, the parachute became entangled in the branches of a tree. A few spry partisans climbed the tree quickly, and found that the parachutist, a young woman, held a loaded gun in her hand; attached to her belt were several hand grenades; and strapped to her shoulder was a perfectly new, shining rifle. Apart from this she also had a large bulging knapsack strapped to her back, which was nothing other than a small radio receiver and transmitter.

Partisans from all sides surrounded the young woman as she finally reached the ground. She asked everyone for his name, and immediately felt at home, as if among her people, even among her relatives — as though she had known the whole bunch of us a long time.

We all sat down on the grass. Our guest handed everybody fresh cigarettes from Moscow, as she told us what was going on at the fronts and in the homeland, and talked about the heroism of the soldiers of the Red Army in their bitter clashes with the enemy.

The next day Anna Petrovna (only after the liberation did we find out that this was only a nickname she had been given before she set out to parachute down behind the lines, in captured territory) was already sitting at her radio set, listening to the news from Moscow, and receiving orders from the overall partisan command staff, located over beyond the front, for our own forlorn staff of commanding officers. She also sent back data about our activities behind the front, and various other bits of information.

Meanwhile the cold weather was getting worse from day to day, and we still had no tents. We slept at night under the open sky, close together for warmth like a pile of logs. We became expert in all kinds of cunning ways and tricks to lighten the pain of the cold, from which we suffered now in the nights, during the hours of sleep. One person would let another, near him, fall asleep first, then pull off from him the heavy coat with which the poor man had covered himself, and the spry clever fellow now covered himself with it. It was only a question of time, however, before this clever fellow also fell asleep; and then a third one came along and pulled away his stolen coat to make it *his* cover for the night ... So one or two or several coats moved around during the night from one place to another, covering people and leaving them exposed; and when the actual owner of the coat woke shivering, frozen to the bone, there was nothing left for him to do but rage, fulminate, and hurl a string of curses into the air ...

And yet, despite the freezing weather, not one of us became sick or even developed a cold. Only the medic of our group grew angry with us for not taking the trouble to set up a tent for him, where he could receive patients and take care of them — and he came down with a cold directly, the very first night that he slept in the tent which we had to erect for him by order of the commanding officer, after he had gone and complained about it ...

Finally, when the bone-chilling weather really became

unbearable, the command staff came to the conclusion at the same time that we would be staying on this island quite a while yet. So we received orders to set up tents of the type we had lived in at the previous base. Once the order was given, within half a day we had whole rows of tents standing. We arranged "paved roads and streets" around and among the tents, and even gave them suitable names.

At a certain distance from the base a huge tent was constructed, that might have resembled a large warehouse. It was intended for a special purpose, but no one spoke about it. Very soon, however, we learned the secret: A distillery was installed there — a makeshift still — to produce the liquor that the men sorely missed.

❦ ❦ ❦

Anna Petrovna's small radio receiver-transmitter was set up not far from my tent. Through the walls of braided twigs I could see the partisans who were assigned to guard it. Seated on a low stool, her back against a heavy tree trunk, Anna Petrovna kept listening and passing on items of information. When the wind blew, she seemed to be shaken back and forth, resembling one of the branches of the wide-spreading tree, as though she was sharing their fate.

Anna Petrovna never seemed to grow tired. She worked without a stop — whereas days of complete idleness went by for us. Only the "vodka" (the "distillery") still kept operating full strength. The men drank without any restraints.

Their capacity or need for it varied from man to man. One became drunk after one or two glasses, another after ten or more. They drank by day and drank at night, and they slept a great deal, before and after slaking their continual thirst.

The harmonica used to pass from hand to hand: They played and danced and made merry. And they set up contests, fighting with daggers. The sportive contestants became wounded in their hands and faces, but they saw nothing wrong or terrible in that: It was only meant for sport, play, entertainment. In one of the contests, Kulya the Siberian made a deep gash into Nikolai Nikolaievitch's hand. Nikolai was the commanding officer of our squad — but they embraced and kissed each other on the cheek. They went on drinking together, and fell asleep arm in arm. In this kind of playful sport Ivan Ivanovitch, Grischa the Siberian, and Anton gave themselves more serious wounds — and went on drinking and dancing together. They gashed one another, shed blood, and embraced as happy comrades.

What about me? Well, I had experience. I knew only too well what such joyful shenanigans in the forest could lead to. So I made efforts not to be found anywhere near them. When my fellow-fighters took to drinking for fun, dancing, and holding their "competitive sports," I didn't just move away. I would leave my tent and disappear somewhere in the depths of the forest. I knew I would need a miracle that Grischa the Siberian or some other drunken partisan should forget that I existed. For hours on end I used to walk around in the forest, as far away from the base as possible. Though I didn't abstain absolutely from drinking, I left for them all the entertainment that went with it: the prancing and the contests with daggers. Let them cavort and enjoy themselves without me, I whispered in my heart. Let them wound one another as much as they wanted — leaving me out.

❧ ❧ ❧

One day a bunch of Ukrainians appeared, who had deserted the German army after serving in it. They told the command staff that they wanted to atone now for the sins and crimes they had committed against the Soviet motherland by fighting on the German side. So they wanted to join the partisans now.

In the first days after their arrival they were treated circumspectly, with caution. Our fighters kept an eye on them and checked their movements. Then, with lightning speed, the relationship to them changed completely: All doubt and suspicion about their loyalty vanished as if there had never been any. They sang patriotic Russian and Ukrainian songs, cavorted in their national dances and poured out expressions of love and tenderness for the dear Soviet Union.

So very soon was it completely forgotten that till only a short while ago these men had served the enemy, had participated in manhunts against us, against all the partisans. They were simply forgiven for their treachery toward the homeland. Everyone turned a blind eye to the fact that these scoundrels had sold their souls to Hitler, swearing loyalty to Nazi, fascist Germany.

They were such a happy bunch, so very jolly. They became so lovable, so endearing for the Russian partisans — for almost all of us.

I seemed to be the only one on the base who could find no happiness in the fact that the Ukrainians had been absorbed into our division. The sight of them only reminded me of the activities of their fellow-Ukrainians in our ghetto and the ghettos of other hamlets and towns in our area. There were reports enough about them and their deeds. They had stained their hands, beyond any cleansing, in Jewish blood. They had beaten and struck us down, shot, burned, destroyed. They had worked hand in hand with the Germans, serving as the main helpers of the "invincible" Nazis. Was I supposed to forget all this now?

"Why have they come here?" my mind asked; and my blood boiled. "Why have they been accepted into the partisan ranks? Why weren't they put up on trial, questioned, investigated, probed? Why haven't they been finished off, gotten rid of — as our men got rid of other traitors to our cause?

"Who will give me his hand," asked my heart, "his word of honor on it, that these men who have come and joined us now didn't take an active part in the slaughters and massacres in the ghetto of Slonim, till it was completely demolished? And now they're going to be my comrades? my fellow fighters?

"Oh no, my hand wouldn't hesitate at all," my thoughts continued, "if I were given the order to shoot them out with my machine gun, in payment for their vicious deeds wherever they were in the past; in payment for doing the dirty work of the Germans, separately or together with them. I would not quiver or shrink back by so much as a hair; my conscience wouldn't bother me a bit."

In those first days after their arrival, some among them tried to strike up a friendship with me. Quietly, calmly I thrust them away. I was unable to listen to the words of flattery that they showered on me. I moved away from them as from some evil — and they wouldn't let go of me. Uninvited, they came to my tent. Their eyes brimming with crocodile tears, they related everything that had happened to the Jews in the ghettos, "on account of those cruel, dreadful Germans"... Here and there, now and then (they added), the Germans had forced them to cooperate; but as much as they were able to (they insisted), they had avoided carrying out their orders ...

And not only that (my uninvited visitors continued): They had even helped many Jews hide out and escape. Very possibly (they continued embellishing) thanks to them some of those Jews could be found today in the forests, among the partisans ...

I couldn't listen to such phony self-glorification. I simply couldn't. "When the Germans fall into our hands," whispered my mind, "they tell the same kind of stories: they were so kind and sympathetic. They never hurt a soul. They were really anti-Nazi at heart, even communists in their outlook on life ... But for them, at least there was a bullet waiting at the end. When they finished their fairy tales they met their death in a thicket, among the bushes ... These Ukrainians who've come to join us, this jolly happy bunch, are making themselves at home among us. They feel fine by now, perfectly all right. Who knows how far they'll get to yet? Maybe they'll be getting decorations, medals of honor ... Who knows?"

However, as their standing among the partisans on the base became more solid and secure, their visits to my tent came to an end. They stopped being interested in developing ties of friendship with me. I wasn't necessary or important to them any more ...

Only one Ukrainian, named Arkady, wouldn't let go of me; and I couldn't manage to push him any distance away. For hours he sat in my tent talking to me, flooding me with tales of horror about the slaughter of the Jews in various ghettos in neighboring regions. Since he described these hair-raising happenings in such detail, I was prepared to take my oath on it that he had taken part in them with his two hands — although he stoutly denied it. Apart from this, I had the impression that his main purpose was to pain and torment me, and I began to suspect that perhaps from sadistic tendencies he was simply inventing gruesome stories that had never happened at all.

His eyes, black as pitch, never blinked while he related his tales of horror. He might have been telling me some anecdote about some character, that had nothing whatever to do with him.

One way or another, though, every word he uttered scorched me. I felt as if white-hot needles were piercing me. And I became more and more convinced that he was enjoying my torment and agony. I tried to hide it from him, to appear completely indifferent to his stories; but he, paying no attention to the face I put on, would sit in my tent till (apparently) his sadistic hunger was satisfied.

I remember one of those days, devoid of any activity, when having nothing to do, the men filled the time with drinking and shenanigan celebrations. Some partisan holiday was approaching, and so the gang had a reason to increase their "liquid rations" — in anticipation. Large bottles were emptied, and they even drank directly from jugs brought from the still.

After a long while Arkady came rolling into my tent, drunk to the world. It was getting on toward evening, but through apertures and holes in the walls, some of the remaining light of the setting sun yet thrust its way into the tent. Arkady lay stretched out on the ground near my straw pallet, and babbled away without a pause. My ears caught only fragments of words, as the white foam at his lips kept spewing them out. He was talking to himself, or to the air in the tent. Finally he rolled over closer to me. From his mouth came a blast of foul breath, with a stench that almost made me vomit.

"Philip ... doesn't ... answer ... me, *ha?* It's not nice ... not proper ... for you to talk ... with the likes of me? ... You're right, you damn devil ..."

He wiped his mouth, grew somewhat sober, and stopped stammering.

"You're so cunning, all of you. We thought there was nothing left of the whole lot of you, not a trace, not a memory. We thought we had gotten rid of you forever, once and for all. Now who knows how many of you will yet come back to life? Who knows?"

He kept talking out the worries that were on his mind, to ease his heart, and I didn't interfere to disturb him. "On the contrary," I thought. "Let this foul murderer reveal his honest self. Only now, when he is thoroughly drunk, will the truth come rattling out of his throat. This is good, very fine."

"And you, Philip — you just shut up the whole time. You don't say a word. No, I'm not afraid of you. I've been hating Jews from when I got born. Do you know? — the Soviet government couldn't find a way to change us Ukrainians. They put a lot of us in prison because we hated both you Jews and their whole regime; and it didn't help them a bit. Now there's a 'new world' waiting for us. We're going to have a whole new Europe, with Hitler the Fuehrer in control; and then we'll be the lords and masters of our soil, our own homeland. And there won't be any Jews on that land of ours. I'm telling you, there won't be any Jews in that whole new world. You understand me, Philip? We'll be free of you. You won't get up alive, never ever again!"

Arkady's mouth filled with white spittle again. He leaned close to me and revealed a deep, dark secret, which no one was supposed to know: When he fell into German hands at the start of the war, he had been taken to Berlin. For quite a while he had walked around there as a free man, having a high time. Then he was sent to a special school for Ukrainians. He received a high-ranking job with special orders, but he wasn't prepared to tell me about that; and besides, that wasn't interesting or important any more, because he had decided to leave the Germans and join the partisans.

So he prattled on and on, till he fell asleep. I left him there in my tent and went looking for Mischa. He was with our unit commander when I found him. I reported to the two of them everything I had heard from Arkady, while the man continued lying in our tent dead to the world from alcohol, lost in sweet, drunken slumberland.

❧ ❧ ❧

The three of us took a leisurely walk down the length of a narrow path, far from the camp. The forest was soundless then; all its living creatures were asleep by now. Not a breeze was stirring. Even the birds on the branches perched without moving, quite certainly fast asleep.

We breathed in the sharp, intoxicating air of the woods. So we continued walking, till we spotted the trunk of a tree. We sat on the ground and leaned against it. As the unit commander kept chatting with Arkady, I moved a bit as though for no special reason, turning my back to them, and stretched out on the ground behind Arkady. To all intents and purposes I was now studying the sky in the night, watching the moon taking its usual, normal trip. In reality I was waiting for a signal from the commander, as we had agreed beforehand. When he gave it, I gently pressed the trigger of my gun. The shot resounded in the air like a short sharp cough, as Arkady fell to the ground.

The earth was soft and muddy. It was no trouble at all to dig a ditch and hide the body in it. The commander and I sat down again, side by side. We rolled cigarettes for ourselves and lit them, and we chatted about this and that, one thing and another, as though we had forgotten what had happened only minutes earlier.

When we returned to the base, before we parted company, I suddenly remarked, "Well, there's one scoundrel less in our ranks now. *Ach*, we could use a much bigger clean-up here. We could really use it ..."

There was no one there to pull me up short and make me think what I meant, whom I had in mind. The commander didn't even answer me. He only responded with a smile, which was also meaningful.

"Yes, Philip," he said before going off in his own direction. "I believe your hand didn't even tremble ..."

❈   ❈   ❈

One morning we awoke and found the forest covered by a dense fog. We could see only a very short distance ahead of us. Only close to noon did the sky clear and the sun become visible; and the farmers' sons among us pronounced their judgment that by all the signs, we were going to have a long, hard winter.

The muddy ground hardened. In the hours of the night the blackberry bushes and the grass became covered with a thin layer of frost that didn't lift till the hours of midday. The rains stopped falling, and instead, strong winds shook the old trees violently. Many trees, without the strength to stand firm, collapsed to the ground. From others branches were torn, as though they were no more than withered leaves. We weren't even certain if our tents would hold out and wouldn't fall apart. We reckoned that the frequent gales would put them to strain and stress every which way, till they wearied them out.

But our lives went on as usual: with nothing to do. The only real work we had was to wash our laundry, such as it was, in the stream that hadn't frozen over yet. There we did our washing, and hung it up to dry on the walls of our tents, on the branches of trees, or on poles that we stuck into the ground, near our big fires.

Our white underwear had stopped being really white a long time ago. By now their color matched, fairly closely, the muddy earth around us. We rubbed and we scrubbed and we rinsed again in the waters of the stream; and when we hung it all up to dry, we saw that our clothes were not a whit whiter than before. There was no real difference to be seen between the before and the after. Yet without this washing operation, existence would have been virtually impossible for us. Through the months of the massive manhunt, little crawling creatures called lice had entrenched themselves uncommonly well in our clothing, and we were desperate for a way to get rid of them. Mischa, for example, had tried every way he knew to fight them to the death — till he gave up in despair. He admitted defeat and surrendered to them. One day he said to me in all seriousness: "First and foremost we have to catch the chieftains among them. They're really in solid, entrenched where nothing can come to them. And they're the ones who are making all the trouble."

Trouble we were certainly having. We were definitely in an unenviable situation. Those "little creatures" kept stealing our rest from us. We couldn't sleep. As we lay side by side in our tent, we never knew where any given bite came from: one of mine or one of his.

The weather outdoors kept getting colder and colder, till we hardly left our tents any more. We lay down to sleep with our clothes on. Most of us had cotton pants, and we covered ourselves with coats lined with sheep's wool that we had "requisitioned" in the past from neighboring farmers. The only trouble was that the wool went moldy soon enough on account of the moisture and dampness in our tents.

For a few days I in turn fought a vicious, battle against the "little creatures" that had entrenched themselves to fester in my clothes. Then I too admitted total defeat. Just like Mischa and others, I used all kinds of schemes and stratagems to get the better of them — and I failed. They got the better of me, till I became sick and tired of the whole thing and simply stopped my one-sided battle against them. I had no choice but to let them spread out and take possession of all my clothes. They didn't hide any more. They simply swarmed out in the open, without fear, day and night. They ruled over me with the tyranny of a heartless conqueror.

"So here we have another affliction come down on us," I groaned, as under my shirt a vicious determined attack by fleas started on my emaciated body. "Evil afflictions, brazen as hell, but decent and fair," I said jokingly. "They don't discriminate between one kind of blood and another. We all suffer from them equally, rank-and-file partisans and the chief of staff, and likewise his second-in-command, Grigory Pavlovitch; the man in charge of the horses and the old medic — even though he airs out his underwear more often than we do, and he examines those garments of his at least about ten times a day."

"It's easier to find a way to live with the devil himself — with the Germans even — than with these fiendish little creatures," grumbled one partisan as he warmed his shirt over the fire, the drafts of hot air opening it up like an umbrella or perhaps a small parachute.

"But when are we going to start hitting the Germans again, as we used to do before that big manhunt? When are we going back into our woods, and take control again there, like in the old days? Hasn't the time come yet to get moving?"

No one knew what to answer; and the questions did not even bother too many of us. But it was not easy to find what to do with the many empty hours of the day. *They* could fill the time with boozing, eating gluttonously and playing at their shenanigans. For me the empty days we had to live through were a heavy burden and a pure trouble. I spent a great deal of time stretched out on my straw pallet and taking walks outside the base. And everywhere, at every time, I was oppressed by aching, melancholy thoughts about my world that I lost, my world that had vanished, and about the bitter fate of the remnants and fragments of the Jewish people who had survived and saved themselves, and fled into the forest to take revenge, to give battle.

Truth to tell, I knew that to a certain extent I had only myself to blame for my isolation and loneliness, because I let my reflections and reminiscences have control of me. I didn't join and blend into the daily life of the partisans. I didn't learn, for example, how to play cards. I couldn't begin to make head or tail of them: I could not tell the difference between one card and another.

Perhaps it was amazing that a person could live so long in the forest among the partisans without learning to play cards.

Yet I was simply not drawn to the play and games of my fellow-fighters. I had no desire for any of it. They played ball games, they had games with guns, and fights with fisticuffs, with each contestant giving the other body blows. I confess that if I had to absorb punches from Grischa the Siberian or Sverdlov or any of the others like them, I doubt if I would ever have gotten up again on my feet afterward. And it was particularly a rousing fight with fisticuffs that they wanted to have with me — a nice chance to settle scores with me ...

A blockhead at card games, I became a symbol of complete stupidity, a hapless numbskull whose like you couldn't find in the whole forest. But in the wake of this development, I drank with them. I didn't try to evade the hard liquor.

All this had started already in the early days, after I had joined the partisans. A few of the fellows who gathered around me asked me very clearly, "What's the matter, Philip? It doesn't suit you to drink with us? Your delicate stomach can't take our special vodka?" And without waiting for an answer, they took me, with my poor bag of bones in my sorry body. Holding me by the arms, they sat me down between them, opened bottle after bottle, and served me "royally": one glass and another. And they watched me, that I shouldn't fall behind in this great spree ...

So I learned to drink. I grew used to it. As the days went by, the whole thing didn't look so skewed and weird to me any more, especially when I learned to know when to stop, when it was time to say, "Thanks a lot, but no thanks."

☙ ☙ ☙

In those days of dreary unemployment, somebody somehow took the trouble to bring to my tent a good, thick book: all the creative writings of the English poet Byron, in Russian translation. I was grateful to the one who brought it. Now I spent most of my free time reading the wonderful poetry of this famed British writer of the 19th century.

I stopped going out of the tent. In the days when Mischa was with me, I shared it with him: my impressions, the feelings I experienced from Byron's lines. I read some of the poems to him. I told him what I knew about Byron, about Goethe, about our Russian poet Pushkin, and about others. Mischa had heard of Pushkin, our renowned Russian writer, but he had never read him. On the other hand, of a poet named Byron he had never heard at all; but the poems I read to him out of the book I held in my hand appealed to him very much.

☙ ☙ ☙

Things began moving ... Under the initiative of a few individual partisans, little groups began to go out on small task missions in the area. Well, our unit was without a medical doctor, as it had been ever since we got to the swamps of Pinsk; so it was decided that we should "borrow" a doctor from somewhere close to the forest.

A detailed plan of action was worked out, and the task of

accomplishing it was given to Volodya, together with one of the younger partisans in our division.

In preparation for his job, Volodya disguised himself as a peasant woman. A farm wagon was made ready, and on a mattress of straw the youngest partisan in the camp was tenderly put down, looking for all the world like a poor sick boy. His face was wrapped in scarves that hid him almost entirely from view. In the wagon's front seat sat the "peasant woman," as "she" drove the horses to the little town of Yanova near Pinsk. There, we knew, a local woman doctor had her practice, particularly for the farm people.

Arriving in Yanova, they found the little town full of German soldiers and militiamen, patrolling its streets and roads. However, when those people saw a farm woman on the wagon weeping and wailing over a sick boy lying on the mattress, they kept away: They didn't come to the wagon to search for the usual things they always seized from the farmers: butter, eggs, cheese, ham, and so forth.

The wagon ambled on at a slow, careful pace, suitable for the very sick youth it was supposedly carrying, till it reached the house where the doctor lived and received her patients. The "visit to the doctor" of this "farm woman with the sick boy" did not take very long; but the very same day the story went through the whole little town that when people entered her clinic after "the farm woman and her sick boy" had been to see her, the doctor simply wasn't there. On one of the walls, however, a large sign had been hung, signed by some partisan named Volodya, announcing that the local doctor, Madame Fyoderov, had been conscripted by the partisans for their needs, and she would gladly continue to treat sick people from the local population who would come to her. She would certainly give "special attention" to Germans who would be so kind as to consult her at the partisans' base in the forest. German patients would be received there with all the honor due them ...

The story of the "kidnapping," how the woman doctor had been snatched away under the very noses of the Germans, when there was so very many of them in the little town, aroused scorn and laughter everywhere, making them an object of derision.

Long after the event, the Germans still grew furious when they heard people talking about the "kidnapping." For many weeks they carried out sudden manhunts and arrests in the market square of Yanova, trying to identify the wagon in which the woman had been spirited away by the partisans. They likewise began interrogating farmers from the villages who aroused their suspicions when they came into the little town. They tried to discover if there were any disguised partisans among these visiting peasants. And their surly anger became a reason for them to rob the farmers of the food products they brought to sell in town — which intensified the hatred that the rural folk felt for the German conquerors.

Two days after the woman doctor came to our camp, I had occasion to have a long talk with her. When I left her, I felt her eyes following me. I had the impression that she had wanted to tell me something, and had drawn back. Then and there I reckoned that she had wanted to reveal to me what my heart guessed: that her name might indeed be Fyoderov, but actually she was Jewish ...

Well, what I thought in my heart, Grischa and Sverdlov argued before everybody: "Are you stupid, or blind? Don't you see she's Jewish? Yes, that's what she really is!"

"Why is she hiding it, then, from me?" I wondered in my thoughts. "Why is she afraid of me, when I'm just as Jewish as she is?"

When I realized how much this meant to Sverdlov and Grischa and all their friends, how much they took to heart the question of the race or people from which she came, as she continued arguing stubbornly and persistently that she was of pure Russian origin, I left the whole matter to them. I washed my hands of it, although there were signs and indications enough to make me agree with them, that this doctor who had been taken and brought to the forest was indeed Jewish beyond question.

❧ ❧ ❧

Some kind of uproar was going on at the base. I detached myself from the book I had been holding, and went out of the tent, to hear people telling how the sentries had seized two strangers armed from head to foot, and brought them to the staff headquarters. In no time the tents emptied out, as everyone headed for the headquarters' tent.

As usual in cases of spies who had been caught, or captured Germans brought for questioning, the gathered partisans waited for the interrogation by the staff to end, so that they could receive the "guests" and take them into their hands for "special treatment"...

Ivan Ivanovitch could hardly keep still as he watched the door of the headquarters tent. He ran back and forth trying to find out details, waiting and hoping for the "prey" to fall into his hands, as though in anticipation of a large, sumptuous meal. Others kept going around and around the tent. They put their eyes to the lattice and peered inside, and saw nothing, because all was hidden from sight. Volodya, Grischa and Sverdlov held gnarled wooden staffs in their hands; others had armed themselves with iron bars, and similar weapons. They all had the impression that this time two important "fish" had been caught, and it would be really worthwhile and satisfying to "take care of them."

To everyone's great surprise, however, the interrogation within the tent went on much longer than expected. No one understood why no raised voices were heard from within, no shouting or vociferating; or why there were no gun shots fired in warning, to cast fear, as we were used to hearing when captured prisoners were questioned. The longer this business continued, the stronger grew the curiosity of the partisans outside, who had gathered in a crowd around the tent. Tempers were flaming, as many lost their patience, demanding to know what in the world was going on inside that tent.

As the many minutes went by, all kinds of rumors began flowing from mouths to ears, changing the atmosphere and the mood among the partisans — chilling it down to calmness. It didn't take long for the fact to become known that the two armed men, whom the sentries around the base had arrested and brought to the command staff, were not prisoners at all and were not spies. They were men of high rank, sent on special assignment, who had gotten to us from the motherland, from the uncaptured, unoccupied territory of "Mother Russia."

As evening fell, the order was given to gather in the area where our battalion always formed ranks. A thick fog enveloped the forest, spread across like a greyish wall. It was only by the bonfire lit in the center of the area, to shine through the fog around it, that we could find our way there.

Division by division, unit by unit, we sat down in a great circle. Then the moment came when we heard the hoarse voice — like a dull, damaged saw cutting wood — of Nikolai Nikolaievitch Bobakov, the commanding general: "Battalion, rise!"

We all stood at attention, including the commanding officers. Our two unknown visitors appeared at the fire now, adorned with medals and decorations that gleamed in the tongues of fire leaping up from the blaze.

"Our splendid army has not forgotten us," the battalion commander's voice filled the empty air. "These two men standing here before us are our brothers, members of our great nation who have been sent from the front to us, to the partisans behind the lines. They bring us word about the cruel, bitter war being fought there by our fellow soldiers, by our justly famed army, to free our homeland from the Nazi conquerors — a battle of life and death.

"Why have they come here? — to demand of us to fulfill our great national duty: to help our heroic men in their fighting, to ease the burden of our soldiers battling at the risk of their lives. They will show us the way how we have to battle the Germans; and we will obey them. So then: Let us take a new oath now and swear that we will follow their orders with our devotion, with our lives, as is right and proper for citizens of the Soviet Union."

Nikolai Nikolaievitch ended his speech with a ringing salute to the life of Stalin, to the life of the motherland, and to victory over the enemy. He raised his two hands high, formed two fat fists to wave in the air, and shouted, "Hurrah, hurrah, hur-r-rah!" And three times the assembled partisans repeated their commander's cry after him, till the whole forest trembled and shook. For a few seconds the echo of the mass shouting reverberated and rolled through the forest. It seemed as if the dense, confined space of the forest, containing the night like a fortress wall, was too narrow for the massive sound, but the volume from the multitude of throats would be able to break through and go on.

After Nikolai Nikolaievitch, one of our two visitors came close, into the circle we had made in forming ranks and standing at attention. Slowly he moved before us, striding from column to column of men, as he examined us with his large eyes opened wide. Then he returned to the center of the circle and stood before us. The flame of the huge fire lit up his swarthy face, his wrinkled forehead, his almond-colored eyes, and even the scar across his left cheek — evidently from a wound that had never healed properly.

"My dear partisans, my friends," the words left his mouth as if he was counting them, one by one, "rivers of blood are flowing now in the battle for Stalingrad. Fifteen thousand human beings — that's the price we're paying every day that we fight the enemy — fifteen thousand lives — a high enough price to pay for our victory in the future — the blood of our heroic brothers. But you have the ability, and you have the duty, to help us save victims and spare them a brutal death. Your share can become greater than ever before in this conflict and in the future victory.

"Already now your share as partisans is great enough, because you force the enemy to maintain a considerable military force to the rear of the battle lines. But with all that, you must get involved more and more in the bitter struggle against the Germans.

"This is the command you are being given: Don't let even one train get through safely over railroad tracks that you can get to. From this day on, from this moment on, you have only one assignment to carry out — to destroy the enemy: to demolish, burn, blow up bridges, roads, installations, and so on."

For a moment he was still, to look at us, at the faces of those who were standing before him. Then he continued:

"No more drinking your 'home-made vodka' till you're dead drunk. No more card-playing and shenanigans. Even robbing and pillaging the neighboring farmers has to stop. Our goal lies now behind the battle lines. Starting directly tomorrow, you have no other occupation, no other job, but to agitate the enemy wherever you can give them trouble, till they absolutely collapse. Only then can you carry with pride the name of partisan heroes … only then!"

We dispersed to our tents. Every man felt that something had been kindled within him, something of what we had known before the massive manhunt and lost perhaps on account of the manhunt, on account of the heavy pressure when the enemy bore down on us, or maybe on account of all the wandering we had to do, or else maybe because we had lost our way, our purpose, as a result of all the heavy drinking, the life of Riley that had become a chapter in the life of our brigade under the leadership of good old Nikolai Nikolaievitch Bobakov.

❖ ❖ ❖

A new order of the day started as our visitor had ordered: no more card-playing; no more drinking for the sake of getting drunk; no more entertainment and dancing to the music of the harmonica day and night; no more antics and games. We began to get busy with destructive materials for sabotage; we took to preparing land mines. We cleaned our supply of bullets, and during the day we polished our weapons.

In the nights we began to make forays into the surrounding areas, like a band of locusts. The Germans in the region began to feel our presence stinging their hides. We knew little about the people in the hamlets and villages around the swamps of Pinsk; but we began getting to them more and more often, to tell them about ourselves, about the partisans fighting a German enemy that was also their bitter enemy. We forbade the farmers to supply the Germans the quotas of milk that they demanded of them. We either took the milk for ourselves or else poured it out of the cans and jugs, just to make certain it would never get to the enemy.

For the most part we gave the farmers signed receipts for the milk, attesting that we had taken it from them; and we told these people that they could present the documents to the local German authorities. The naive farmers used to ride into town and bring the receipts, whereupon the Germans beat them severely or put them under arrest, arguing that the peasants were fooling them, that they had given away the milk and other dairy products to the partisans out of their own good will, instead of obeying the strict orders the Germans had given them.

Three days after our two important visitors reached us, I returned to the woman doctor Fyoderov the books she had lent me. Under my pillow still lay the book of Byron's poetry in Russian translation, but who had time now to read it? Everything had to give way to the work in hand: to get our arms and ammunition ready, and prepare to go out over a wide area for the purpose of inflicting some kind of damage.

It became known that one of these two high-ranking visitors was a VIP (Very Important Person) in the military-political hierarchy of the Soviet Union, and he planned to stay with us for an unlimited time. But all we ever learned about him was that he was named, or nicknamed, Maxim.

In the very first days after his arrival, he began strolling around the camp, going from one tent to another, taking an interest in what each and every one of us was doing. Actually he was on the lookout for loafers and good-for-nothings, individuals who were hiding away in their tents, drinking or playing cards. If and when he met any, there was nothing to envy them for. A few days later they were not to be seen idling anywhere on the base. Maxim sent them out on dangerous missions and serious work. Having come back from some assignment, before they had hardly had a chance to rest, he sent them off on some other task.

We were amazed and impressed by his charismatic personality; and I spent a great deal of time studying his outward appearance. There was something singular and striking about him. His thick mustache was rather a mixture of dark brown and light yellow, with its two tips well brushed, sticking out stiffly over his cheeks. He wore a Cossack hat, striped green, yellow and purple; and beneath the hat his curly russet hair stuck out. His brown boots were rather short, with the uppers turned back — typical Russian footgear. Above all, however, his eyes made the strongest impression on me: brown, with thick brows that hooded them, keeping them hidden from anyone who wanted to look into them. When the brows lifted and the eyes opened wide, something gentle could also be found in them, as well as a piercing, examining look, which made you feel that this man standing before you could read your thoughts; you would not be able to deceive him or evade him.

The first action he took stirred us up powerfully: He destroyed the "vodka" still. One day he went out to the spot early in the morning, and he found the "operation" going full blast. The vats were gurgling; the bubbling liquor sent up steam, as though a bathhouse was in operation; and a number of barrels full of cooled liquor stood before the still in plain sight, ready for drinking.

Maxim did not hesitate for a minute. He took the automatic rifle off his shoulder and sent a spurt of bullets flying into the barrels, into the vats, and into the pipes that carried off the liquor. In a very short while he turned the place into a ruin; and this done, he went back to his tent, which stood near the tent of the command staff.

When the matter became known in the camp, they went to the spot as if to a funeral. They came together to lament the destruction and mourn their loss. The scent of the liquor pouring out of the pipes, and mainly out of the barrels, spread everywhere, reaching the camp. It tickled the nostrils, teased, made tongue and palate feel dry and thirsty. Close by the still, this savory fragrance rose even from the grass and the low thickets. You could become intoxicated from the scent alone, without drinking a drop ...

"*Ai*, just one little glassful to pour down the gullet; just one last shot," groaned the "professional" drinkers, as they went scraping and foraging among the shattered barrels and vats, all so empty and desolate now. They assembled like mourners around the grave of someone dearly beloved. Not one of them had ever imagined that their precious still could be destroyed so finally, so absolutely ...

Grischa, Sverdlov and Ivan Ivanovitch got together at the spot for a meeting of minds. In whispers they discussed the tragedy and attempted to formulate plans, thinking that somehow they would find a way to salvage something, make repairs, and partly restore the still at some other spot, in secrecy. Alas, they finally had to admit defeat and concede that there was nothing to be done. Nevertheless, before they left, they searched out every broken vessel, sniffed, upended barrels, sucked at moist pipes — and couldn't find enough drops to wet their throats properly.

❦ ❦ ❦

For a few days we didn't see Maxim ever leaving the headquarters' tent. It was told that he could be found inside, leaning over a large map spread out before him, with cigarette butts strewn on the floor all around.

We reckoned that we could expect to start some large-scale operation very soon. We had only our own guesses and thoughts to go by, which passed along from one partisan to another. Yet in any case, we felt we had to be ready for some big action, or a series of specific task missions, against the enemy — about which we would be told very soon.

At that time the anniversary of the October Revolution, a

national holiday, was coming close. Every one of the *politruks* (political agents or officials of the Communist Party) gathered in the divisions the people in his unit and lectured on the significance of the October Revolution for the status of the workers.

Before the arrival of Maxim, a different "order of the day" had been planned for the October Revolution holiday. The still had been expected to supply a large quantity of liquor, for really great drinking. The celebration had been planned to last a full week, featuring ceremonies, speeches, fulsome feasts, competitive games, dances, and so on and on. Then Maxim came and changed everything. Instead of wild celebrations, they now spoke of serious, heavy attacks where the enemy was concentrated, about acts of sabotage — specifically during this national holiday.

For me, though, nothing changed. All the fine talk of the *politruk* in my division made no impression whatever on me. I doubted if he himself believed what he said. But apart from that, there was something I could not get out of my mind: While the massive manhunt was going on, this very *politruk* happened to meet a Jewish partisan, and he took away from the man his boots, his rifle, and his gold wristwatch; then he told him, "Now go to your Jews." And this Jewish partisan indeed went to his people; he shared the fate of his fellow-Jews: for after the *politruk* spoke to him, someone shot him in the back — and it was never known who it was who ended the life of this Jewish fighter after he was robbed blind and left defenseless.

There was something else, too, that I couldn't forget: When Grischa the Siberian dragged me out of my tent by force (not long after I had come into the forest and joined the partisans), and he stabbed me with his bayonet, I had called to this *politruk*, resting then in his tent next to mine, to come and help me — and he had never stirred.

So I had my reason for listening with scorn and contempt as he spoke about the brotherhood of people and nations as *the* basic, ultimate principle of the Bolshevist October Revolution. This *politruk* had shown me just how much brotherly love he had. He was the living denial of it.

☙ ☙ ☙

One evening I went out of my tent, and encountered Maxim. I saluted, and felt his glances cutting through me. I was ready to walk on, but he signaled me with a gesture to stop.

"You're our machine-gunner — right? What's your name?"

I didn't answer immediately. Instead, I examined his thick mustache, whose tips were quivering; I was surprised at the whiteness of his teeth, that gleamed as in a dark-skinned face. "He is laughing," I thought in silence. "It is a good sign."

"Yes, comrade commander," I hurried to answer now. "I'm the machine-gunner. And my name is Philip Shulimovitch." I had the impression that Maxim was annoyed because my reply had been late in coming; or perhaps he was angered because I gave special emphasis to the name Shulimovitch. He measured me with his eyes from head to foot, and his glances seemed razor sharp and furious. My feet began trembling.

"Come, Philip; let's go."

I was ready for anything that might happen now.

The night was only beginning. Before I encountered Maxim, I had planned to walk over to the team of partisans with whom I was to go out later on a task mission, to blow up a large bridge. Now that I had met Maxim, all my plans were shot to pieces.

We were walking further away from the base, and the truth was that a small terror kept gnawing at me, some kind of fear of being erased from life. "Look," said my mind: "In just the same way, while we were taking a pleasant walk and having a quiet chat, on orders of the command staff I once shot and killed Arkady the Ukrainian. Not a bird was terrified. No one heard anything. The forest swallowed the sound of the gunshot. By the time they found out at the base, Arkady's body was already rotting away, and no one became excited particularly. "Well," asked my mind, "how much less will it bother them when the same thing happens to me. Who will care? Who is going to lament my death? ... All right, then: just be prepared. Your name is Philip Shulimovitch, isn't it? Isn't that enough reason to expect the worst?"

I became more and more convinced that my intuition was right. Our dear commander Nikolai Nikolaievitch Bobakov would certainly want to get rid of me. I was one of the old-timers in the division, one of the first men to join. I knew too much about what had happened; I knew about all the things he had done. For him it was far better that the living testimony of a Jewish partisan should not survive.

We kept walking, with only the night's stillness for company. I felt the skin of my body burning, as though it had been singed by fire. And after a few minutes I grew cold, as goose pimples covered my shivering body.

"What is he waiting for?" my mind wanted to know. "Let him pull out his gun and be done with it ..."

Above us the sky became free of clouds and grew clear, as though it wanted to look splendid for me, in honor of my death. In its halo the creamy-bright moon sailed calmly along. From its lofty heights it looked down into the forest, searching, searching, till it found us. Perhaps it wanted to be present at the special event that was soon to take place.

A light wind stirred the branches of the trees. A star, a small splinter of gleaming cold, tore loose in the sky and flew off into the far distance, to expire and disappear in the black void of night.

I felt Maxim breathing near me. I could not get his stare off me. I could only keep in mind that I had to watch every move he might decide to make. Dark, pessimistic thoughts flooded my consciousness now, swelling up like a pustule. They were painful.

Impatiently I waited for Maxim to start talking. I wanted to hear his first words, to get some inkling of the point he was aiming at, the reason why he had taken me out of the base when — as I told him — it was my duty to get ready to go with the whole task force, to blow up the bridge. What was it then that he really wanted? Why had he taken me on this long walk, keeping me in suspense? — for what confounded reason?

I suddenly thought of my good friend Mischa, sleeping by himself now in the tent we shared, snoring away as usual, with no one to disturb him. He had known I was to go out on this task mission with the group, and hadn't waited for me. By his reckoning, I was to return in the early hours of the morning; and then I was to wake him so that we could share the tobacco and other items I might have with me, as we ordinarily did when either of us came back from some action or a visit to some farmers in a village ...

This coming morning, though, when he would wake from his sleep and not find me lying on the other pallet of straw, he would not know at all that I hadn't gone with the action group, that I hadn't taken any part in blowing up the bridge. It would never occur to him to think that my body, like so many other corpses, was rolling somewhere among the bushes and thickets, its life erased by orders of the command staff. Only later would he find out, and he would be the only one on the whole base to shed a tear or two over my end ... the only one ...

"And then," went my thoughts, "another partisan will move into the tent in my place. Will Mischa become friendly with him, as he became with me? Will he tell him, too, in roundabout ways, about the letters he had gotten from his fiancée? — about what she wrote? Maybe he will, and maybe it won't be like that at all. Yet nothing will really change. One man will replace another. One will clear out, go off somewhere, leaving his bed free, and another will take his place. It happens all the time, doesn't it? ...

"A day or two will go by, and the naive, unsuspecting partisans will ask, 'What happened to Philip? — you know — that machine-gunner?' And they'll get a very simple answer: 'Why, nothing ... that Jew? — You know: he's just gone; he isn't here anymore ...' "

Wrapped in my thoughts, I had forgotten entirely that Maxim was sitting beside me. When I remembered, it suddenly occurred to me that his silence was deliberate, for a specific purpose. But who knew what that purpose was?

My mind took off again on its pulsing train of thought: Taken all in all, there wouldn't be anything special or important in my being "erased": One day or another, someone walking in the woods would stumble on some rotting human bodies: the remains of spies, traitors, captured Germans whom the Soviet partisans killed out of hand. And perhaps among all these corpses there will also be the remains of a man who had borne the name Philip while he lived in the forest: A Jew who had served as a machine-gunner in the partisan unit headed by Nikolai Nikolaievitch Bobakov. Well, what would be so special about that? Would this be the only instance of a Jewish fighter being erased? Would it be anything exceptional?

"Let a little time go by," said my mind, "and as with the others, nothing will be left of me — nothing ... Only some bones will go rolling about, to get broken, stepped on, trampled underfoot ..."

"No, no, no!" suddenly screamed a voice within me. "It will never be! *Never — do you hear?* Keep your eyes open and be ready to face whatever happens!"

I moved a bit away from Maxim. His two brown eyes were shining like phosphorus. I felt his stare that never left me ... And finally he broke the silence.

He asked me to tell him about the way we had been living, day after day, till he and his colleague had gotten to us. He wanted to know about the relationships between the officers and their units ... a host of questions came at me — to which I didn't think I particularly owed him any answers. Why should *I* be his source of knowledge? I was very doubtful if he was being straight and honest with me. If he really needed this information, I thought, he could get it from certain officers easily enough. An ordinary partisan of the ranks, whoever he might be, should not answer questions of this sort.

I didn't stop staring back at him, straight into his eyes, while he spoke to me. In the look of those eyes I kept searching, trying to fathom something of his real motives. What he was saying, I hardly heard, I kept watching the movements of his hands, while with one hand of mine I wiped the sweat that kept falling from my wet brow, to appear again and again on my cheeks. Droplets fell on my clothes and coursed over my body.

Maxim rolled a cigarette for himself, lit a match, and began puffing. One hand of mine stayed the whole time in my pocket, caressing my small revolver. Not for a second did I draw my fingers away. "Let him make one move," whispered my mind, "with that loaded Mauser on his belt, and my gun comes out. I'll be able to fire ahead of him ... We'll see who shoots first."

❋   ❋   ❋

A morning breeze ruffled the pine branches. Stripes of blue stretched across the brightening sky. Wearied out, I reached my tent and lay down on my pallet of straw. I tried to fall asleep, and couldn't.

It had not been enough for Maxim to ask about the way we had been living in the forest, about the wholesale, unbridled drinking, about the way we sat around with nothing to do. He also asked about the attitude of the partisans toward the Jewish fighters; he wanted to know everything that happened to *us* till he arrived.

My answers were very detailed. I did not forget even one incident. It all came out with a clarity of precision, just as when I had spoken openly to Grigory Pavlovitch, the lieutenant of our squad. I told Maxim of the hatred for the Jews that was the inherited stock-in-trade of so many of the partisans. I told him what had happened in the wake of all the baseless criminal accusations that had been made against the Jews in the forest.

I cannot say that he wasn't startled, taken aback by what I told; but in no way was I convinced that he hadn't known of it all before.

"And so, what now?" I asked myself. "Now that he knows it all, what will be the fate of the poor, miserable Jews hiding out in the forests, with or without weapons? Will they be able to come out of hiding? Will they be accepted into the fighting units? Now that I've spoken to Maxim, will they no longer be open game for anyone to kill?"

My head was spinning. I knew sleep wouldn't come. Then dawn forced its way into the tent, flooding it with more light than the space could hold, so that the light thrust its way back out through the walls, into the open woods. I myself felt no need for it.

"Suppose there is a change for the better now," went my thoughts, "through Maxim. Who is going to benefit by it? There used to be twelve or thirteen hundred Jews concealed in the forests where we were originally, hiding in constant fear of the Germans and the Soviet partisans. In the organized active units, a few hundred Jewish fighters used to serve. Out of them all, a few dozen are left: no more. So who can benefit if there is any change? — those who aren't here any more? — the few isolated souls who have remained alive?

Everyone who is now in an active unit keeps fighting relentlessly in any case. In general he pushes his way out front in every battle, because he has such a powerful desire for revenge against the Germans — and because he doesn't want to give anybody an excuse to put a bullet in his back, when and if they decide to deal with him!"

I had told Maxim that a little while before he and his fellow-officer came to us in the forest, a group of Jewish partisans turned up, trying to find us and join. From farmers in the neighborhood they had learned where we were, and along they came in anticipation of finding their journey's end. When they were already close to the base, they encountered partisans from the Voroshilov Squad, and these partisans simply killed them all out — all. Not a soul was left of them.

The head of this group of ill-fated wanderers had been a young man from Slonim named Bobletzki. I had known him well. He was among the first to start the rebellion in the ghetto. From the ammunition warehouses of the Germans he had taken out a great deal of weaponry and supplies, which was then transported into the forest for the partisans. He was always a courageous, loyal fighter, till he fell dead in the forest — not in combat, but by a spray of bullets from the partisans ...

In the heat of the conversation I asked Maxim, I begged him, to somehow explain to me what in the world could be the background of such an attitude, such a relationship to fellow-fighters, who were combating a common enemy together with them. So many of the Jews in our forest had been killed in the same way as the Germans we took captive, or even more shamefully. Who would demand justice, revenge for us? (I asked him this.) And of whom would we demand it?

Maxim gave me no answer. We sat a long while after that without exchanging a word. In silence we stood up at last and returned to the base. We parted with a warm handshake, and that was all. With this our whole encounter ended.

Now I could only envy Mischa. He didn't even hear me come into the tent. Nor did he stir when I lay down full length on my so-called bed. He was snoring away properly, covered by his coat. Only his disorderly mop of hair stuck out, lying on the straw mattress like a bunch of bright-colored cords.

"It's just hell," I muttered to myself, "sheer plain hell for me to bear all this pain. Who is going to remain alive to tell it all? Who?"

☙ ☙ ☙

Evidently, though, in spite of everything I fell into a deep slumber. When I woke up, it was broad daylight. I tried to bring back to mind the few things that Maxim had said to me — and I couldn't remember them.

An autumn sun shone on a thick pine, tangling the treetop in its rays. I had the pleasure of welcoming into the tent two strips of golden sunshine, which found no more comfortable place to rest than on my blanket. But as it seemed, those strips of sunshine didn't feel good next to me, and they quickly stole away out of the tent.

They left me to myself, with my soul for company, and my soul could find no peace.

CHAPTER SEVENTEEN

The Spy We Caught

E WENT BACK TO THE WOODS where we had lived
until the massive manhunt. It was Maxim's decision, because he
hoped that there we would regain our vigor and go back in full swing
to fighting the enemy, especially in those regions where we had been
active before. These were the stretches of land where the German
forces were strongly spread out, where there was a great deal of
enemy movement on the roads.

Not one among us felt any pain at the firm decision. We knew
we were not going to miss either the swamps or their mosquitos that
always plagued us. Nor would we miss the constant lack of food that
we had to suffer because the neighboring farmers themselves were
impoverished enough, often going hungry for a bit of bread.

On the way back to our own woods in our own forest, we passed
through many villages where we used to visit before the ferocious
general manhunt. Many of those villages were scorched earth now,
wiped from the face of the world. The Germans had paid the farm
population back for the good help those people had given us.

In the woods, the Germans had sent up in flames large areas of
forest, so as to thin out the cover of the trees and make it difficult for

the partisans to settle back in those parts. Nevertheless, we felt good at "coming back home" after such a long, enforced absence, and we were happy to find whatever there still was in the old camp site.

For two or three days we were busy putting up tents where we had decided to settle. Immediately after that a few teams were sent out to neighboring villages that had not been stricken, to organize food supplies for the whole squad. The rest of the fighters were dispatched on missions of sabotage, to derail trains and carry out a few other hit-and-run operations.

During the early days of our renewed activity, I came back once after dawn, dreadfully tired from the successful placement of land mines on a road that was heavily used — an assignment given a small team of us. A truck carrying German soldiers had then ridden over a mine that we had planted under the cobblestones, and it blew up. Not one of the soldiers in the truck had survived.

As soon as we returned to the base, I didn't wait with the others for even something hot to drink, but hurried off to my tent, lay down on my straw mattress, and went off into long hours of deep, total slumber.

Suddenly, I awoke. Like a strong, loud cough cut short in the middle, an outburst of raucous laughter rolled into the tent. I opened my eyes, and couldn't grasp what was going on. Valentin was one of the regular messengers of the command staff, and there he was, dragging me out of the tent by my feet. Still half asleep, I could make no sense out of anything. How was it that my head was entangled in the straw of my pallet, as it was being strewn about in the tent, while my feet were outside the door, as Valentin held fast to them?

"Get up, Philip," he roared. "Get up fast. You have to come to headquarters. Maxim ..."

When I heard that name, I woke up completely, gathered my still-weary bones together, and set off quickly to the headquarters' tent.

Our conversation was short. I received an order from him to clean my machine gun well, and make ready to set out on some mission (not a word about it did he say) with Maxim alone. I held back from asking him where we were going, and what we were out to do. Shortly before we left the base, however, Maxim told me that lately, in the nearby villages, a certain man had been seen moving about: a suspicious character who presented himself to the farmers as a partisan. His story was, apparently, that he had become separated from his unit during the large general manhunt, and had lost his way, and now, he claimed, he was trying to find his unit and rejoin his fellow-fighters. According to information given the command staff, however, the man was actually gathering details about the strength of the partisans in the area, and the kinds of weapons they had. It seemed he was particularly interested in the various ways of approach to the camps of the partisans, since (as he said) he hoped to find his unit in one of these bases.

"We know further," said Maxim, "that the man appears in the villages mainly in the daytime. At night — when the partisans appear on the roads in the area — he disappears. He hides out in the house of a collaborator. That's the house we have to get to ...

"Do you think," Maxim asked me, "we have some kind of complicated job ahead of us?" Then he added immediately, "It only needs good planning and a little intelligence, plus a little luck ... With all that working together, the man will fall into our hands."

I felt his laughing eyes all over me, while I kept taking bites out of the chunk of bread I held in my hand. When I finished swallowing I answered him: "Look, there isn't any need to talk about difficulties. We'll get the man. We'll bring him here. And when it becomes clear that he's really a traitor, we'll get rid of him — as he deserves. After that it won't matter one bit if this was an easy job or not."

"You're right, Philip: we'll get him here. That's sure. But we may have to move on the paths leading right into the village of Kossova, and the area is full of German army forces. Still, let's not lose our calm and get into a panic." He laughed and added, "Remember, Philip: If we get him, the first thing to do is to give him a few good punches. Understand? He has to get hit right between the eyes, so that he doubles up and doesn't know what's going on with him. Then we overpower him easily and take him with us. That will be my job. My hands are experienced ... they're a little different from yours ... All right, then: You just gag him, stuff a good piece of cloth into his mouth, and I'll do all the rest. Agreed?"

"Of course, comrade Commander. Just as you say."

☙ ☙ ☙

As Maxim's companion on the task mission, I was given one of the best horses in the unit, and I received the lithe animal saddled. I only had to mount, and would be ready to go.

We waited till the hours of evening, and then left the base, riding slowly. There was no reason to hurry. From time to time partisan guards stopped us to demand the password; and as we gave it they let us continue our journey, while they wondered what sort of adventure was under way that brought Maxim, the top commander, riding off with me ...

In a short while we reached the village of Volchy Nury, nestling in the forest. Before the massive manhunt, the population there numbered a few hundred. The first partisans who reached it in their flight from the Germans had found refuge and safety there. The villagers gave the fleeing fighters hospitality, provided food, and directed them on to the small handfuls of partisans who had settled deeper in the forest. A long while later, when the first partisan units had reorganized under one command and were settled on a proper base, a "recruitment center" was set up at Volchy Nury, where young people could come to join in the war against the Germans.

From that time on, the villagers were under the protection of the partisans. The fighters became responsible for their safety. And the Germans, fearing the partisans' strength, made sure not to come into the village. Over the roof of one of the cottages fluttered a red flag, adorned with a hammer and sickle. This house served as a sort of official partisan headquarters, and there members of the various units sat — among them, some of our information people. It was a small partisan dominion inside the German empire of evil that spread over their captured territory.

In the early days of the widespread manhunt, yet before the Germans came into the forests in force, they overwhelmed the villages around us and cut them off from us. We lost these precious sources of our survival, that we could depend on for food. But more important, we lost our precious sources of knowledge, the farmers who had always kept us informed of the enemy's movements.

Along with other villages, the German armed forces had barged into Volchy Nury too, and made a shambles of it. They were vicious. A few hours after entering the village, they rounded up all the people and chose a large number of the men to dig large pits at the end of the village. There they threw in men, women, and children — the greater part of the village population — whom they massacred; and before they left, the Germans set the whole village on fire. Not one house was left standing.

After what happened in that village, I thought, no one could ever again voice any real complaint against the Jews for having gone to their doom like sheep to the slaughter — for having gone to die in the Holocaust without any resistance, without any strong attempt to fight back. Here were about two hundred farmers; the forest was their home ground; and these farmers, half-partisan fighters, were armed. And they let the Germans get the better of them. They went to the pits they had dug, to be turned into corpses, without lifting a hand against their murderers. What, then, should the Jews have done? — the Jews who were locked up in the ghetto; who before being taken to their death were subjected for months, months on end, perhaps a year or two, to persecution, privation and hunger? — when they were made to suffer every kind of humiliation?

As we reached the village, Maxim's face became contorted. Instead of cottages, we saw mounds of stones, and household goods singed and scorched, lying scattered at the roadsides, on the village grounds. We made our way over the farmers' fields: The wheat had not been cut. The stalks had turned dark grey, covered with dust, to bow their heads to the earth. Even the birds, as it seemed, had no great appetite for the kernels, to come pecking for them; they passed them by.

Midway in our journey the dark of night came down on us. It glided off the mountain tops, came out from the ruins, rose from the fields of withered wheat, and filled the narrow path where we were riding steadily, slowly, without a word between us.

❈   ❈   ❈

Through the fields we made our way to another village, where we wanted to stay a while. We went according to the signs we knew, and arrived exactly at the home of Gavrilok, a peasant who worked for us and served us as a loyal, devoted contact man. This Gavrilok was consumptive, miserably poor from generations back, without a strip of land of his own. Only a few months earlier, he had lost two sons: The young men led a group of partisans on a route that our fighters didn't know. As they walked ahead along a river bed, the two ran into a German ambush, and met their death together with part of the group.

In his village Gavrilok was very wary of informers, but everyone knew he was helping the partisans in their battle against the Germans. By orders of the command staff he came under our protection. The villagers were warned against harming him in any way. If anything happened to the man, they were told, the whole village would soon go up in flames.

Gavrilok lived in a miserable little hut, with almost no furniture. We found his wife, dressed in rags, sitting and spinning thread from wool that didn't belong to her, to earn some money for food for herself, or for her children if they needed it more.

Two small emaciated creatures, aged about seven or eight, peered down on us from the oven on which they sat. They stared more at our weapons than at us, actually. The urchins didn't seem frightened of us at all. They even smiled at us, as though to say, "We know everything. We're not scared of *you*."

Leaving me sitting at the table, Maxim spoke with Gavrilok in whispers, till the peasant made off somewhere in a hurry. As we sat together, we emptied a flask of liquor that we had with us, and finished the *ogurki* (cucumbers) that the woman had set on the table. While we waited for Gavrilok to return, we took off our boots and dried the heavy stockings wrapped around our feet.

One by one, people began stealing into the little house: people called to come and meet Maxim, people we knew to be secret sympathizers and supporters of the partisans' war against the Germans. When all were there, inside, the door was shut. Maxim presented himself to the men as a paratrooper who had parachuted his way down from a Soviet plane into the captured Russian territory. He told them of events and developments on the battlefront, of the courageous fight that the Red Army was waging, till the Soviet men had begun meting out stunning blows and defeats to the enemy, in a relentless barrage of combat that would continue till the Germans would be completely driven out of the entire Soviet Union, including Byelorussia.

His words made a strong impression on the peasants, lifting high their morale. Maxim demanded of them to help the partisans in every possible way. He urged them to vanquish by themselves, on their own, the traitors and collaborators with the enemy who lived in their midst.

A lively discussion followed, and as the people there were embroiled in their talk, the two of us stole out of the little house and continued on our way without arousing anyone's attention.

Around midnight we reached the approaches to the hamlet of Kossova. From afar we identified the local church, as strong lights illuminated the entire area. By the maps we had with us we knew where the fortified positions and bunkers were, in which the German soldiers were entrenched. There was a time when a Jewish partisan group had waged a strong battle against the Germans in the hamlet; and paying a heavy price in fallen men, they had overcome the enemy and captured the place. But this group of fighters didn't remain in our forests. They moved on eastward, closer to the front; and many of them fell, as we later heard, in actions against the Germans.

A long time had gone by since then, more than a year. Now the whole region was swarming with informers and spies. Collaborators, both local people and others brought in by the Germans, were helping the enemy in their grim fight against us. They gathered details about our movements in the region; they got onto the tracks of those who were helping us; they took part in ambushes and other enemy actions against us.

Silently we dismounted, and walked the horses, holding the reins loose. The machine gun was in my hand now, my finger on the trigger. I was ready for any surprise. Colored rockets sailed through the dark of the night — the Germans' way of telling the partisans in the operating area that they were not asleep, and our fighting men had better not get too close to the borders of the hamlet. Somewhere a solitary dog barked, and one or two others kept answering — probably, I thought, to show their friendly feelings for each other in these lightless hours of the night that cast fear on them too. Directly afterwards we heard outbursts of gunfire coming in spurts, as narrow bands of light swept across the black sky.

⚘ ⚘ ⚘

We tapped lightly on the cottage door, and a deep, bass voice broke through the silence within: "Who's there?"

"Open the door!" Maxim roared. According to the information we had gotten from Gavrilok, this was exactly the house where the suspected man we wanted often came.

We went in and closed the door behind us. Only a few words passed between us before we gagged and sealed the peasant's mouth and bound him well, then threw him into the cellar under the kitchen, so that he would not disturb us at our work.

We knew the man we wanted was in the habit of coming to this house regularly, just before the end of the night. So it was now clear to us that we had arrived much too early. It was, all in all, only a little past midnight. Maxim stretched out on the bed, while I sat down on a stool by the window, to watch whatever might happen outside.

Our horses stood placidly in the stable, chewing the oats we had put before them. As I sat by the window, I heard them neighing and whinnying in pleasure — quite certainly because they weren't standing now, as they always did at our base in the forest, under the open sky, exposed to wind and rain.

A strong wind beat on the windowpane, making the whole cottage shake. I saw that Maxim had fallen asleep in earnest, lying there on the bed. As for me, my heart was pulsing strongly within me now — not because I felt any fear, but because, sitting there alone in the intensity of night's darkness, I was flooded by haunting thoughts. My own harrowing mental, psychological wounds opened within me, till I almost forgot where I was ... What was I doing here, in this poor, miserable cottage? Why was I sitting on this stool, letting my tired eyes stare out into a night darker than blackness?

To rouse myself free of my oppressive thoughts, I rose and

began pacing lightly, softly back and forth across the room. The moment came when I went back to the window, and to my surprise I became aware that the dense darkness had evaporated. Night was ending at last, as a pale, wan beginning of the light revealed the large stretch of ground behind the cottage, the granary and the barn. On the cover of the well in the middle of the grounds, the pail stood upside down. A bird was perched on it, its beak hidden out of sight, tucked into its feathers. For some reason it had forgotten to wake up.

I heard footsteps approaching, and my heart clammed up in me. I felt his heavy treads like beats of the wind on the windowpane. Then I tugged Maxim by the feet, till he rolled silently off the bed.

Three taps sounded at the window. We knew this was the signal of his arrival, and we were completely sure now it was the man we wanted. I crawled on my stomach to the door. My hands and feet were shaking as though I had just risen from a sickbed, but I mustered my strength and flung the door open wide.

With his full body Maxim fell upon our "visitor." He pressed him so hard against the wall that there was nothing left for me to do. Yet I had to have *some* share in the job, for the sake of my self-respect; so I gave the back of his head a good tap with the butt of my machine gun, and on receiving this little "gift" he groaned. Maxim turned to look at me, and smiled — as though to tell me, "Well, I see you've learned something by now."

Whatever we had to do after that did not take long. We took a wagon out of the stable and harnessed the farmer's horse to it. There we put our captured suspect, having tied him up well. We left only his hands free, so that he could drive the wagon. Then we led our horses out, and mounted them. We were ready now for the trip back to our base ... but there were still some details that we had to attend to ...

On all four sides we set the cottage's thatched roof on fire. We had barely moved off when we saw huge flames leaping upward, adding their glow to the morning light.

This was not the only house we set on fire. There were others that we reached on our route, or turned out of our way to get to them. These were the homes of farmers whose sons served in the German militia, and whose owners, as soon partisans appeared in the area, would generally go and alert the Germans. Thanks to them we had lost quite a few of our men. Now we were settling the score somewhat.

We traveled on steadily, at a good pace, till we were close to the forest, when we heard the distant echoes of gunshots. The Germans, we reckoned, must have turned out to hunt for the partisans who had come in the night and operated directly under their noses, on the outskirts of the hamlet of Kossova. They could not know that all in all, only two men had come "visiting" in the area, and the two alone had done the whole job ... But we were safely away from them by now.

"Maybe we can stop and rest a while," said Maxim when we were well inside our forest. "Yes," I replied at once, "and get some food inside us. In this freezing cold," I added, "it wouldn't do any harm to put inside us a fair amount of liquor — but pure, strong stuff — to warm up the bones."

I finished off a quarter of a large loaf of farm bread. From time to time I washed it down with swallows of whiskey from a small flask that I had with me. Maxim did the same. We soon felt properly warm, with a pleasant glow in the heart.

We decided to make a thorough search of the man we had captured, who until now had been inclined to tell us nothing about himself except that his name was Volodya. We undressed him completely, and I saw that Maxim really knew where and how to search. His deft fingers soon found a message hidden within the man's shirt collar. He slit the collar open and took the thin, well-folded paper out, only to find that it was in code, which he couldn't read. And Volodya had no wish to help us.

As a sort of advance payment, on account, Maxim gave him a resounding slap across the face, so stinging that the man's skin burst in several places and blood ran freely. Not wanting to lag behind my commander, I slammed my hand into his other cheek; but compared with Maxim's blow, my effort seemed like a love tap, or like an attempt to wipe his face a bit ...

We demanded that he tell us about the Germans for whom he worked, and what it was he did for them, but the cat seemed to have swallowed his tongue. We could not get a word out of him. "Oh well," we told each other, "there's no need to hurry. We'll get back to the base, and then he'll find his tongue where he lost it. He'll talk, he'll sing. Our boys will take care of him. We're going to have fun ..."

By midday we were back in the camp. Volodya stared in terror at the men who came hurrying out of their tents to form a welcoming committee. Seeing that I was no longer needed, I looked at my two hands and saw that they were stained with blood. I went swiftly to wash them clean.

I rinsed them a long time, and dried them, but for some reason it seemed to me that the dark red-brown stains would not leave. I went back to the well and washed my hands with strong, coarse soap, as farmers always did. I poured heaps of water over my palms. I rubbed them with sand. And still I felt, disturbingly, that this blood — a human being's blood, even if the man was a traitor and an enemy — stuck fast to my hands. And who knew how long it would remain there?

❧   ❧   ❧

After a long sleep I woke. At the big, blazing fire around which the men were seated, I was told that the "boys" who had taken charge of Volodya had done wonders with him. Their fists went to work beautifully, and he soon opened his mouth and found that he had much to say.

He came from Dunevas. At the beginning of the war, as a soldier in regular service in the Red Army, he had gone over, of his own free will, to the side of the Germans. Very pleased with him, they sent him on to Berlin, and from there he was despatched to Borisov, in the captured territory of Byelorussia, where the Germans ran a special "school" for the training of spies to deal with the Soviet partisans.

It soon became clear, though, that our command staff was not going to learn anything startling, or even new, from Volodya's story. As it happened, the Soviet partisans had their own men planted in this "school," and whenever a training course ended there, every command staff would receive photos of all the men who had just been "graduated," along with full particulars about them. The information even included every man's destination — exactly where he would be sent — and details of special assignments that each one was given.

Volodya's picture too was on file at our headquarters, and so there was no need to learn anything more about this Cossack from Dunevas. That being that, Volodya was taken a distance away from the base, where some of the men attended to him. They tied him to two trees like a hammock and lit a fire beneath him to warm his hide properly. Only then did his tongue really loosen up, and he revealed details that were of considerable importance for us.

Toward evening the men brought me Volodya's suit and Cossack hat — a gift — for my help in capturing him and bringing him to the base. Happily enough, I took off my tattered, patched-up trousers infested with vermin, and threw them straight into the fire. Then on went my "new" clothes. For the first time in Heaven knew how long, perhaps since I had first fled into the forest to survive, I was wearing a whole suit, that was still fairly new. I had the impression that I must look like a character from the city who had lost his way and wandered into the forest, or else like a partisan all dressed up in this costume, waiting to be sent into the city on a special mission.

On the right lapel of the jacket there were a few bloodstains. I rinsed them off with water; yet I avoided looking at that lapel, even now that no trace of blood was left. "Well," I thought, "if I ever win any medal or decoration, I'll pin it on right there, and I'll never take it off ... so that I won't touch that spot again ..."

CHAPTER EIGHTEEN
The Cement Factory

THE DRY, COLD WEATHER pinched and bit at our hands and faces. The real winter, though, was yet ahead of us; this weather was still "mild"; but some among us thought it would be well to prepare bunkers for ourselves now, in good time — underground rooms, in place of the tents we had erected on returning from the swamps of Pinsk. The men argued that the tents would never hold up in the heavy snowstorms that were sure to come. Moreover, in the conditions of the forest, it would be a great deal warmer below the ground than above it.

The matter was argued back and forth, till it reached Maxim, and with a wave of his hand he squashed the whole idea: "What? — spend the winter months in nice underground rooms? That's not for partisans. It will be a kind of vacation camp, so that you can enjoy a bit of winter in the wonderful forest air ... What's the matter with you?" he added immediately, talking seriously. "The devil won't take you if you'll sleep in the snow. It happens to be healthy, in fact. But in any case, don't worry: I'll make sure you don't stay very much here on the base, to sit around idle at the big, warm fire. You're going to warm yourselves in the fire of action against the enemy ..."

Our renewed activity in the region raised our prestige among the local population, especially among the farmers in the villages. The missions we carried out put fear into the Germans. They had thought at first that the forests had been emptied of all partisans, that their valiant forces had gotten rid of us all in the widespread massive manhunt, exterminated the last one of us. Now their nervous systems knew that they were mistaken.

And Maxim was pleased as punch with the change that had come over us. He chortled with joy. At her transmitting equipment, Anna Petrovna sent her messages on to the main partisan headquarters in Moscow, giving precise details of our actions — mainly exact information on the losses we were inflicting on the "gloriously victorious, futuristic" Nazi enemy.

❀ ❀ ❀

After my "joint effort" with Maxim that captured the spy, the Cossack Volodya from Dunevas, I was given two days of freedom, to spend them as I pleased. I was in a state of elation. I was simply not accustomed to such "upholstered" treatment. So I rested in my tent as much as I could. I felt no great wish even to go outside and warm myself at the big fire. I enjoyed the stormy, restless wind shaking the tent back and forth, trying to take me flying off somewhere into the wild blue yonder ...

Yet the moment came when I was suddenly fed up with all this idle, pointless resting. I stood up on my two feet and went out. Ambling over to the big fire, I added a few logs to it, and the flames came to new life. One of the men on the base had forgotten a thin little book there, and I picked it up and began reading it. Over the flames I had set some water to boil, with a large dollop of honey mixed into it. So I sat by the fire now, reading and sipping my hot drink.

Someone had evidently sent Nikolai Bachor on to me, with the idea that I would be a perfect customer for him. I looked up and saw this old farmer from the village of Volchy Nury standing there, waiting to talk to me. He took out a thick, heavy book from the inside of his winter coat, and whispered into my ear, "The New Testament, and the old one, bound together — in Russian."

"It doesn't interest me, Bachor." As it happened, I knew the old farmer quite well. In his free time he would always come looking for me, to sit down beside me and draw me into conversation.

"Listen, Philip," he said now. "Listen to Bachor the old farmer. From a few sentences in this book, that your own prophets spoke, I can show you when this damned war will end. I can tell you the exact day, the hour ... It's all in here ..."

I put on an appearance of listening to him, of being interested in the prophecies he had found, while actually I kept glancing aside and reading the little book in my hand, as I was right in the middle of it. Meanwhile, however, the leaping flames of the big fire had gotten to the little book and begun making an end of it.

"Look, Philip: You're a religious man, aren't you? You believe in G-d. You can tell me; I won't give you away. I know I'm not mistaken about you."

I did not see why this old farmer should be interested in my faith and religiosity. I saw no reason why he needed any kind of answer from me — and I remained silent. Under the conditions of my existence, living as I did among Soviet partisans, subject to the authority of the Soviet military command, the wisest course for me was to keep silent, to remain anonymous and unknown, revealing nothing to anybody about my private thoughts and beliefs.

Bachor waited patiently for me to respond to his question, but my eyes kept watching the flames licking at my little book, till the last lines on the final page turned to ash.

The name of the author stayed in my mind. He was an American writer. Well, I thought, if he was still alive, I was sure he could never imagine that his modest book, good or bad as it might be, had found its way into a Russian forest where human beings were living as well as wild animals. This little book of his must have passed through many hands. Many must have lived through the adventures that he spun and wove, and either praised the book or found it distasteful — till it reached the end of its existence at this fire. In another minute the strong wind would scatter its ashes every which way, and nothing would be left of it ...

Old Bachor was evidently hurt by the fact that I would not comply with his wish, that I would not answer his questions, and I refused to accept the Russian *biblia* that he had taken the trouble to bring me. With his gnarled, withering fingers he scratched his wrinkled face and scraggly beard; then he hid the volume under the woolen vest that he wore beneath his heavy farmer's coat, and he left me in peace.

❈ ❈ ❈

On a moment's notice I was called to headquarters. When I stood at attention before him, Nikolai Nikolaievitch, the commander of the squad, ordered me to choose a few of the men and go with them out to the hamlet of Ivtzevitch. At its outskirts there was a cement factory. Everything it produced was transported to Germany; our mission was to explode the factory, so that it would not exist anymore.

"But," I protested, "we know the hamlet is full of Germans. How am I supposed to get into the outskirts with a small force like this?"

"Come on!" interrupted Maxim. "You know that area well. There's no reason why the operation shouldn't succeed. And you have your own friendly farmers in the area," he added with a smile. "As I'm told, they supply you with special tobacco and a little good liquor. They'll help you. They'll guide your team and give you all the information you need."

I saluted: "Right, Commander. The orders will be carried out, and I have every hope we'll succeed."

Late the next day, as we waited for night to fall before setting out on our mission, we sat around the big fire, cleaning our weapons. Every other minute Sonya came over. This spunky partisan was herself a native of the hamlet of Ivtzevitch, and she wanted to know all kinds of details about our assignment. When she saw me attending to my machine gun, she asked me if it was in good working order and was not giving me any trouble. Then she took her automatic rifle completely apart and cleaned every last bit and piece of it thoroughly, as she kept humming and softly singing Russian and Yiddish songs.

The men were under tension, though. We did not talk about it. We even made jokes and put up a show of laughter and good humor, but every member of our team, set to go out on this assignment, felt how serious was the job ahead of us. We knew the danger we would face if the enemy got on our tracks too early, or if we should have to wage even the smallest armed conflict with the strong German forces.

We checked one more time to make certain we had forgotten nothing out of all the items we had to take with us: bottles of benzine, explosives, matches, grenades, and so on. At last we left the warming fire and went from the base quietly, as the mantle of darkness covered us, absorbing us into the night.

For a good few hours we rattled around in the silent dark, riding in wagons and walking, till we came close to our destination. We skirted the villages and the paved roads, giving them a wide berth. We preferred to avoid entering even the friendly villages, although we had to make some exceptions and find our way to a few cottages where contacts were waiting for us: men with whom we had made arrangements beforehand.

On our way we continued, following our own twisting, winding routes. This made the journey take longer, but so we had planned it; and the result was that we did not hit any land mine or fall into any ambush.

Sonya and Yanek, a young Pole who also came from Ivtzevitch, knew better than I did all the roundabout, turning pathways and byways, and the two served as our scouts, taking the lead. When, finally, they were a few meters away from the cement factory, Sonya made Yanek go flat down on the ground. "All right," I heard her tell him, "now crawl forward on your belly, like a frog ... *nu*, like this, like this ... Don't tremble; go with confidence. You won't come to any harm ..."

Yanek reached the fence. Carefully he checked everything he had been told to check, as he scanned everything going on within the factory area. Only a few seconds went by, and from his narrow throat came a soft low whistle, as though from a hollow reed. This was the signal that we could move up to the entrance.

At that moment Sonya appeared at my side. I took out a few bottles of kerosene that I had been carrying in my knapsack, and gave them to her; but for her this was not enough. She pleaded with me to let her be the first to break into the plant. "Look," she argued, "I know this factory. I know every inch of the grounds. I know every part of the place, every structure and piece of equipment. I knew this factory inside out before the war ever started."

I gave my consent. With her in the lead, the whole team made its way into the factory grounds, and there we paired off. Each pair of men had a specific task to carry out, as we had decided only moments earlier, lying near the gate hidden from sight, before we broke through.

"All right: put your hands up!"

"Don't move. Everyone is to stay just where he is!"

The workers were stunned, struck dumb. They thought a whole unit of partisans had come to capture the place.

At our orders, the work in the factory came to a halt. All the men that the partisans found in various places in the area were gathered into a large meeting room. I explained to them the purpose of our "little visit," and assured them that in a little while, as soon as we were finished with our business, they would be able to go home and get a good long restful sleep, because there would be nothing more for them to do here.

While I was dealing with the workers, Sonya was busy on her

own. She learned that the German supervisor was due to arrive at any moment, so she asked us to wait a little bit with the explosion of the place, to give us a chance to capture this "big fish" beforehand.

Sonya hid in the sentry booth at the factory entrance, in place of the guard who had been on duty. When a horse's hoofbeats told her that its German rider was arriving at the gate, she leaped out to meet him, her automatic rifle in her hand with her finger on the trigger. As he came to a full stop, she informed him that the entire factory area was under the partisans' control, and she ordered him to dismount. Otherwise, she added, her finger would press down, and he would fall off the horse, alive no more. The well-disciplined German officer obeyed instructions and surrendered to her.

Meanwhile, the other partisans had not been idle. They dragged wood logs and placed them very close to the flammable storehouses that took up most of the grounds. Under the big furnace itself we placed two heavy masses of explosives, and poured kerosene liberally in the spots that we wanted to be sure that the huge bonfire would reach.

As for the "boss" himself, the Nazi supervisor whom Sonya had captured and disarmed, we tied him well, as though he was to be sent through the mail as an insured parcel; and we put him tenderly into the furnace. Then we sent the workers home, to spend the rest of the night in peaceful slumber; and we ourselves dispersed, each to the spot that he was to set on fire. And so we finished our job.

The entire area went up in flames. From the great furnace rose a huge column of smoke that twisted and buckled, like a vast emission of dirtied absorbent cotton that floated upward toward the sky.

On our way back to our forest we waded across the little river, as explosions continued to echo in the night's atmosphere.

At the cement factory the tall chimney of red brick suddenly collapsed and came crashing down with a mighty roar. Apparently this woke up the Germans in the hamlet of Ivtzevitch, for now the air became decorated and filled with rockets. Machine guns spattered bullets without a stop. Grenades kept exploding in every direction. But the shells and the bullets were all aimed upward into the air, as though the men who had sabotaged the factory were flying overhead now and had to be shot down.

As it happened, though, we were not flying in the air at all. There was nothing for us to do up there. We were merely sitting on the other side of the river, not far from the hamlet of Ivtzevitch. We kept laughing at them in scornful glee; and the night laughed with us.

A bright moon made its way through some clouds and appeared in all its splendor, and it too smiled to us and chuckled heartily. I could have sworn it appeared overhead now in order to thank us and congratulate us for the good, clean job we had done.

In my heart I gave thanks to Heaven that there had been no mishaps ...

CHAPTER NINETEEN
The Night of Yom Kippur

THE DAYS WERE RAINY and grey, the nights very cold. Yet nothing hindered us from going out on our missions of sabotage against the enemy. On the contrary, our activities grew more forceful with every passing day. Teams of partisans competed among themselves in their ambition to outdo one another in the number of successful strikes against the enemy.

The Germans paid us back, of course. They did everything possible to hamper us and restrain our movements on the roads. They increased their forces that guarded the routes, and waited in ambush for us at the bridges — and so inflicted heavy losses. The number of our wounded men increased, and we weren't always able to save their lives. Only a few of the men severely injured were fortunate enough to be brought to other partisan bases, where to some extent Soviet planes waited to transport them across the front lines to hospitals on free Russian soil, so that they could receive healing treatment or undergo emergency operations.

Our supply of ammunition diminished and became pitifully small. There were those who kept a few dozen bullets in their pockets, and others had not even that much. And so they began stealing from one another. At night, as the men slept in their tents or near the big fire, bullets would be taken stealthily even from a knapsack tied to a partisan's body by his belt. When morning came, shouting, cursing and execration filled the air, over this business of the bullets. The amazing thing was that no thief was ever discovered. Nor was it possible to identify the stolen ones: Everybody's bullets were rusty, and a great many were damaged.

Nothing was more precious to us than a bullet. How often could such a little object save your life, if you used it swiftly enough to finish off someone who wanted to finish you. And everybody took special care to guard the very last bullet he had. In the critical moments of intense, severe battle, every one of us made sure to have that last bullet with him — for insurance against capture. Quite a few courageous partisans used that insurance: The last bullet went by their own hand into the head or the chest, to bring a quick painless death that put them beyond the reach of the enemy ...

※　※　※

On one of those grey stormy days of bleakness, a new partisan appeared in our squad — a Jew. I did not know from where he came, or how he had been accepted into our ranks. I refrained from getting into conversation with him: I had no wish to rattle him. And so I waited for the right opportunity.

Two or three days later we happened to meet and talk. Coming from the command staff, he took a path that brought him to my tent, as I was standing outside it. He came close and told me that he had just now been given some mission to carry out, and he wanted to ask me to join him, along with two other partisans whom he would get. From the details he gave me I realized that we would have to cross the railway track running from Slonim to Byalistok, and that track was extremely well guarded by the Germans. It was regarded as too dangerous even just to cross. I asked him point blank if this did not make the task impossible.

He admitted that the track was very well watched by the enemy; but, he said, our assignment was not to damage it but only to get across, so that we could meet someone who would be there on the other side, waiting for us, and he would give us something for the squad. Chayim (that was his name, as he presented himself to me) added not another word. I was left with no idea of who that someone was, or what something he would give us for the squad.

And I did not ask. Seeking no further details, I consented to go with him.

Before we parted company he asked me for my first name; and I told him how, in my first days in the forest, the name Philip was pinned to me, and how it had permanently stuck.

I wanted to know what sort of partisan this was, who had only now come to the base and joined us, and here he was already being sent out on a mission. He was a tall man of about forty, broad boned, with a mustache adorning his lip. Looking at his eyes, I could not tell if they were black or brown, and I finally decided they were a mixture of both. He seemed to me a courageous man, of strong character, who would be ready to risk his life if and when it might be necessary.

All well and good; yet how did he get himself accepted into the squad, when so many other Jewish partisans had been driven out of life in the forest? — after so very many had been abandoned to an unmistakable fate, or had been murdered outright? I was not brazen enough to ask him, but from others I learned that for over a year and a half the man had lived in our forests, and during the whole time (as Yosef Rachmilevitch had done in the past) he had maintained a close connection with our command staff. With his dauntless courage he had roamed the villages in the hours of the day, dressed like a farmer; and from the local people he collected weapons and ammunition of all kinds — rifles, guns, bullets and so on — paying for them when necessary. By means of couriers and contact men he passed everything on to our squad. Lately, however, the situation became too hot for him. Informers and Nazi collaborators got onto his tracks and began giving details to the German militia, which were passed on to enemy intelligence.

The result was that the Germans began looking for him. They set traps for the man, hoping to catch him in one of the villages. So he was forced to come out of his obscurity and get, with all speed, to the squad that he had been helping till now.

"He is very lucky," I thought in my heart, "that he didn't come to join us before Maxim arrived to take charge — because Maxim holds the reins over almost the whole command here. And it was a pure miracle," I thought further, "that neither of those two charming Siberians, Grischa or Sverdlov, ever came across him in the village or the woods where he used to spend his nights. They would never have given a thought to all he has done for the squad, all the ammunition he has gotten for us. They would have finished him off, once they discovered he was a Jew."

❦ ❦ ❦

The two other partisans who joined us to form our small "task force" were also newcomers to the squad, like Chayim, having been accepted as partisans only a short while ago. They were young men from a village near our woods, with no combat experience whatsoever.

We had not yet left the camp area when they were seized by fear, and the further we moved away from the base the greater grew their sheer anxiety. Every whisper of a leaf in the breeze, every echo of a tread on a bough that fell from a tree, made them quiver. They went arm in arm and kept up a patter of talk the whole time, to abate the fear that they could not hide.

We too struck up a lively conversation: Chayim, the older man, veteran of the war years, and I, the young partisan on the threshold of adulthood. Our talk, however, was not out of fear. On the contrary, it livened our pace, as we paid no heed to the rapid rate of our walking. It seemed as if, on our long trek through the forest, we wanted to be able to tell each other everything that had happened to us until we met.

There had been a family in Chayim's past, with children who would have been about my age were they still among the living. They had been a source of pleasure and satisfaction to him. They did well in their learning, as they received a traditional Jewish education in his home. He earned a good living, and his income improved with the years. He lacked for nothing.

When the day of the slaughter came to the hamlet, by the decision of the "heroic" Germans, Chayim happened to be away in a village, to trade some expensive cloth for food supplies, that he planned to bring home for the family. He returned to find that he had no one to come home to. Not a soul of his family was still alive. They had all been taken to the pits and shot to death.

"I was spared," he said. "I stayed alive; but I'm like a tree that's been pulled out of the ground: It keeps knocking around from one place to another, and will never find again a fixed place for itself, because it's been pulled out of its source of life. Nothing can ever give it new life."

I put my arm through his, and somehow it felt so good to be together with him, in his presence. I felt warmed inside, and the thought flashed through my mind: father and son. It was a burning, painful sensation ...

The sun went down. A short while back, the trees had seemed to blaze in a golden light, and now they turned black as coal. The forest became dark, as though it shut its gates on us, so that we could not get out.

Chapter 19: THE NIGHT OF YOM KIPPUR / *189*

And so the night of Yom Kippur had come.

Before we left the base we had spoken about it, remembering that with nightfall, the most holy day of the year would come upon us, while we went walking in the forest. How good it would be, thought my mind, if we could be alone now; if the two of us could stop walking for a while and rest, just by ourselves, to pray and pour out our hearts before our Maker.

I wanted to rest my head on Chayim's shoulder and weep, sob out my pain into the darkness of this special night. Yet the words that I wanted to well up from my heart and flow from my mouth, to scatter and fly through the forest air till they reached heaven — those words never came to my lips. They remained imprisoned somewhere within me, and disintegrated.

We went on walking. Our goal was still far from us, and our feet continued moving. The mantle of darkness that covered us seemed to make the forest more intense and concentrated, as though it were filled with blank walls of such utter blackness. A pack of wolves was on the move somewhere not far from us, howling in the night. And we found it hard to keep going. In my imagination it seemed certain that the route we were taking would bring us not to the railroad tracks but to a different site that we were really seeking: the synagogue in the locale where I had lived. There, I expected, we would meet them all — all the people I had known and loved.

Somewhere in my mind I already heard the great blend of weeping and sobbing by all the worshippers on the night of Yom Kippur. With every step we took, the crying came closer; the murmur of prayer became clearer. I wanted to ask Chayim, to plead with him, to stop for just a bit. Perhaps we too could say the *Kol Nidrey* prayer, and entreat the Almighty to "let our supplication go up at evening, and let our outcry arrive at morning." I seemed to be confused. Everything appeared to be getting out of joint. My whole body was shaking. A fire was blazing within me, burning up the tears and the words of prayer together.

Then something strange happened. I suddenly noticed that the two young partisans who had come with us were gone. They weren't there. Perhaps they had lost contact with us on account of the dark; or else they were possessed by such terror at the thought of what might happen when the time came to cross the tracks, that they decided to return to the base. They would probably find some excuse, some way of justifying themselves, and they wouldn't come to any harm.

The truth was that I too was filled with terror over the task that awaited us. I argued with Chayim that since only the two of us were left, perhaps we weren't duty bound any more to risk crossing the tracks: We would certainly not be able to defend ourselves if we were ambushed, or if we had to face any kind of encounter with the enemy. I had the impression, however, that my words never reached Chayim. He did not want to hear them, and they never registered on his mind — perhaps because he thought it was not worth listening to what I said and responding to it. His eyes looked straight ahead and he hastened his footsteps. The glance he gave me seemed to tell me, "Every word you say is wasted. We have to get to our destination at any cost. Just don't consider your life so very precious."

As a seasoned partisan I felt as though he had slapped me across the face. I was ashamed of what I had said and thought, and tried to forget it all.

At last we were there, with the gleaming tracks in full sight. And at that very moment, not far from us, the earth seemed to fracture. It trembled and shook, as though from a powerful earthquake. The night's darkness was torn to shreds by a tremendous explosion, while a mighty flame lit up the air.

As I learned later, about a hundred meters from us, perhaps nearer, a team of partisans from our squad had found a new spot on the railroad line that was not so well defended, and had worked to derail a particular train — with astonishing success. The cars of the train now went rolling swiftly down the incline, enveloped in flames. The explosions kept going off in rapid succession, evidently because the train had been carrying a good amount of ammunition to the front.

As a child pleads with his father, I begged Chayim to let us leave the spot with all possible speed, because German soldiers would be arriving immediately from all sides, and they would fill the whole area. So in any case, I argued, we would not be able to carry out our mission; and if we did not turn back at once and get as far away from there as possible, what would we do with ourselves once we were surrounded by the enemy?

This was a man of steel. No matter how I talked and pleaded with him, he made not the slightest reply, gave not the slightest sign of softening; and finally he rebuked me: "You idiot! Right now is the very best time for us to go across the tracks. The Germans that get here will be all bothered and busy over their heads looking for our fellow-partisans. And besides, do you think it would ever occur to them that at a time like this other partisans might be floating around in the area, preparing to cross the tracks?"

His face was beaming, and his brown-black eyes shone with a brightening smile into the night.

Quickly we climbed to the top of the hill and crossed the tracks in safety. Choosing our direction, we rolled down the incline on the other side. With careful steps, but with greater confidence, we headed now for the spot where a certain man was supposed to be waiting for us, to deliver "something" to us for the squad.

Thank Heaven, all went well. By a thick oak tree we met the man, and shook hands warmly, and we took from him what we were to get. My hands were occupied now, holding two boxes of bullets that were quite heavy, and Chayim's hands too were laden. He had been "honored" with the same "gifts" as myself, with the addition of a new machine gun that had been "lifted" only a few hours earlier from a German military post in the area.

Now came the problem of getting back. We were able to cross the railroad tracks again without mishap, but only with great difficulty could we manage with the burdens we were carrying. It had been planned for four people to take them, and we were only two. When we were deeper into the forest we put our loads down and sat leaning against an oak tree.

The hour was very late. Soon the night of Yom Kippur would be drawing to an end. The boxes and our weapons lay at our feet. The wind that had accompanied us all the way grew tranquil. It was quiet in the forest now. And we also, two Jews sitting there side by side, were still.

Resting against the tree, I remembered little chapters of *Tehillim*, Psalms, that we used to say in the synagogue after the prayers on the night of Yom Kippur, and my lips began moving softly:

"*Hashem* (L-rd), how great are my troubles; so many rise gainst me. So many say to my spirit: There is no rescuing help for him in G-d ... Yet You, *Hashem*, are a protecting shield for me ... Rise up, *Hashem*, help me, G-d; for You have struck all my enemies down ...,"

I don't know if Chayim heard me murmuring these words of *Tehillim*; I don't think he did. Yet he suddenly bent his head down and burst into a flood of tears that he could not control. My heart tore within me at the sight of this strong man of dauntless spirit weeping now, broken inside. Yet I knew that his tears were mine as well; this was the agony and suffering of both of us. This was the weeping and lamentation, of a world that had been torn out by the roots. These were tears on a Yom Kippur night that had brought two surviving Jews to a tree in a lightless forest ...

Dawn came up slowly and illuminated the east. We loaded the

boxes of bullets on our shoulders, each took his weapon in his hands, and we made our way back to the base. We found the men there waiting for us, eager to receive the bullets that the whole squad needed so badly.

CHAPTER TWENTY
On the Way to the Airfield

THIN SNOWFLAKES WERE FLYING and swirling in the air, leaping upward and settling slowly. They came to rest on our clothing and clung to our faces. Before us lay a pure, white carpet of snow; but with our large, heavy boots we trampled it, leaving behind us blotches of mud and puddles of water.

"Why don't they tell us where we're headed for?"

"We set out on this mission when evening fell, and now night is here. How long do we have to keep walking like this?"

These were the kind of questions we kept asking ourselves. Whenever we set out on a task mission, we would always calculate, like thieves in the night, how many hours of darkness we had at our disposal, to fulfill our assignment before dawn came. Here we had been going steadily since evening fell, and were not getting nearer to any destination that we knew of.

What was going on? How did they suddenly discover so many twisting paths in our woods, so that we could make this night journey on them now — this journey without an end? Where did these convoluted little ways come from, that were tripping up our legs and wearying out our feet? Till this night we had never known of these sinewy pathways and never trodden on them. Who discovered them, with the old broken trees lying across them since heaven knew when? We simply found them in our way, lying one atop another, one beside another, linked together, like limbs and parts of a body; and we were forced to crawl on hands and knees to get over them.

We had gone out from the base riding on sleighs that the horses pulled. In the hours of night that were now behind us, a number of times we had to get off, unhitch the horses, and carry the sleighs on our shoulders; and in the darkness we had to help the horses get across the obstacles, together with ourselves. So in the process we had our clothes almost torn from us, and our faces scratched, as though we had gone scrapping and wrestling with one another.

All at once I became aware that we were approaching the town of S. — and a short while later I realized we were at the fence of the Jewish cemetery. It was there that a labor crew of young Jews, myself among them, had been put to work breaking tombstones, so that they could be used for paving roads. Afterwards, in the forest (but still a long while ago), I was told that a road had been paved right through the cemetery itself. For part of it whole tombstones had been used, and if you came there you could still read on them the names of people long gone from the world, with personal details.

If no one ever thoroughly plowed up the earth, the dead were still there in their graves, underneath the paved road. Yet perhaps the bulldozers had even plowed over the huge pit, the mass grave into which the bodies of thousands of Jews, from the town and its surroundings, had been thrown. Perhaps over that too a new road had been paved. On the other hand, it might still be open — a huge, gaping wound of my people open to the sky — just as it had been on the day I fled into the forest. It was reasonable to believe the Germans had left it as it was — so that they could use it for Jews who would be found in hiding, in bunkers — to bring them there, mow them down, and throw them in.

I dragged my feet forward with difficulty. Minute by minute my steps became more and more twisted. I fell and picked myself up. There were moments when I thought this whole trek of ours was only one long exercise of walking over tangles and stumbling blocks, till the end of the night; and once the dawn brought the first light of day, we would go back to the base and spend the day recovering.

We halted and leaned against the cemetery fence. Some squatted in the snow, to rest a while. And in me, memory was alive now:

❦ ❦ ❦

One day, while we were toiling away at breaking the gravestones, a wagon drew up not far from our working site. The German soldier escorting the wagon ordered the two people in it to get down. The two were Jewish, already virtual skeletons: an old man, and a woman of about thirty. The pieces of tombstone piled all about did not let the wagon get too close to the huge pit, so the soldier harried and hurried them forward to that enormous mass grave.

They passed almost directly before us. The old man was limping on one foot, and the young woman, who didn't seem to be a relative at all, held him by the hand and led him along — as a daughter might hold her weak, aged father by the hand for fear that he might stumble and fall on a way full of obstacles.

The old man's face was calm, and his lips kept moving in whispers the whole time. Every so often he lifted his eyes heavenward, as if he wanted his Maker on high to know that if it was all right with Him, as far as he was concerned he was ready to return his soul, without any complaint or grumble, to the place in eternity from which it had been taken.

All of a sudden there was the small explosion of a shot, and the old man, standing at the edge of the pit, slid into it. Uncommonly calm and serene, the woman remained standing alone now at the edge. The German was in no hurry. He had time. He fixed his clothes and shook some dust or fragments of earth out of his uniform, and only then he shot her. And she too rolled into the pit.

And we continued with our work, breaking and smashing the stones. But our hands were reluctant now. The sledgehammers they held would not obey them. We were terrified of the Germans who guarded us and continually drove us, with their curses and shouts, to work faster ... faster ...

Groans reached us from the pit, and almost drove us out of our minds. Someone among us mustered up his courage and stealthily went to the edge of the pit. He was soon back, to tell us that the woman had not been killed by the second gunshot, and she was thrashing in dreadful agony. Lying with her back over the dead old man, she had looked at him — the young fellow peering over the edge — with her eyes wide open, and asked him to beg the German soldiers to put another bullet into her body, to end her unbearable suffering. She had spoken to him in Yiddish, her mind fully clear.

Well, we begged and pleaded with the Germans to do this poor, unfortunate woman a favor and end her death agonies with one more gunshot. They laughed at us and chortled with glee. These guards of ours were no young soldiers, but German citizens getting on in years. Some were well over fifty. They loved to shoot at birds when they were in flight or perched on trees. They loved to shoot down wild pigeons and roast them over a fire. But they felt it a pity to waste a bullet on a woman half shot to death, whose screams filled the air of the cemetery. We pleaded and pleaded with them, begged and cajoled; and they would not budge: It wasn't worth it, they said. She would die in any case. Why waste a good German bullet?

After we finished our work we went to the huge pit; the screaming and shrieking had ceased a few hours ago. We covered with earth the body of the woman who had covered with her back the body of the old man.

☙ ☙ ☙

What in the world were we doing now? We seemed to be going yet once more around the area of the Jewish cemetery. I had lost count of how many times we had made the circuit; and still we were not moving closer to the town itself. At times we even drew back, moving closer to the thick forest. And meanwhile trucks rode along the main roads, filled with heavy loads covered by yellow-green tarpaulins on all sides. Other trucks were filled with German soldiers, and some were towing tanks or cannon. All the vehicles traveled eastward, toward the front.

We were moving now on winding, twisting paths. In the darkness of night's ending we must have seemed like shadows climbing walls, appearing and vanishing, now there and then gone. At long last we reached a vantage point from which we could see the houses at the edge of the town, that still lay wrapped in its mantle of sleep. Only a few outbursts of gunfire marred the silence. Perhaps on their rounds, patrolling the dark, desolate streets of the town, the German soldiers were firing into the air as they often did — to alleviate their boredom, and to throw an extra bit of fear, for no particular reason, into the local population.

We were wearing white coats over our clothing, to which we had attached white hoods that veiled our faces. The wives and children of friendly farmers near our base had worked long and hard sewing them for us, out of their own linen cloth. Many were the nights they had not slept, till the coats were ready for us. We for our part had spurred them on to work without slack, because we knew that without this white covering, we could never go out on our task mission in the season of heavy Russian snows — although what that task mission was, only the command staff knew.

We looked like creatures from another world, like demons or dead souls perhaps, that had left their graves dressed in their burial clothes, to find a healing repair for their existence, or merely to move to another burial ground.

"Philip!" Mischa broke the silence suddenly, putting his hand on my shoulder: "What's your idea about all those circuits we made, going around and around in the outskirts of the town for so many hours of the night? Now the night is about to come to an end, and the dogs have taken to barking without any let up, trying to tell their masters about us, I suppose. Don't you think we'll be discovered before the dawn comes up? Where we are now, it's so easy to kill us all out — do you hear? — till the very last one of us!"

I had no answer for him. We continued winding our way slowly, like a flock of wearied, worn-out sheep. If one of us collapsed, he dragged down with him a few others, before and behind us. We marched with difficulty among the broken trees and the mounds of branches. The twigs and tree limbs stabbed us, wounding us in the hands and feet; and not an outcry did we make. No one dared break the silence. We felt how great the danger would be if we were discovered too soon. Nor did the stillness bother us. In the long time we had spent living in the forest, we had learned to walk a good many kilometers without a single word spoken. We learned to be as silent as the night that accompanied us — the dark night that concealed the secret of our mission through the many hours since we had set out.

A sleigh came along beside us, and Mischa and I jumped on and found places to sit. We found Semyon — the one who always looked after the horses — in the driver's seat, lost now in a strong, sweet sleep. Our partisan horse moved on steadily with confidence, in the path of the sleighs riding ahead of us. Its ears were drooping. Perhaps it was likewise cantering on, half asleep, wearied out from the hardship of our long journey.

I thought about that poor creature pulling us along. My mind dwelt in general on all the animals that served us with so much devotion. More than once it happened that a partisan came back from an assignment seated in a wagon, and slowly but surely he fell fast asleep. Nothing mattered to you any more at that point. You trusted the animal harnessed to the wagon. Alone, without anyone guiding it, it would bring you back to the base. And if it encountered an obstacle that it could not cross, it would stop, stand still and wait till you awoke; or it would start neighing till you *had* to wake up.

One fearless partisan, a Georgian named Fyodor Shukrashvili, worked for weeks on his horse, till he trained it successfully to know how to act in an emergency: if it was caught in armed conflict or in an ambush. He trained it that at the sound of the outcry *Germans!* it should began prancing and galloping furiously, as if facing a fire.

Other partisans followed this Georgian's example, and imitated him in the training of their nags, till the shout *Germans!* became for our horses too a word of fear and alarm, that was meant to send them flying off in a demented fury.

Snowflakes covered the mane of the thin, bony animal that was pulling us: the sleeping Semyon, Mischa and myself. We were in a world of white now, with only the wind stirring the trees and their boughs, occasionally shaking off their mantle of snow, to reveal the grey bark that merged with the dark of night's ending.

An incident out of the past came to mind: In the past summer a small group of partisans, including me, went to a hostile village to stock up on food supplies. We loaded all sorts of good things on the wagons: white flour, barley, potatoes, dairy products, and even clothing; and a few animals as well — cows and lambs that we led out of the barns and tied to the wagons. Some of the sheep we put inside the wagons. And while we were at it, we took some honeycombs out of the beehives and ate the honey, spitting out the bees.

Satisfied with the success of our venture, we made haste to leave the village. As we passed by a cottage, we suddenly heard the door creaking open, and the old villager who lived there, a wagon-driver by trade, came close to us. "Little pigeons of mine," he pleaded, "dear children, I'm the only one in this whole village who is sympathetic to you. Believe me, I'm your friend. So listen to me: I heard people talking, saying that the Germans are preparing an ambush to trap you near the bridge. Listen to me and don't go that way ... Take the route that circles around the village of Domenyavitch. It's a muddy side road, but it's safer. The Germans won't be waiting for you there, and you'll get back alive and well."

We were five partisans in all, some of us drunk, and all feeling good; so we scorned the man's story and laughed at him, refusing to believe it ... And we fell into the trap. It was only with difficulty and with the aid of a miracle that we escaped. This is how it went:

We came safely, without any mishaps, to the bridge at the fork in the road. In the usual way, we got off the wagons before crossing the bridge, and let the horses go on by themselves; and we trailed behind slowly, at a little distance from them. We held our guns at the ready, as well as hand grenades, prepared for action. I won't say that in our stomachs there was no fear at what might happen; but we had Sonya Mayevtzevitch with us, a brave partisan who knew the region well. In the squad she was known as a dauntless young woman. And she gave courage to the rest of us, spurring us on.

"Stupid idiots!" she called out to us as she lead the way. "Why are you crawling instead of moving forward with your heads high, afraid of nothing?" She strode ahead, and we followed, like children trailing after their mother.

We crossed the bridge without accidents or surprises, and were certain that the danger was over. And so we went back onto the wagons and burst into song to greet the morning that had just risen, waking the birds from their slumber as we went. An indescribable fragrance rose from the plants and grasses around us, and spread through the fresh, dewy air of the new day.

And then we caught it.

We were already near the entrance to our forest, riding along on a dusty side road, when an outburst of gunshots suddenly rained down on us. For a second it even seemed that the earth was spitting them out at us. There was no time to return the fire before our trained horses began running off in a frenzied haste. We leaped from the wagons and did our best to get out of their way, out of the path of the galloping animals. There was only one thing that every one of us wanted: to get as fast as possible into the cover of the nearby fields of rye. The grass in a rye field grows tall, but those bullets were chasing us with terrifying whistles. Whichever of us was still breathing was certain that he was the only one of the team left alive.

Later, much later, we found ourselves at the spot where we had planned in advance to meet, should any trouble befall us. Only then did we appreciate the warning we had been given by that old farmer in the hostile village. Only then did we realize what a favor he had done us, trying to convince us not to go by the road we had taken. And we would not listen to him.

On the ground bedecked by wild grass we now stretched out to rest, put shredded tobacco into thin paper to roll into cigarettes, and smoked. The sun-drenched morning smiled at us and shook away layers of dust from our eyes, as it removed from our nervous systems the remnants of terror that still lingered in us. Our hats were full of holes made by the rain of bullets; our rifles were damaged; but by some miracle we had emerged unscathed — except for one partisan who had been struck by a bullet in his leg. To escape discovery by the enemy he had lain in the rye field in his wounded condition without making a sound. We went looking for him, and when we found him we took him with us.

Sonya was still quite stunned. From her automatic rifle only the metal part had remained in her hand. The wooden butt had flown off in the exchange of gunfire. She had actually been the only one to snipe back steadily at the Germans who had ambushed us, while we scampered off trying to elude them by some kind of wild, hasty retreat. The Germans had thereupon aimed all their fire at her — and couldn't vanquish her. Her forehead was grazed and scratched, but she insisted that it was not true that a bullet had struck her. Those scratches, she said, came from fragments of glass that had injured her when she went crawling on the ground.

Coming for a moment out of that incident in the past, back into the present, I studied the horse that was dragging our wagon with difficulty, stepping along with the speed of a turtle. And my mind went again into that experience of the past. I remembered that as we came close to the region of our camp, only a few dozen meters away, we became aware of a wagon laden to the hilt with valuable provisions, moving slowly down the road, without a living person in it. It was one of the wagons we had abandoned when we had been suddenly ambushed. We recognized it by the heads of the lambs that we had loaded on it in the village. Those heads were horribly dislocated now, their tongues hanging out, moving and wagging this way and that. The lambs were all dead.

We leaped down to the ground and surrounded this wagon that the lone horse was pulling without a driver, and we were ready to swear that the animal recognized us. It whinnied and neighed as though to show its pleasure that we were all together again.

In those first moments we didn't notice that this devoted horse had an open wound in its underbelly, from which blood had been dripping the whole time. As we reached the base, just before we could pass the entrance, our horse collapsed and fell. We undid the harness quickly, but it doubled up, straightened out its body, and lay there breathing heavily, while its death throes began. Tears ran from our eyes as we all stood there, not moving. At last it opened one eye wide, and gazed with a frozen stare. From its mouth ran a foam of white saliva. It turned over, and with its feet in the air turned its head aside. Its life was over.

❈   ❈   ❈

One way or another, I found my mind dwelling time and again on the animals in our partisan corps. Invariably when we went out on a task mission, they went along as faithful companions, at times to share our fate with us. Some returned to the base; some remained on our small impromptu battlefields, their life gone. Or they might fall from the fire of a sudden ambush, with some of us. But while we made every effort to get our fallen men out of the combat area, to take their bodies back to the forest, give them a proper funeral and bury them in the partisan graveyard, our fallen horses were left lying on the scenes of combat. They could be seen lying here and there, their bellies split open, the birds pecking away at their flesh. At times a bird flying overhead might come down and perch on one of the limbs of a horse that a bullet had killed, and the little winged creature would sing to it, chirping away heartily, as though it were sitting on the chimney of a house or the branch of a tree. Flies kept swarming about, and foxes and wolves invariably came, each to take its share ... until on some forgotten day you could come and find single bones scattered around, so white they might have been sticks of marble ... just bones, that did not remind you of anything ... bones that would not tell you how they might ever have been connected to life ...

On our sleigh, Semyon continued to hold the reigns in his hands, his head bent forward, and still fast asleep. It seemed to me that not only the men on the sleighs were dozing but even the partisans who were dragging themselves along before and behind us: They too seemed to be dozing off as they walked. For some reason I felt that even the night was in no hurry to come to its end, but sluggish and lazy, it too kept napping like us, and it simply felt good, comfortable, going along with us on our journey.

I stretched out in our sleigh, next to Mischa. Through the hood that covered my face I saw no more than his eyes, and I recalled that I still owed him an answer on his fearful complaint earlier in the night: about the danger that was lurking for us if we kept on wandering close to the town. I saw he was tired out, half asleep, and I thought it better just to ponder about him, my only friend in the whole partisan camp, rather than start a conversation with him.

From time to time he used to tell me about his parents and the village in which he grew up. He had hardly known his father. The man had worked in a nearby town, and used to come home very seldom. Mischa never knew the reason for this. He thought his father must be a "city type," of the bourgeois, who could never adapt himself to country life. Nevertheless he would ask himself, "Yet after all, what is the matter with Father? What is he really like? Why is he so different from the village people, and even from me, his own son?"

When he was a grown boy, Mischa was told that his father was a Jew. In those days he did not understand what it meant. A number of times he spoke to his mother about it, but she never had a clear answer to give him. She found it hard to explain, or she evaded the matter.

In one room of his home there were various pictures and portraits hung on the walls, and among them were photographs of his two grandfathers. On one wall he saw his father's father, with a long unkempt beard. On the wall directly opposite he saw his mother's father, also bearded, and with the edges of his mustache twirled upward and around like rings. It had always seemed to Mischa that the eyes of these two men avoided looking at each other.

In all the years that his father was alive, Mischa wanted to feel closer to him, to get to know him better, and he could not achieve it. One day the man was arrested in his office in the town, and exiled to Siberia. A relatively short while afterward, an official letter arrived, informing the family that his father had died from an illness he had contracted. To this day he did not know what the crime was for which his father had been arrested and exiled, nor what the real cause of his father's death might have been.

In one of our actions against the enemy, Mischa showed extraordinary bravery; and he received a medal for it, for which many envied him. The day it was awarded him, he went looking for me; and when he found me at the big fire, he dragged me off to the tent we shared, sat me down with him, and spoke softly, so as not to be overheard.

"Instead of awarding me honors, I would rather that they should change their attitude to the Jews, root out the hatred they have for them. Don't think, Philip, that I don't ..." He did not finish the sentence. The rest of his words remained within him. But I understood that he wanted to convey somehow the anguish and bitterness he felt at the acts of murder that fellow-partisans had committed against the Jews in the forest.

I did not react, however. It was in my mind to tell him that he was not making himself clear; he was not calling by their right names all the rotten, abominable deeds that had been committed against the Jews; he was being too careful and circumspect ... But I had no wish to pain him. And I knew that if I ever brought up the false accusations which had been made against the Jews in the forest during the massive general manhunt, I would erupt in rage like a volcano. I would list in detail every vile act that had been perpetrated. I would tell him how members of the Soviet army, ordinary soldiers, low-ranking and high-ranking officers, had all adopted the Germans' hatred of the Jews and had become no less heinous and horrible in their anti-Semitism.

I kept silent, however. And as it seemed, the good-hearted Mischa understood what lay behind my silence.

Our sleigh seemed to be inching along now, and I thought that Mischa must have fallen asleep as soundly as Semyon the driver, indeed as much as the horse itself, which almost seemed to be pawing the ground in one place. All at once Mischa raised his head a bit and turned to me. "Philip," he exclaimed, "you never gave me any reply when I said that if we kept wandering around till the morning, who knows if we won't get killed out during the day? Well, what do you think? Do you know? — for some reason I just don't believe I'll ever get another medal or decoration in this life of mine."

I was surprised at this black mood of Mischa's, and didn't know how to answer him. "Look," I told him: "Everyone who goes into any kind of warfare knows the fear of death. It gnaws away at the heart of the most courageous fighter, who knows how to lock it away within him and hide it well. There isn't any doubt that you have courage — plenty of it. You'll never be afraid to expose your life to danger in combat. So how can you bring yourself to talk like this?"

Were I able to, I would have told him, without any shame or embarrassment, that every time I was about to leave the base on some task mission, I would always lift up my eyes to heaven and ask, "Master of the world, is this the last time for me? Will I perhaps not be coming back any more? Am I going to remain out on some field of combat? Or will my comrades bring me back and put my body in the common burial ground of the partisans?"

I would not have restrained myself from telling him, my Mischa, even more: that in general I would always turn to the Creator in prayer and beg Him to let me go on living, so that I could take revenge on those vicious, bestial Germans, to make them pay with their lives for the Jewish blood they shed. Nor was that all: From time to time I would implore Him, my Maker, to grant me one additional day of life after I saw their downfall — just one more day ...

But of all this I said nothing to Mischa. The truth was that all of us wanted to live, yet life kept slipping away from us, one by one. Our numbers kept getting smaller, ever smaller. Death lurked and waited for us everywhere, at any and every moment of our lives. Sometimes a bullet came and shot out the life of a person who was completely certain he was not going to lose it; he was absolutely sure he would go on living; he even made plans for his future. And the bullet came and cut everything off.

On the other hand, you could find someone going around with the feeling that for him it was all hopeless, just one lost cause: He did not stand a chance of evading the fatal end that was pursuing him ... and he stayed safe. He went out on a combat mission and came back alive — or at most slightly wounded — so that he could go out on a "job" another time, and another time — to encounter death face to face over and over again, and triumph over it. For the grim reaper always went looking for someone else from the start, never for him.

How many of us *had* fallen, though. How many of our seasoned veterans were gone. In the region where we had operated, in the various places we had stopped at in all our wanderings in the forests, the earth had absorbed so many bodies of our fighters. Not a day went by without victims; not a day. It was true that our tents did not stay empty. They filled again and again with new men who sensed that the Germans did not have victory in their pocket yet, no matter how convinced they might still be (if they ever were) that they were "the wave of the future."

Yet where were the two of us now — Mischa and I? Was Mischa right perhaps in asking if our turn had come? Heaven knew.

Through my hood I saw Mischa looking up at the dark, cloudy sky. I had the feeling that he was shivering with cold. Was he chilled, or was there another reason?

We moved onto a flat, smooth surface of frozen snow. Our sleigh moved easily now, as if by itself, indeed as if it was pushing our horse forward, against its will. From time to time the animal turned its head around, as though it wanted to see just whom it had the honor to be taking across the frozen plain.

Something was troubling Mischa, though, pressing down on his heart. He evidently felt a need to talk, to get something out of his bitter heart.

"Do you see, Philip? From our base to the partisan burial ground, the distance is very short. Ten times a day, maybe more, we pass by the location, and we never notice how it keeps getting bigger, keeps biting off more bits of the forest. We uproot another tree and another tree and another, and in their place we put the bodies of our men. Next to every grave we plant tender young pine saplings. Some of them have grown nicely. They get nourished through the soil, from the bodies of our partisans. Are you listening, Philip? Maybe in the course of the years, big, tall pine trees will be over us too. They'll spread their boughs wide, as their roots dig into our bones. We'll rot away, and they'll grow, getting bigger year by year. And one day our men will cut them down too and pull out the roots, our roots ..."

I could not believe it was Mischa telling me this. I was astounded to hear such black, melancholy thoughts from him. Yet his talk became only more impassioned:

"This cursed, confounded war is to blame for it all. It takes a person out of his home, out of the warmth of his family. It takes him far away from the people he loves. And it turns him over to the tender mercies of bombs, shells and bullets. Only a personal miracle, if it happens for you, can make them all miss you, pass you by and let you live. And if you don't get the miracle, you stay in a furrow of a field somewhere: food for the wild animals hungry for meat. If you're more lucky, they gather your body and bury you, and the vultures and wild animals lose a meal ..."

He suddenly burst into tears. "My poor mother must have started mourning for me long ago, giving me up for dead. And what about Marussia, my fiancée? What do I know about her? Can anyone tell me for certain that she's remained faithful to me? — that she's still waiting for her beau who went away to war? Maybe she went and married someone else? But it would be just another accident of war, Philip: just another accident; this too."

How well I could understand what he was telling me. Yet what could I say in response?

"Look, Mischa," I said at last. "Your mother is alive, isn't she? Let's assume that till now nothing has happened to her. Well, if she's alive, it's natural for her to worry about her son, gone off to the front. Of course she worries. But the day will come when the war will end, whatever the outcome will be. You'll go home then, and you'll see your mother and she'll see you; and then you'll both be overjoyed. You'll weep and cry, both of you; but it will be from sheer happiness, and you know it.

"What about me?

"If I die in the next bit of combat, or in the one after that, today or tomorrow or the day after, who is going to miss me? And if I stay alive, if I'm lucky enough to go on living, who is going to be overjoyed about it? Do I have anyone left? Anyone to be tremendously happy to see again? Will I be able to shed tears of happiness?"

Mischa opened his eyes wide. I saw them gleaming through the hood that covered his face. His look swept over me, covered me. And I went on talking:

"Don't be amazed at what I'm saying, Mischa. The words come straight from reality, and reality is as bitter as wormwood. Look: Not one of us Jews has a family anymore. Every family has been wiped out, murdered. Now the war is at its height. It engulfs almost the whole world. And wherever German boots trample and tread, there is no hope for the Jews. The Germans eliminate them. So it means that if a Jewish partisan stays alive, he is all alone in the world, without family, without close kin. And what is our status in the forest? Where are all the Jewish partisans who were fighting with us two years ago? Where are the Jewish family camps that we used to have?

"Just for a minute, Mischa, refresh your memory. While that big manhunt against us was going on, one morning, in the course of a half hour, over sixty Jews were put to death: men, women and children, from the Jewish family camp that was right close to us. Tell me: how did the Germans get to that camp? How did they know exactly where it was? Who told them? Wasn't it said openly among us that the information came from our squad? Didn't you hear, just as I did, that there were partisans among us who gave the facts to the militiamen among the local population, who work for the Germans?

"And I'm sure you remember" — I was talking now straight into Mischa's eyes as they glared at me through his snow-covered hood — "when the attack started against the Jewish family camp, a few small units of our squad took up their weapons, gathered around the staff headquarters, and waited. That's all they did, Mischa. They waited. At the headquarters they knew very well whom the Germans were attacking. But the commanders of the divisions and the units were making jokes and laughing — at the expense of the Jewish victims at the neighboring camp. So tell me, Mischa: Why didn't any people from the squad go out then to help those Jews, when they were attacked so close to our base? What made those partisans just stand about waiting, without any reason? Why did they set out to encircle the Germans only after those 'visitors' had finished their attack? Wasn't it all planned like that deliberately, from the start, to give the Germans time to massacre the Jews with such great success?

"Do you remember? When we came to the Jewish family camp, we found it a shambles. At the entrance was the body of a young girl, shot to death. She had been tortured. The arms were twisted, the eyes put out, clothes torn. Grischa the Siberian didn't hide his sadistic joy. 'Look at that Jewish heroine,' he said. 'She fought the enemy with a thick stick in her hand, and she fell in the war.' Sverdlov, Ivan Ivanovitch, others, just laughed and laughed along with him — barbaric, brutal animals."

My voice had turned to a blaze. The words came pouring out in a stream. I forgot about our long trip through the night and our task mission. My voice grew stronger, as though I wanted others also to hear me, not Mischa alone. It seemed to me that I wanted the night's end to hear me too, as it was folding itself up, and the sky, which appeared to bend down to us to pour out its snow and listen to my scorching, painful conversation with Mischa.

"You know as well as I do," I continued, "that the group of Jews there did not have even two decent rifles that could be properly called rifles — not because they didn't know how to get hold of weapons and use them, but because partisans from our unit and other units in the forest came and confiscated their weapons from time to time. They simply took them, for their own use — even the arms that those Jews themselves made, in the workshop that they set up, where they used to repair our weapons also, whenever it was necessary."

Our sleigh continued gliding and racing over the frozen snow, though the great majority of us still did not know what destination we were aiming to reach, and what we were to do when we reached it.

I moved closer to Mischa. There were moments, as my words assailed the hood over his face, when it seemed to me that my voice was tearing its way to the heavens, that everyone must hear me shouting. I was frightened that at any moment Sverdlov, Grischa and their like would come laughing at me in gleeful, cackling scorn, enjoying the anguish that was making me writhe, proclaiming that I had gone out of my mind.

"Do you want to doze a while?" I asked Mischa. "Should I stop talking to you?" My heart drove me on, though, and I did not wait for his answer.

"On that awful morning of horror," I reminded him, "we pursued those Germans. We ambushed them on the road, in the woods. And we also saw them from afar, exulting with joy. They were triumphant. It was no small 'victory' for them to kill off in such a short time, in the very heart of the forest, such a large bunch of Jews — without any interference by the partisans.

"We attacked them in force. We put them under strong fire. Our bullets rained down on them. We encircled them and killed as many as we could. Do you remember? Nikolai Nikolaievitch Bobakov, our valiant squad commander, sat down on one German and killed him by sheer pressure.

"But couldn't all this have been done *before* the Germans had a chance to slaughter the Jews? What would it have mattered to our command staff if sixty Jewish souls, saved from the ghettos, leftover fragments of families that perished, had stayed alive? It would have been so easy to protect them and save them."

I realized that Mischa was not dozing at all. His open eyes were ablaze with emotion, and I knew that I was getting not only on my own nerves but on his as well. I was letting him find no peace.

His hand rested on my head and patted my hair, in the gesture of a mother trying to calm her grieving, raging child. I began to feel better, but after a moment of silence I had to continue:

"Mischa, each of us two must remember what happened that day, and on other days. I mean that if either of us remains alive, he has to tell not only the courageous deeds and exploits of the partisans against the Germans. He also has to tell about the fate of the Jews in the forest. I'm sure people won't find it pleasant to hear or to read, but we have an obligation, a duty to make it known. For this reason alone it's worth remaining alive — to fulfill this human duty."

The snow continued falling, piling up layer after layer. Everything was sheathed in white. The forest all around looked so pure, unsullied by a stain.

"And you know, Mischa," I went on, "with this the story of that day isn't ended yet. It was a day of tragedy upon tragedy. If you remember, a number of Germans and Ukrainians were taken captive. In one of their wagons lay a woman all bound and tied. Her legs had turned blue-red, all swollen from the cold. One of our men asked the Ukrainian driving the vehicle, 'What is this person doing in your wagon?' He answered that this was a Jewish woman who had led them to the family camp, and afterward she was supposed to lead them to the partisan base headquarters. Those who heard him were astounded. The woman herself burst out screaming, denying to heaven what this captured Ukrainian said. It was a damned lie, she insisted. She had a daughter in the family camp, she said; and both had been living in the forest for over two years.

"The truth is that the partisans didn't believe the Ukrainian. They couldn't. What he said didn't make sense. They had found the woman bound hand and food, about to be brought by her German and Ukrainian captors to the nearby town, probably to be questioned, tortured and killed.

"And still, when the men of the squad returned to the base, the Jewish woman was placed in detention, together with the Germans and Ukrainians. I was there when she was questioned. She related that as soon as the attack began, she managed to escape from the bunker together with a few other Jewish women, just before grenades were thrown into it. The attackers pursued and shot at them. Her companions fell dead, but she continued running; and when all her strength was gone, she stretched out flat on the ground and pretended to be lifeless. The Germans, or perhaps the Ukrainians, kicked her and stomped on her — till she couldn't bear it any more, and she uttered a cry. It was then they had taken her and bound her hand and foot.

"In that Jewish family camp a few survivors remained, a precious few who had managed to stay hidden from the Germans. The squad's command staff brought them in for questioning about this woman. With tears in their eyes they declared that what the Ukrainian said was a malicious lie. She was a woman named Schalk from the city of Lodz, Poland. She had been with them in the forest from the moment they had escaped there from the ghetto. Her husband, a watchmaker, had been shot by the Germans in the great massacre that they carried out in the ghetto. The young girl who was found dead at the entrance of the Jewish family camp had been her daughter. She had stood guard there, with the stick in her hand as her sole weapon of defense.

"This was the testimony that was given for the woman whom

the Germans and Ukrainians had tied up, planning to take her captive. And the testimony was of no help to her. The command staff decided, apparently, to believe the Ukrainian's cock-and-bull story. Or maybe they had other considerations in mind in reaching their verdict. For two days Mrs. Schalk of Lodz was held in detention and subjected to severe torture. Then she was taken out and killed. The Russian woman who did the cooking for us pulled hair out of her head. Other women, all Russian partisans, beat her with iron bars or with logs of wood. Only when they realized that what one was passing to another was no longer anything more than a bag of bones, they threw her body into the bushes somewhere near the base. Days afterwards, when we passed by that spot, we could see two feet jutting out of the ground like two logs partly broken off a tree, waiting for a storm wind to come and wrench them off completely.

"All I'm asking, Mischa," I demanded of him once more, "is that if you'll be among those who come out alive, you should know you have a moral duty as a human being to tell about this Jewish woman named Schalk. Let people know what was done to her by partisans of the squad under the command of Nikolai Nikolaievitch Bobakov, an air pilot and captain in the Red Army, a member of the Communist Party in the Soviet Union. If you'll disclose only this episode and make sure it becomes known, it will be enough — enough."

I may have suspected Mischa before of hiding his head inside that hood of his and shutting his mind, if not his ears, to my bitter, harrowing words. Now I saw it was not so. I could clearly see the tears running down his cheeks, to be absorbed by the white cloak, while he remained silent, never uttering a word.

I felt I was suffocating. In the atmosphere of the open forest I suddenly needed air. It was as if I had been handcuffed and thrown into a cellar without a spark of light, to have the door locked shut on me.

❈ ❈ ❈

"Everybody off the sleighs. Lie flat on the snow!"

The command went from mouth to mouth, as the night was rapidly withdrawing. The sleighs were driven off to the sides of the road, and we stretched out on the snow, as though it was one huge mattress. A sharp wind shook our white cloaks, till they seemed to be the fluttering wings of demons. Minutes went by, and perhaps more minutes, and no new command reached us.

For some reason, what Mischa had said about the war came to my mind. People of other nationalities who were fighting in the forests, I mused, would go out to freedom one day. They would return to their homes, to the places from which they had come to the forest. They would work on their farms again, or go back into business as before. They would raise families and live normal lives.

What was to become of *us*? Where would we go? If the Germans won this world war, it was possible that we might never be able to leave the forest: never. We might have to live here till we died. The price of a Jew captured alive would become very high. The Germans would pay a small fortune for him and kill him, so that in the world they dominated not a remnant or trace of this people would remain.

These thoughts were not new for me. They had been coming into my mind for some time, over and over again. On days of freedom, holidays, I would go on brooding and dwelling on these dark, pessimistic ideas. I had visions of Poles, Russians, Germans, going out at daybreak to hunt, as it was their custom. Well, they wouldn't go hunting only four-footed animals: wild boars, foxes, wolves, and so on. They would work to ferret out a Jew in hiding. They would get on his tracks, trying to sniff out the spot where he could be found. They would come into the forest with dogs specially trained for the job. How exultant they would be when they caught a Jew alive: a rare, bizarre creature that was becoming extinct in many regions of the world; a creature hardly to be found anymore.

"Can it come true?" I asked in my heart. "Can such a situation ever become reality?" The questions stayed soundless. These black, bitter thoughts I did not share with Mischa.

        ❦   ❦   ❦

"Stand up, stand up. Everybody up."

We stood at attention in rows. Ivan Ivanovitch rose from his prone position, and collapsed again at once. He had been drinking right properly, so the story went. And so he received a right proper kick in his rear from his commander, making him turn over twice. Those around him helped get him up, and they stood him straight in the ranks. The only trouble was that his feet were like wobbling wheels: they refused to carry him, and he found it hard to keep straight and steady. From his mouth poured an endless stream of curses, and it was not often that one heard anything so juicy and original.

Mounted on a white horse, Maxim stopped at our unit, and out of its members he chose ten. He ordered them to saddle horses and go out on patrol, in advance of the squad. To give the men protection, he ordered me to join them, with my machine gun.

As luck would have it, I was given a tall horse that was easy to ride, and was told to hurry up and saddle it. Well, I was no great expert at the saddling business. I knew how to ride a horse, but not how to deal with it. I had never managed to learn how to tie the stirrup strap, the backstrap, and so on. My fingers kept becoming entangled in what I was doing.

Well, now too, when I had to hurry and get done with it, so that I could go with the group, it did not go particularly well. Again and again I went beneath the horse's belly, from side to side, almost dead with the fear that the horse might become angered at someone it did not recognize, and fell me to the ground with a hoof. I envied Semyon, who always took care of our horses. He knew this business so perfectly, and he dealt with these animals as with little children, literally playing with them.

The team was waiting for me now, watching the pathetic spectacle I was making of myself, and rolling with laughter. I tried all kinds of ways. I spoke to the animal earnestly, heart to heart. I spoke tenderly; I flattered it. I pleaded with it to lift now its tail, now this foot, now that foot; that it should move forward, turn back. Of course the animal did not understand a word of the strange phrases it was hearing; or else it thought, rightly for sure, that there was no reason why it had to obey my orders. I reckoned that not only my companions but the animal too was laughing at me. Feeling utterly helpless, I lowered my eyes to the ground, my face flushed red with shame.

I finally overcame the difficulties, however, and somehow managed to get into the saddle and set off riding. The group had set out before me, however, and for a good while I lagged behind, till, in the course of time, I caught up with them.

Only now did it become clear to us that we were headed for the air field near the town. All weariness and indifference left us. The feeling of boredom evaporated. In our eyes blazed a fire of eagerness that could easily have burnt up the entire town, whose outskirts we were now approaching.

Slowly, slowly the sky cleared overhead, revealing the airfield to our eyes. There it was, spread out before us, entirely surrounded by a long, high fence of barbed wire. The aluminum wings of civilian planes and bombers gleamed like polished mirrors in the morning light.

Thirty meters away from the field we halted. We could see clearly all that was going on in the area. And now we had to decide quickly but carefully what to do and how to do it. We were the advance team, and the partisan groups behind us were waiting for a signal from us. It was our job now to gather information on the size and strength of the military force stationed at the airfield. We had to learn, generally, what means of protection and defense the site was provided with.

One by one we crawled through the snow, till we reached a large pit that was half outside the airfield and half within. The snow covered us almost completely. We inched forward under the barbed-wire fence, and found ourselves inside the bounded area.

Two German soldiers on sentry duty were marching back and forth. They clapped their hands together, struck one foot against another, glowered, roared and fumed. They were evidently angry at their superior officers for having turned them out of their warm beds into this dreadful cold, like a pair of dogs, to do a turn of guard duty that they thought altogether unnecessary. They kept throwing frightened glances at the nearby forest, as they obviously waited for the sun to rise and the light to grow stronger, so that their hearts could stop turning over ten times a minute in terror of "those terrifying bandits," the Russian partisans who filled the woods in the neighborhood (as they believed) in the tens of thousands.

We held our breath, waiting for the exactly right moment when we could start "playing" with them.

My eyes caught Mischa's glance on me, and I saw there was a smile in it, as much as to tell me, "Forget what I told you, Philip, about being afraid of death. Forget about those worries of mine that I shared with you. My mood has gone and changed for the better. We'll live. We'll live. You'll see."

The two German soldiers reached the edge of the pit in their patrolling, and stopped. They noticed nothing at all suspicious. They took out some shredded tobacco from their pockets, and Russian style, rolled it in some pieces of newspaper, calmly, serenely, into the shape of cigarettes. Before they had a chance to strike a match we moved, and dragged them into the pit. They practically rolled into our hands.

Without much ado we "persuaded" them to open their mouths and talk, and received precise answers to our questions. Our interrogation finished, some of the men put them deep into the snow in the pit, and sat on them.

At that very moment a choir of crows came to settle on the fence that surrounded the airfield, and broke into wild, raucous cawing. Now that we had the information just extracted from the two German soldiers, one of our team of ten clambered out of the pit and climbed up a tall tree that stood midway between us and the partisan units. From there he gave them the signal that it was safe for them to advance onto the airfield.

While our fellow-fighters prepared themselves for a swift move to this final destination of ours, we made a rapid search through the pockets of the two Germans, who had gone to sleep forever beneath our seated men. We pulled out bundles of letters from home, from the "motherland." In one letter that I was able to glance through in a hurry, a woman described to her soldier husband how hard her lot was now, and she implored him to keep sending bundles of clothing and other valuable goods regularly. Only thanks to those packages, she wrote, could she manage to support herself and their child. A similar letter was found in the pocket of the second German; but there it was his girl friend who begged him to send her more valuable things, so that she could sell them for a higher price.

I translated the letters, written in German, for my companions. One thing I knew well enough: The contents of all the packages and bundles that these two soldiers had sent their women had come from Jewish homes. It had all been taken as loot, either during or after the massacres of whole Jewish communities. At that moment I felt sorry that I could no longer make these two Germans talk. I would have wrenched details out of them about all the looting they had done in Jewish homes. And I would have paid them well for it, given them everything they deserved, and more.

Meanwhile the partisans had arrived on the airfield en masse, and the real work began in earnest. The electric wires and the telephone were cut. The field had connection no more with the outside world. Patrols from the various units taking part in the operation went scouring buildings, to rid the airfield of any and all Germans who were quartered there or were serving in some capacity. Many were found sleeping, and they remained asleep forever. They had certainly never imagined that the new lovely day, just begun, would turn out like this.

I saw Sverdlov carrying a dead German on his shoulder, and when he grew tired he threw the body away and continued walking. As Ivan went running through the area he discovered another German soldier. He killed him on the spot and pulled off his handsome boots, and these he threw nonchalantly away — hitting one of our commanding officers on the head. Another German soldier came bursting out from somewhere, tore open a partisan's belly with his bayonet, and shot himself to death.

Everyone was rushing about, as though the airfield was going up in flames. We forced our way into a warehouse, and each one of us dragged out one long, narrow box that contained one bomb. We knew that when we returned to the base, we would take out the innards of these bombs, and with this material we would make ourselves a fresh supply of mines and other bits and pieces of explosive hell, since our own supply had run out. We learned now that this was the main purpose of the whole task mission: for good explosives were essential, indispensable, in our damaging strikes against the enemy.

I myself ran across the breadth of the airfield with a frenzy of energy, a box on each shoulder. Each box with its bomb weighed over a hundred kilograms (over 200 pounds), but possibly I didn't feel the weight at all. I knew that every man among us was carrying on his shoulders a quantity of death for German murderers.

With relief I placed my boxes on a sleigh; and as I ran back for more, I was amazed to see how many partisans were there, involved in the operation. I saw faces I didn't recognize, people I didn't know at all. Only afterwards I learned that to make sure the operation succeeded, and to let others share in the booty, additional squads had been brought to join us — squads named Voroshilov, Kirov, Bodyonov, "Stalin," "Death to the Conquerors," and so forth. This is why it was no wonder that for a long time afterward, the farmers in the region told stories about paratroopers flown in at night by the Red Army, sent specially from Moscow to destroy the airfield. It was a beautiful fantasy that we loved to hear about in those days, and we took no trouble at all to deny it.

The operation went off splendidly, without any obstacles or interference. We could do exactly as we pleased.

I saw Sonya, the young Jewish woman partisan, moving swiftly somewhere ahead of me, whereupon she disappeared in a stormwind. Directly afterward I saw her trudging with her heavy boots as fast as she could through the snow, which had turned into muddy slush. "What's all the burning rush?" I called after her in Yiddish. "You're likely to fall if you run like that, and with a bomb on your shoulder in the bargain." She had no time, however, to pay attention to my words, let alone give me an answer. At that moment nothing in the world existed for her except the job of getting bombs out of the warehouse and loading them on the sleigh.

When we were ready to leave the site at last, Ivan Ivanovitch came looking for me. "Here you are," he exclaimed; and putting his bony, heavy hand on my shoulder, he told me about Sonya:

"Did you ever see a young woman like that? She really has spirit. She's a devil, I tell you. She's got more courage and spunk in her than a whole lot of us." Then he related what she had done on the airfield: Our squad was the first to get there. One of the buildings had to be searched, because there was reason to suspect that armed Germans were lurking inside. The commanding officer asked if anyone wanted to volunteer to go in at the head of a small team and scour the building thoroughly. The officer hardly had a chance to finish talking before Sonya was there, standing at attention before him and singing out, "I'm ready, Commander!"

Accompanied by two partisans, she strode ahead into the building, taking the lead. The three were there only a short time, then out they came, with Sonya leading a wounded SS man by the arm. "I'm sorry, Comrade Commander," she said, saluting, "but there was only this one in the building — nobody else."

❦   ❦   ❦

In the small city of Slonim the sirens wailed, but as the inhabitants woke from their sleep they could not reckon the reason for these piercing cries. The mines we had put under every building and in every underground storage place of ammunition at the airfield kept exploding for a whole hour after we were gone, sending up billows of clouds to the sky. Our last achievement was to block and seal up the road to the airfield, using anything and everything we found. We set up barriers and roadblocks of all kinds, which were not going to be easy to remove.

Our work done, we withdrew to a nearby village, to keep track of the enormous conflagration from there, as it spread to the town. We ate and drank, happy to hear the wild outcries that reached our ears: Sounds of confusion and fear that tried to mar the beautiful, dry, winter day so full of the bright sunlight that drove and dispersed the clouds in the sky, as it cast a rare sheen over the white snow, bringing music to our hearts.

CHAPTER TWENTY-ONE
The Conflict on Friday Night

INCE THE HOURS OF THE MORNING a heavy warmth filled the air. We lay entrenched in the moist, clinging earth, letting the blazing sun heat our bodies, which had not been washed for weeks. Rivers of sweat ran from our faces.

The night before, we had crossed the highway leading from Brest-Litovsk to Moscow; and thus we soon found ourselves, a team of partisans with a special assignment, back in the forest of Polessya, in the region of those swamps of Pinsk. At the edge of the forest, we left behind us — I think it would be better to say, abandoned — our wagons with the horses still harnessed to them, and tied to trees. We wanted Germans passing by on the highway to notice them and seize them for themselves. They would sit down in the wagons to ride off with them, but they would not get far: In every wagon a bomb lay hidden beneath the straw, set to explode and kill or maim anyone riding in the vehicle.

The swamps of Pinsk hadn't changed; perhaps they never would; but we knew the region well, having lived there long enough, and we were able to take care not to sink deeply into the liquid mud at any danger point. We watched over one another very carefully, making sure to use only the smoother, drier paths.

It remained, however, a world of swamp and mud. As far as the eye could see, it was an endless earth that resembled unkneaded dough, rotting away consumptively.

We kept walking for long hours, till we reached the area where we had stayed during the massive general manhunt. Every village we passed on our way seemed like an island shut off from the rest of the world; yet all had one thing in common: poverty. In all of them there was the miserable appearance of the huts and cottages, and of the farmers themselves. An air of gloom and sorrow emanated from everything: from the soil, from the livestock that looked so gaunt and starving, from the people we saw dressed in rags and tatters, with all the light of anticipation and hope gone out of their eyes.

As we moved along, mainly on our feet, we learned that in one of the villages in the region of Pinsk, the Germans had parachuted down a considerable number of armed men; and there, in the village, those paratroopers had entrenched themselves, with the purpose of taking action against the partisans in the region. We learned further that every single day some part of the local population, which in general was hostile to the German conquerors, was taken out and shot; and at night the cottages and huts of these unfortunate victims were set on fire, to turn their meager, miserable belongings into smoke — to teach others to tremble with fear before these "heroic conquerors."

On this assignment of ours we had to continue onto a route that led close to the front. We had no choice but to go across the village of Ignatovka, that bordered on the highway we had to use; and it was there that the Germans had stationed themselves. The only alternative we had was to go back to our own woods and not carry out the task which our division had been given. If we did not want to do that, we had to go on toward the village and try to cross it, even if it meant a clash with the Germans.

It was hard for me to drag the machine gun on my shoulder, but I trudged along — till I suffered a peculiar mishap. By mistake I veered off the proper route, and my two feet became stuck in the mud. Only with the help of others could I be dragged out, but both of my boots had to be left behind in the swamp. Try as I would, I could not get them out.

I felt miserable, desolated. What could I put on my feet in their place? Then I remembered that when we had been in this area during the large, widespread manhunt, I had seen the impoverished farmers wearing sandals made out of wood; and to keep the sandals from slipping off their feet, they would wrap around them long strips made out of reed bark, that reached almost to their knees. Well, I thought, having no choice, I would make myself such a pair of sandals, measuring and whittling to make them fit me.

When he saw me in my quandary, however, my good friend Mischa consoled me: "Don't worry, Philip. You'll finish off a German, and measure his boots; and if they don't fit, you'll finish off another one. One way or another you'll get yourself a better pair of boots than the ones you lost back there in the swamp."

So it was that I waited impatiently to encounter the Germans. I looked forward to scoring some good hits, so that my poor feet could stop suffering. And I didn't have long to wait.

We had barely reached the outskirts of Ignatovka when a strong barrage of gunfire came down on us. It seemed that the Germans had been on the lookout for our arrival. Perhaps they had received information on our movements around the villages. Perhaps they had noticed us as we came close to this village, and put themselves on the alert. At any rate, a battle broke out between us, with light weapons and machine guns.

The truth was that we were ready enough to retreat; but we reckoned that it would not be easy, and they might even mow us down, to the very last one of our men, if we tried to sneak away. So we continued exchanging gunfire.

Right at the start of the armed conflict a few of our men were wounded, and we were unable to help them, because they were in open territory. The bullets in our pockets became fewer and fewer, and I began feeling more and more desperate as the minutes of sharp fighting sped by. Only the onset of night could help us, I reflected. The darkness could be our ally. Yet nightfall was nowhere in sight. Even the hour of sunset was still a good way off.

I received a command to move with my machine gun to the center of the gunfire. Unfortunately, just on the spot I reached by crawling stealthily, sharpshooters seemed to have their weapons trained; and when I reached my new position, they aimed their bullets directly at me. I squeezed my poor body into a thicket, and from there I let my machine send some spurts of fire toward the snipers and sharpshooters. Their bullets and mine crisscrossed in the air, whistling and shrieking dreadfully, blending in a symphony of gunshots, a devil's concert of fire.

Arkady of Odessa was sent to bring me a full packet of bullets. He crawled closer and closer to my thicket till, from a short distance away, he threw it, and it found its path into the thicket. I was grateful to him for the wonderful gift. But just then, at the very moment he carried out his task so well, he caught a bullet and fell, seriously wounded. He remained where he was, unmoving, groaning hard, as the blood flowed from him. I was desolated to see him lying there like that, so badly injured: a handsome young man of only twenty-two, with life now seriously in danger. Only a while ago we had gotten to know each other. He had escaped from a German war prison and managed to get to our woods. For weeks he had wandered over paths, villages, forests, till he found us. And now this.

I threw a glance at him. His eyes were bulging from their sockets, soundlessly pleading with me, "Save me, Philip. Pull me over to you. I'm already so close to your thicket ... so close ..."

Yet in those minutes there was nothing I could do. I did not even dare lift my head up above the thicket: The German snipers were only waiting for me to do just that. Any sudden, careless move on my part, and they would have their wish. My machine gun would be silenced; I would double up and roll over in the thicket; my life too would be finished.

Yet Arkady's face looking toward me, his red tearful eyes, were driving me out of my mind. There was a weeping misery in his eyes, but also a powerful pain, and an anger clenched up in him because I wasn't hurrying to help him, to save his life.

"I must do something," whispered my mind. "No, not something. I have to save him from dying; or at least, get him out of danger of being taken alive by the Germans."

I sent a few more rounds of gunfire toward the snipers, and the barrel of my weapon became too hot. It had been racing back and forth as though driven by a mad spirit. Then I breathed my thanks to Heaven: One of the snipers doubled over and fell full weight on the muddy ground in front of the hut, where he had found a place of concealment. One half of his rifle remained sticking up out of the soft earth, like a marker on a freshly covered grave.

Now I smiled, stuck my head up a bit, and exchanged glances with Arkady. In his eyes flashed a gleam of hope — the hope of life.

Crawling, I came in reach. He grasped my machine gun with both hands, and so I pulled him back into the thicket. He tried to say something, but the words only changed into tears — tears of happiness.

With her knapsack of medicines, Anya managed to reach us by crawling across. This was the "sister of mercy" who was rumored to be Jewish, although she would not admit it. She tore the sleeve of his shirt and dried the wound with it. All in all, the bullet had pierced one of his lungs and sped out. A partisan in the forest would not collapse and die from a wound like that.

It was fairly quiet now around us. Either both sides had become tired out or had grown fed up with the indecisive battle, which neither side could win. Or again, the thought came to me, perhaps both sides preferred to wait till the bloody day would end, and we could get away from each other.

I suddenly felt a powerful desire to roll myself a cigarette and smoke. My pockets were full of shredded Bessarabian tobacco, and I kept fingering it now the whole time, with unusual pleasure. The urge to smoke was plaguing me like an itch demanding to be scratched, till I almost went out of my mind. I felt the taste of the tobacco, the curling, billowing smoke, not in my nostrils but with all my senses, with my whole being. My lips began becoming moist and puckering in by turns.

Then a thought cut through me with the sharpness of a knife: "Shabbos, Shabbos!" Once Friday's daylight went, the holy Sabbath began; and then, no matter what, I would strike no fire and burn nothing, unless I had to, to stay alive.

But no! The sky above me was still aglow with its own red fire. The flames of ebbing sunlight leaped above the clouds that were sailing along to some unknown destination, and tinged them red. Somewhere in the east another wave of clouds was moving slowly, as though it had set out to extinguish the fire of sunset that was enflaming the last remnant of the day.

"Hurry," whispered a thought in my mind. "Roll yourself a cigarette fast. The sun is already ..."

"It's Shabbos!" another thought cut in.

The aroma of tobacco rose up in my throat now, in my palate, intoxicating me like strong drink. I was dying for at least one puff: just one good, long draw on a cigarette, and no more ...

At my left Vassily was lying on the ground, resting — a middle-aged Russian, a partisan. When I asked him for a small piece of newspaper, to roll my shredded tobacco in it, his two eyes opened wide at me in a penetrating stare: "What?" he asked in a quiet but forceful voice. "Have you gone out of your mind, Philip? Now is the time to smoke cigarettes?"

It was as if he had struck me across the face with a whip. I felt that not Vassily but someone within me had rebuked me, scolded me aloud, to put me to shame.

The sun seemed to be staring at me with a red, swollen eye that had taken a punch in a fight with the encroaching darkness. "It still hasn't set altogether," I told myself calmly, as my fingers went on caressing the tobacco as though it was a precious object. In my fantasy I sensed the enormous pleasure of smoking away there in the thicket, without any gunshots to disturb me.

"Forget it! Take that hand out of your pocket. Just lift up your eyes and look across the sky. *Shabbos* has come; the holy Sabbath is already here!" I could swear I heard those words whispered in my ear.

"No: you could have finished a cigarette long ago, you idiot. And it still isn't too late."

"Just one good long draw, and I'll throw it away. Just one puff ..."

The sun was still enmeshed in its struggle. It spat and shook out the last fragments of its fire, till it was gone, vanished over the horizon. I shut my eyes. Forgotten for the moment was the armed conflict that was not finished yet, along with everything else around me ... In one swift movement I emptied out all the tobacco that had filled two pockets. With my boots I mixed it well into the mud, so that I should never see it again; it should no longer exist for me.

Relief came — a great relief. I felt freed from a powerful pressure, as though a stone had rolled off my heart. Yet with all my good feeling, my moral or spiritual happiness, there was a pain in me too — all mixed together — pain that I had reached such a state, when a cigarette could mean so much to me.

I didn't start to doze. I didn't see any visions of hallucination. There was no room for such things during a battle, even if no one was shooting and the rifles stayed silent. Still my eyes closed of themselves, and into my mind came the scene of the *shtib'l*, the modest chassidic house of prayer and study, as it looked on a Friday evening, filled to the brim with the worshippers, the local people dressed in their Sabbath clothes. The faces shone with the glow of the Sabbath, with such an aura of splendor and grace spread over them — pure Sabbath radiance.

They were happy faces. Gone by were the six working days, filled with cares, anxieties and troubles. Now the holy evening came; peaceful rest arrived. Before the prayer began there was time to study. Volumes of Torah learning were opened, to be studied with age-old chanting. Adults, youngsters, and even schoolchildren — I saw them all now in my mind, before my eyes, poring over the words. I saw those little children so clearly now, with their shining ruddy cheeks, and their curly *peyos* (side curls) swaying back and forth, as the older ones studied with them, the parents watching and enjoying the sight, enjoying the rare atmosphere of this time of week.

The prayer was melodious, especially the poetic stanzas of *Lecha Dodi*, the half-mystic prayer-poem that envisions the Sabbath as a heavenly bride to be welcomed in: "Come, my beloved friend, to meet the bride; let us welcome the presence of the Sabbath ... with singing too, and exultation, among the faithful of this precious people ...

Come, O bride; come, O bride, O Sabbath the Queen."

In the memory that I saw so clearly, my father served as the cantor, the *chazzan*, to lead the prayer, and I stood by him to help him, to sing with him the wondrous chassidic melody that carried the words of *Lecha Dodi* — so heartwarming, caressing a melody that set the heart singing.

✶   ✶   ✶

Smashed was the silence around me, as bullets began whistling in the air over my thicket. I harnessed on my machine gun, put in the cartridge of bullets that Arkady had brought me, and fired away without a stop. More and more I aimed my fire at one German sniper who would not let me alone, and at last the moment came when one of my bullets struck him. He managed to cry out something in German before his hand released his rifle and he fell to the ground, like a tree cut down by an axe that chopped into its roots.

Without any particular difficulty we withdrew from the scene of battle. Only a few bullets were left in my cartridge; it was almost completely emptied. And the situation was the same with the other members of our team. But we succeeded in getting all our dead and wounded men off the battlefield. Someone carried Arkady on his shoulders, as the poor fellow's pains made him groan with a pitiful sharpness. We finally reached a patch of ground that was more or less dry, and there the doctor who accompanied us began dealing with the seriously wounded. With a plain, ordinary farm knife he cut away limbs that had become partially detached, hands and feet that bodies only dragged along, which could not be saved.

I sat down on a rotting log of wood, and looked at the dusky sky. Now I knew that *Shabbos* had descended into the world: Sabbath the Queen, reigning through all the realms of the Creator's universe.

I thanked Heaven for the kindness I had found this day of heavy fighting, this day I had spent between life and death. Nor did I forget the trial I had undergone — the test to which I had been put by my tobacco — and went through it successfully. It was a trial that brought me back to my own true world, so precious to me: my world that I kept alive in my imagination and memory: my world whose reality I still felt with all my being.

CHAPTER TWENTY-TWO
Sonya

BECAUSE I WAS CARELESS, a bullet shot out from my gun. It was my pure good fortune that it didn't strike anyone; but I was still sentenced to seven days in confinement.

Pavel, a Byelorussian country boy with a doltish face, was assigned to keep guard over me. Before he put me into the tent that served as the guardhouse, he took my trousers belt, my pocket-knife, and the sewing needle, threaded with black thread, that I always kept stuck into the back of my jacket lapel.

He kept marching constantly around the tent, without a stop, all tensed up, his rifle loaded, his face dead serious. Every once in a while he lifted the flap that served as the door of the tent, to make sure I had not absconded. I could only assume that he did not rely on my decency, and he was not sure whether I might not be concocting schemes and plans of escape from this confinement. It seemed to me that he was trying to learn the truth about this from the expression on my face and from my movements inside the tent.

So Pavel kept guard over me according to all the accepted rules of incarceration under the conditions of the forest. He made sure that from the kitchen that served the base, no cooked food should reach me — nothing but boiled water and a ration of bread. This poor fellow never found out that the scrupulous, punctilious watch he kept over me was not really so very effective — because whatever I wanted, even a little hard liquor as a bonus, came into my tent by stealth.

After three or four days of this detention, I found this very special guard of mine quite unbearable. I could not stand his stupid face anymore, nor his idiotic habit of lifting up the tent flap every once in a while to see if I was still there. I was amazed that he hadn't become fed up with his striding around and around the tent, hour after hour, kicking with the tips of his boots the blackberry bushes that grew close enough to touch the tent — like a horse kicking its heels when it stands too long tied to one spot and becomes bored by having nothing to do.

"Idiot!" I had such a strong desire to shout the word in his face, at one time when he raised the tent flap. As usual, he struck his witless face inside and stared at me, more with his nose than with his large watery eyes.

The truth was that I had no right to be angry at him. Nor did I have any reason to rail at him with any complaint. After all, he was only a tyro, a beginner. He hadn't even gone through any "baptism of fire" yet. He still didn't know the taste of battle; he had never been tested in any armed conflict. He was assigned to guard duty, and he was doing his job properly, according to the rules. He was watching me as if I was a very precious treasure. What complaint could I have against him? What was he guilty of? Till only a short while ago he had lived in his village, safe behind the stove, enjoying his food prepared with dough and sour cream, his sausages that were kept in the cellar or hung on hooks in the entrance hall of the cottage; while we in the forest had already gone through vicious bloody encounters in our constant war against the Germans.

Not far from my prison tent sat Ukrainian partisans, singing their beautiful, haunting songs filled with yearning. I wrapped my head in my blanket to shut out their melodies from my ears. I remembered the songs they had sung when they were posted at the barbed-wire fence around the ghetto where I had been forced to exist. I did not need any reminders now of those days, with all the cruel, inhuman things those Ukrainians had done to us.

The fifth of my seven days of detention went by, and I was still in the hands of Pavel, the big simpleton who was keeping such careful guard over me, although his busy watchfulness was not so very effective.

Evening was approaching. Only now had the sun finally set behind the clusters of tall oak trees. Unintentionally, without thinking, I made the tent walls move and shake. And Pavel came running, distraught, pointing his rifle at my stomach. Frightened that he might get addlepated and fire at me, I fell upon him, to try to hold him captive; but he seized me by my foot and remained staring at me with his mouth open, not knowing whether he ought to shoot me or not. The poor fellow was shivering with fear, with his inability to decide what to do with me. His sheep's eyes almost bulged out of their sockets. Only their pupils were still, not moving at all, as if frozen.

"I'll shoot you if you move!" With difficulty he got the words out, his teeth chattering and knocking together.

Well, I explained to him that I had meant no harm, and still meant no harm; and I certainly had no thought of running away. What had happened to me, I went on explaining, was that I was seized by strong stomach pains. If, I continued, he was a decent, good human being, he would see to it that a pot of hot tea was brought me from the kitchen — strong tea mixed with honey, and properly laced with good strong liquor.

Pavel took seriously this story that I had invented. His compassionate face wrinkled up over the stomach pains that had not stricken me. He released my foot, which he had kept firmly in his grip the whole time, and began talking gently to me. To reward him for his kindness, I moved back further into the tent, so that he could be very sure of me. Once I was out of his sight, the laughter burst out of me, and I could quell it (as I had to) only with difficulty, after covering my mouth with both palms.

Only a few minutes went by, and at Pavel's request a pot of tea was brought me from the kitchen — mixed with plenty of honey and high-proof liquor. It revived me. Then I took to smoking cigarettes, one after another, till at last I fell asleep in a cheerful mood.

❧   ❧   ❧

Later that night I was woken from my sleep, as orders came for me to report to headquarters. As I left the prison tent, Pavel turned his head away from me, muttering resentfully. I didn't know if it was because I hadn't finished my full seven days under his tender loving care, or because he had not been ordered to escort me down to headquarters. I waved to him with my Cossack hat, that I wore winter and summer, sporting all the colors of the patches that I had sewn into it to mend it.

"Be well, Pavel," I called out to him from a distance, in the hope of pacifying him; but he did not even bat an eye at me; and when I looked back for a second, I saw him marching his beat around the tent as though I were still inside, kicking with the tips of his boots the blackberry bushes that almost clung to the canvas.

At the headquarters, Commander Bobakov sat at the table with several partisans, among them Sonya, taking the main part in the discussion that was under way. In great detail she explained the various possible approaches to a certain hamlet she had learned to know well yet before the war. She was quite sure that by the route she wanted to use in leading the team of partisans, they would be able to penetrate into the little hamlet even in broad daylight, without being discovered.

I listened to the discussion, and learned that Globshevitch, the place under consideration, was a hostile region, where a wedding was soon to be held; and according to information received at headquarters, Germans and high-ranking militiamen of the Byelorussian population were invited to the celebration. The plan was that our fighting team was to penetrate the village suddenly, surround the house where the wedding was to take place, kill whoever had to be put down, capture anyone who had to be taken prisoner, and return to the base with the weapons and ammunition that would be seized from the enemy men.

From all Sonya said I realized that despite her confidence, the assignment held considerable danger in store for us, nevertheless. Even if we succeeded in getting into the little hamlet without being discovered beforehand, it might still come to a brutal encounter, even face-to-face combat, between us and the Germans, plus the militiamen helping them in that hostile area. We knew this could definitely happen; it was clear to everyone in the room. But we were also well aware that there was no partisan action without its element of danger. The order was given that this mission was to be carried out — and no further questions were to be asked. Only one thing remained to be done: to get the task accomplished successfully.

As we left the headquarters tent, I attempted to exchange a few words with Sonya about the plan. There were a few thoughts and reservations about it that I had, which I had not brought up inside, during the discussion. Along the way, however, she disappeared from my sight among the tents. When I caught sight of her again, she was far ahead of me, with her new automatic rifle slung across her shoulder — a present that had been awarded her in recognition of the bravery she had shown in the invasion and capture of the airfield. The polished steel of her weapon shone in the night's darkness like a sharpened sword. And onward she strode.

❀ ❀ ❀

We left the base in the final hours of the night. By the time we reached the edge of our woods, dawn was on the verge of breaking.

At headquarters, the responsibility for carrying out the mission was placed not on Sonya but on a division leader in our squad. Nevertheless we well knew that it was she who would take charge and lead the team, directing the operation as we went along.

The sky above us began to grow clear, though our footsteps were still embroiled in the dusky dimness of unfinished night. It was still enough to stumble against something, to see some odd piece of wood at a bit of a distance, and we were ready to imagine something suspicious there, that we had to beware of.

The entire time, Sonya went in the lead, "sniffing" and trying to detect whatever might lie ahead, and forever growing impatient with us for lagging behind, for treading the ground without moving forward faster. "The devil knows what's happened to you today," she shouted. "You see a log of wood, a broken branch on the ground, and right away you stop. What sort of fear has gotten into you? What are you? — partisans, fighters, or just a bunch of bewildered children who lost their way in the woods?"

She flung the words at us like slaps across the face. No one opened his mouth to reply. We were too ashamed to lift our eyes. We could only trail after her like sheep. As for the division leader, she pulled him along by the sleeve, scolding him for not marching in front, at the head of the team — for not being a proper leader at all.

When dawn came, we halted our marching and stretched out under cover of the wide-branching trees, so that we should not be discovered. From their knapsacks the men took out chunks of bread and ate their fill. I noticed a well with water, and crawled to it. It was refreshing to wash my hands and face.

From various directions young shepherds began arriving with their sizable flocks. Alongside each flock romped a large shepherd-dog, that would not let any of the creatures under its charge roam too far from the flock. The shepherds themselves gathered at their regular place and stretched out on the ground, not too far from us. They collected twigs and small logs, and made a fire to keep them warm. And there they told their stories, played their shepherds' pipes, and sang their heartbreaking shepherds' songs.

We kept a sharp lookout over the area, focusing our eyes in a specific direction, till we noticed a hand raised high in a distant wheat field. A farmer who served us as a contact man, gathering information in the area as well, was hidden there in the field, as planned; and this was his signal to us that the way to Globshevitch was clear now, free of any danger. Throughout the hours of the night there had been no movement of Germans or militiamen in the region.

At the moment, however, something entirely different caught and held the men's attention. Some of them noticed that I was moving my lips and whispering. Sergei was the first to break out laughing. "Look," he chortled, "look: Philip is saying his prayers!"

I turned a blind eye and a deaf ear to his gleeful laughter. I continued praying unabashed, being in the middle of *Shacharit*, the age-old morning worship to the Creator that I remembered by heart from all the years of growth to adulthood, when I said it faithfully from a *siddur* each and every weekday. This was the first time in the forest, however, that anyone had noticed me at it. As a rule I managed to do my praying discreetly, keeping it hidden from everyone's sight.

Perhaps it was the morning songs of all the birds, perched on the trees or flying overhead, that filled my whole being with a surging wish to pour out my heart's woes and needs. But evidently this time I had not been careful enough to keep it unnoticed. Seemingly I forgot about the persons around me, and the age-old words of Jewish prayer came about a bit more loudly than usual, so that I too could hear them, and not my Maker alone. Evidently I became virtually unaware of my surroundings, letting it all fade out of my mind — the wedding in the hamlet of Globshevitch, the task mission we had to accomplish — as my private, whispered worship transported me to another world — so that in the instant that reality broke in, I did not know why all that laughter was going on around me. I could not understand why people should jeer at me when they saw me in prayer in the early hours of the morning.

❀ ❀ ❀

We made our way from several directions into the center of the hamlet, and opened up with our guns. The peasant men and women who were standing in their doorways or lounging just inside, disappeared deep inside, in utter confusion. The village became emptied of people, looking as if all life had suddenly stopped there in midday. Here and there a dog barked; and in a few minutes all the dogs of the village decided to be heard, and were not to be quieted.

We surrounded the house where the wedding was going on, and prepared for quick action. After all our calculations, after all the steps we had taken with so much thought and care, we reckoned on a dazzling success. We were certain we would capture such a great number of Germans that we would have to share them among us. Each one of us would get at least one German — alive or dead. And we calculated and reckoned how much ammunition would fall into our hands — automatic rifles, and those polished, shiny hand-guns of theirs ...

Fate reckoned otherwise.

It fast became clear to us that not one German had come to attend the wedding, and not even one militiaman. We could take it for granted that this beautifully planned operation had been revealed to them, somehow they had learned of it; and those who should have been there for us to terrify had decided they would rather not put themselves in danger, or endanger the whole village and its people who served them so faithfully.

Dark clouds of gloom settled into Sonya's face. She was grief-stricken by the disappointment. In a mad frenzy she ran through the rooms of the house, searched through the cellars, the barn, the stable — and found nothing suspicious. When she came back into the large parlor where the guests were sitting, she seemed ready to burst into tears: Despair flowed into her disappointment.

The thought flashed through my mind that if only two or three of the "boys" went off down the road and set an ambush for the Germans, and then actually captured one or two of them, we would literally bring her back to life. We ought to do anything we could — anything — so that she should at least not have to return to the base empty handed. But it was only a thought.

When there was nothing left for us to do there, the commander of the division gave the men permission to take anything they wanted from the people in the house. At that I blithely made my way into the kitchen and asked the mistress of the house (the mother of the bride) for a large needle and thread. When I was freed from detention, I had neglected to ask my guard Pavel to give me back the ones I had had before, and now was my chance to make up the loss. I sat down at the window and went to work mending my torn clothes.

While I was busy at my tailoring, young Sergei passed by before me — and I almost didn't recognize him. He was wearing a dark suit, and a dark hat perched on his head — items he had taken from the bridegroom, leaving the young man in his underclothes. Sonya decided she liked the stockings that the bride's sister was wearing, so she took them for herself. Others of our team followed Sergei's example, whereupon several of the guests also remained in their underwear. From the bridegroom's brother the division commander took off a pair of new boots, and then he decided to take away the pair of stockings from Sonya, because he wanted them for his fiancée, a girl in one of the villages near Globshevitch.

When all this activity was over, the men sat down at the table and helped themselves liberally to the good food that had been prepared for the guests. They sang Russian ballads and partisan songs, while the guests trembled in fear. For good measure a few shots were fired into the ceilings and walls of the rooms, to frighten them a bit more.

Half drunk, the "task force" left the village, after taking horses and wagons from the farmers, that would bring us back to the base in relative comfort.

❈ ❈ ❈

Eight routine, normal days went by. The ninth day after our action in Globshevitch, we were called to staff headquarters. As we stood at attention, a letter was read aloud — a letter signed by one of the farmers in the hamlet, which complained of the acts of robbery and looting committed by our task force during the wedding that took place there.

Every one who had been there, in the action, was now questioned by the command staff. They wanted to know about the objects and the clothing we had taken from the people at the wedding, and so forth. When my turn came, I turned over the lapel of my jacket and pointed to the threaded needle stuck there, and then I showed them the patches I had sewn on my clothes at the time of the wedding. Sonya told about the pair of stockings she had snatched from the bride's sister, which the division commander had then taken from her, while they were still there, for his fiancée. Young Sergei, on the other hand, did not have to say a word: He had come to the headquarters wearing the bridegroom's suit.

To justify ourselves, all the partisans argued before the men asking the questions that it was the division commander who had given them permission to take from the people at the wedding whatever they needed, and that he too had made off with what he wanted.

The interrogation went on for several hours. When it ended, we were sent back, each man to his unit. And with that, we thought, the matter was over and done with.

❈ ❈ ❈

One day the division commander who had headed our task mission was ordered to gather all those who had gone with him, and to take them again to Globshevitch. We could not imagine what our assignment might be this time. We had heard, however, that in recent days the Germans and local militiamen had stepped up their activities on the roads and paths around this hamlet that was hostile to us, and it had cost us some partisans' lives. It was possible, then (so we thought), that we were being given the "honor" of finishing our "business' in the hamlet that hated us. We would apply the standard treatment to a hostile locality that bred informers and collaborators: We would sent the whole locale up in flames — so that others would learn a lesson and fear to oppose us. In this way, too, we could open up the roads and paths again, and move about with greater safety there.

Some of us tried to pry some details out of the division commander about this new action that we were going into, but he managed to parry the questions and avoided giving any answer. "When we get to the place it will all become clear": this was his blank, pointless answer, that did nothing to satisfy our curiosity. We desperately wanted to know what was going on in that village.

The only one who did not badger the leader with questions was Sonya. She was seemingly confident that the team was heading now toward a difficult and dangerous mission, and it would be best not to talk about it and not to probe for any details beforehand.

When we reached Globshevitch, the division commander ordered his men to go to the houses of the little hamlet and tell everyone, men and women, to assemble immediately in the courtyard of the school. So our curiosity became all the stronger. It was completely unusual to leave the members of a small task force in complete ignorance about their assignment, knowing nothing about what they were to do until the very last moment.

The farmers who came to the school courtyard crossed themselves, in their great fear. So frightened were they that they burst into tears. Mothers came, holding little children in their arms, and they could not look at us directly. They didn't know what we had in store for them, and were simply terrified. Sonya came late, arriving with a bunch of local people who had been hiding in their homes. She ferreted them out and brought them to join the rest.

To quiet down the large crowd of people in the courtyard, pressed together and almost hysterical, the commander shot a few bullets into the air, and immediately took out a sheet of paper rolled up like a scroll. He opened it and began reading:

"By order of the command staff of the Marshall Rokosovsky Partisan Squad, the partisan named Sonya from the hamlet of Ivtzevitch is hereby sentenced to death by a firing squad, for the crime of looting that she perpetrated among the populace of Globshevitch on the day of ..."

No!

I heard not a word more of this sentence against Sonya, as it was read to the villagers. I fled. I forced a way through the densely packed crowd, and ran. I couldn't bear to be a witness to the dreadful crime that my fellow-fighters were going to commit. It didn't matter where I was heading, or into whose hands I might fall. I sprinted across the village like a madman.

But the words kept echoing in my ears: "… the partisan named Sonya from the hamlet of Ivtzevitch is hereby sentenced to death by a firing squad …" I still couldn't believe I had heard the division commander saying it in the school courtyard. There were moments when I told myself I was only having delusions, waking visions in a nightmare, and it wasn't truly real. So I ran without stopping, feeling over and over again that I was being struck across the face by a leather whip.

I stumbled over a fallen tree and suffered deep scratches, and there I lay, not moving. I yowled, tore my hair, screamed into the air like a dog wailing into darkness of night.

"Why? Why was *Sonya* picked out to be the scapegoat, the sacrifice to appease those people, this treacherous bunch of traitors? Why didn't the command staff sentence Sergei to death? He put the bridegroom to mortal shame. He humiliated him in the sight of everyone, taking off his fine new suit and putting it on, leaving the poor young man in his underwear. Why wasn't the division commander ordered to be shot? He was the leader of the task force. He set us to do the looting. He urged all of us to take whatever we wanted from the wedding guests.

"What did that command staff find about Sonya to accuse *her* of? What," I asked myself, "except the single fact that she had born into the Jewish people? This alone was enough. For this they chose *her* to be the scapegoat — this alone and nothing else. This was enough."

❧ ❧ ❧

The division commander needed three bullets to kill her. The first two were defective. In fact, the second bullet jammed his gun, and it took a while till they could get it out of the barrel. So twice Sonya collapsed on the ground in hysteria. It was later, at the base, that I was told about it. The partisan standing guard over her had to lift her and get her back on her feet.

At the last moment her mind went. She tore at her clothes, wrestled with the partisan who was standing guard over her, railed at him for not letting her go and set fire to the whole village. "Look," she screamed: "The village people have surrounded us. They want to shoot us. They want to murder the partisans!"

The third bullet struck her in the head, and she died instantly. The division commander told the villagers to take her body and bury it in their local cemetery. And the partisans returned to the forest immediately. This time the leader had carried out his assignment in accordance with the orders of the command staff.

❧ ❧ ❧

At last I also returned to the base. It was late at night when I arrived, after a day of aimless movement. I must have covered over thirty kilometers on foot.

Wherever I had gone, running or walking, I saw her. Every sound I heard, everything that reached my ears, seemed to be Sonya's voice — coming from this brave Jewish partisan, this singularly courageous girl who had no equal in the entire squad.

I didn't know what to do with myself. No place that I turned to seemed to be the place for me, where I could settle down and be still. I felt ready to wake them all from their sleep, to rouse and shake the whole forest with my screams of protest. I thought of dragging the men of the command staff out of their beds, to ask them, to demand an answer to my question: "Why did she deserve this? What you pick *her* as the sacrifice, the victim?"

Yet all I could do was suffer, thoroughly ashamed of myself for feeling and being so utterly helpless, for doing nothing more than go into my tent and lie down on my pallet. My eyes didn't close. I didn't fall asleep. But I had no wish to look at the clear moon strolling along up there in the sky. I drew back from looking into the dark eyes of the night that surrounded me.

No, I did not wake anyone from his sleep. I did not bellow or scream. I only spoke with myself, soundlessly. I spoke to my heart, giving it a solemn promise that if I remained alive, I would not be still. I would find some way to make Sonya's story known, to cry out for justice for the vile death of a brave girl no more than twenty years old, the last remnant of a Jewish family in the hamlet of Ivtzevitch, killed by her fellow partisans when she was innocent of any crime.

CHAPTER TWENTY-THREE
Liberation Day

THE SUN OF SUMMER DRIED the damp earth in the region of the partisan camp. This didn't make us very happy, however. We had been in the forest almost three years, and for reasons of security we had always preferred damp, swampy areas. Of course the swamps and the mud burdened our lives and hampered our movements, and they were richly supplied with mosquitos that tormented us without mercy. Yet at the same time they were a natural hindrance and obstruction against a sudden invasion by enemy forces into our territory.

The days were very hot now; and like us, the birds looked for shady spots. They hid where they could, becoming loth to fly, and even to chirp and trill.

So the ground dried, and our sources of water dwindled; but the base was still full of plaguing mosquitos and flies. We could find no peace either inside the tents or outside them. Those little creatures were everywhere. Swarms of them would fall upon us, humming, to nourish themselves on our blood. Keeping up a steady droning sound, they would bite away freely, till our faces and entire bodies would be a mass of swellings. To protect ourselves we set fire to moist, rotting roots of trees, and distributed them at various places around the camp. These roots didn't burn. They only sent up enough smoke to choke you till you were ready to vomit; and the smoke drove the tiny, flying parasites off and kept them away — but alas, not for long. Once the billowing smoke became a little weaker, they were back in droves, evidently coming straight out of their hiding places; and they would attack us with yet greater zeal, biting viciously as they hummed and droned. Evidently the sound they made was like a war cry: It drove them on to attack our poor human flesh with greater fury.

The high summer heat, almost tropical in its intensity, made the bark peel from many of the trees, like skin on a sunburnt face. The tall grasses and small, tender, scrub bushes bent their heads to the ground, as if they were fainting. Overhead a blue sky blazed, with hardly a cloud in it. And if a wispy strip of cloud appeared anywhere, the rays of sun located it immediately and attacked, till it melted away like snow on white-hot metal.

❧ ❧ ❧

Then the day came when Anna Petrovna caused a storm in the base. On her radio receiver she picked up a brief message that sent her running across the base with it in a fine frenzy, to deliver it to staff headquarters. From hints which she herself let out afterward, we gathered that the message she delivered was not bad at all. A while later we all knew that the Red Army had opened a major offensive against the Germans, at its front, and our striking forces had begun advancing westward.

The same day, another message came through: In many locations, sizable enemy forces were surrounded, and German soldiers were being taken captive in droves. People among us made a reckoning, and reached the conclusion that our day of liberation was not far off. It was too early to calculate just how long it would take till this day came for which we were waiting in longing, but at least we began to believe that now there was a solid basis for hope. We just had to have enough help from Heaven to hold out, to stay alive until that day of wonder came.

"Liberation": We did not have the word yet living in our minds. It was not really there yet in our thinking. It was still alien to us, strange, somewhere off in the distance. But there was something so unexpectedly beautiful about it, like a bit of a dream that gladdens the heart. Our hands lost some of their tension. Our minds began working more loosely, more irrationally. We became different from what we had been till now. And we had no words to put together with this one special word: "liberation." We simply developed a tendency to unusual emotions. Men embraced, kissed one another on the cheek, danced — in anticipation of the day that was certainly on the way.

I too was happy. I also had such moments. "We're going to leave the forest," went the thought in my heart. "We'll return to normal life, some in the city, some in the village. We'll start living again among free human beings. We'll surely have a roof over our heads again, a place to live, with a table, a bed, a proper chair to sit on, household utensils ... People will go walking in the streets, out-of-doors; they'll sit in the parks and the gardens. There are going to be shops and stores again, people selling, people buying, people smiling, laughing, singing, playing music. It will probably be just as it was before ... before this nightmare ... relatives, friends ... just as it all was before."

Yet the plain truth is that this lovely word "liberation" also frightened me, afflicted me with the pains of an inferno. Someone inside me asked, "What normal life are you talking about? To what homes, what streets, will you go back? Where in the world are *your* relatives, *your* friends? They're all in the ground, in the pits, returned to the earth — all of them. And who is going to give *you* a roof over your head? — the *goyim*? Your non-Jewish neighbors are going to have compassion for you? — those who helped the Germans? So what is all your happiness about?"

The good news, however, continued to reach us every day, and then every few hours. "The Germans have begun retreating along all the roads and highways," Moscow Radio informed Anna Petrovna. "Our forces are advancing rapidly." Anna passed the news on to us. "Do you know, fellows?" she added: "It could happen tomorrow, or the day after, or maybe in a few days. The whole thing will be over. Now anything is possible — anything."

For long months, however, Anna Petrovna kept sitting and sending messages on the transmitter that she had brought with her from Moscow. She kept striking the keys like a bird pecking away at the branch of a tree it was perched on. And all the time she had not a bit of good news to tell us, not one happy smidgen of information about the front. Nothing was moving; nothing was changing. The whole situation was frozen.

Then the day came when new information came through every few minutes: a fresh triumph by the Red Army; whole stretches of territory recaptured from the hands of the conquering Germans, whole areas set free. Enemy forces were being demolished; their ranks were disintegrating.

How different the situation was now; how different the morale of the partisans.

Two years earlier, during the fierce battle over Stalingrad, a number of Soviet partisans deserted from our ranks. They went to town, to live under the German occupation, to cooperate with the conquerors. I remember a Ukrainian, a full member of the Communist Party, who had been a high-ranking officer in the Red Army in the past. One evening he was sitting with us as we listened to the gloomy, sombre news bulletins that our radio — a simple receiving set, the only one we had — brought us from the front. Suddenly the moment came when this Ukrainian gave the radio a kick that broke it into pieces, and off he went. He disappeared from the forest. Like others of his kind, he had run out of endurance. He could not bear it any more. So he too went off to serve the German forces of hell that had conquered his country, his homeland.

And now the day of liberation was drawing near, the day we would be set free from enslavement by war, the day that we had never been certain if it would ever arrive. They were all happy now — all of them.

"And you?"

I had no answer to give myself. My bitterly melancholy reflections weighed heavily on my feelings of happiness. I could only let both sets of emotions live in me, mixed together however they might be.

We felt the effects of the enemy's retreat, as the battlefront moved back and came closer to us. The Germans began combing the woods and clearing them out, as they needed them now for their way back. In these enemy actions hundreds of partisans lost their lives. Death fell upon us just as we were anticipating a return to life. Our woods became filled with people in flight from the forests of Bryansk, Nalyvok, regions beyond the Neiman River, regions in the environs of Grodna and Novogrodok. They were fighting units and non-Jewish family camps, who told us of dreadful atrocities that the Germans had committed before they withdrew: wholesale murder among the partisans and civilian populations.

Well, I reflected, this meant that my chances of staying alive were getting smaller. Now, when I was so near the passageway back into life, the door might shut in my face. The danger was lurking that just now, before the liberation we craved so strongly, after we had traveled so long a road of combats and conflicts with the enemy, we had a good chance of finding our lives ended while still in the forest, never to make it back to freedom.

❧ ❧ ❧

We left our boots on when we went to sleep. We made ourselves ready to face enemy action. By our reckoning, we would still have to wage some bitter combat, against German forces on the retreat. On the other hand, plans were made for our own retreat, if necessary, to the swamps of Pinsk.

And meanwhile we found it hard to get provisions. In the course of almost three years we emptied out the food supplies of the farms in our vicinity. We took from the farmers whatever we needed, and a good bit more. And now, having impoverished them, there was no more point in searching on those farms. There was simply nothing more to find. Having no alternative, we began to seize chickens. Yet how many chickens could the indigent farmers of Byelorussia raise? What could they feed them, when they themselves never had enough to eat?

The partisans went deeper into the woods and began hunting wild boar and other forest animals. One day Volodka, a first-rate sharpshooter in our squad, sent a bullet into a wild boar, hitting it in the belly. The animal was shaken for a moment by this unpleasant surprise. It let out a mighty roar. And it continued running on its way, as though nothing important had happened. Volodka took an oath that he would never have anything more to do with wild boars.

In the clear summer nights that came down to us, the stars sparkled in the sky, and the moon seemed to be doing exercises to pour its full light down on us, in this last period of our time in the forest. We felt good. Soviet planes began flying overhead, over our clusters of trees.

Then the day came when we heard faint, distant echoes of the exchange of artillery fire. Our hearts both gladdened and trembled, but the joy overrode the fear. From the command staff came an order to dismantle the tents. I could have blown my tent down with one strong puff of breath, but I was so very reluctant to fold it away out of existence. How many hours had my poor bones rested inside it, on the pallet of straw that always had a musty smell from the damp earth beneath it. How many tears had fallen from my eyes in that tent. And how many moments of solace had I known in talking with my friend Mischa. The whole ground area of the tent was barely six feet by six, yet it had been large enough for us to knit and develop a true friendship that made us boundlessly devoted to each other.

Yet just now, so soon before we were going to be set free, Mischa was not with me. He was neither inside the tent nor outside it — in fact, nowhere on the base. All I knew was that he had gone off at the head of a selected team of fighters, on a secret mission. Before he left he confided to me that the men were being sent to operate behind the lines — right at the back — of the retreating enemy. I fell to wondering: Would I ever see him again? Would I know what became of him? Or would he have the good fortune to come out alive and go back to his village, to his mother, to the girl who was engaged to him? I wanted to be able to embrace him at the moment of liberation, at the moment when our roads into life would have to separate, as he turned eastward, back to his motherland and his home, and I ... I? Who knew?

We dug pits in the earth and buried all the things we would have to come back and retrieve after the Red Army captured the region and my old city of Slonim. Among those things we concealed the documents of every partisan unit, with the lists of names of the fighters: those who stayed alive, and those who had fallen in combat or died otherwise in the forest.

In the last few days a list was sent to the chief partisan headquarters, on the other side of the front: the names of the partisans in our squad who were recommended for distinction and marks of honor. I was informed that my name was on the list.

A few of the men were given the task of burying for safety a number of boxes containing the documents and papers of the command staff for the entire period of our combat in the forest. Among those papers were assignments received from the main headquarters in the last few days, through Anna Petrovna's radio equipment, appointing various leaders and captains in our squad to official positions in the council of Slonim — the local government that was to be set up immediately after the liberation.

Among all the orders came also the command to bury our printing press, that had been parachuted down to us a long while ago. With this small press the command staff had been able to issue a newspaper in Byelorussian, for which I had written articles under the name of Philip Philipov, a partisan who was, supposedly, Russian by birth. The newspaper's editor had once received a request from the editor of the main, general partisan journal (issued at the central headquarters) for information about this Philip Philipov. The man wanted to know who this writer was, and so on. As I later learned, in his letter of reply our local editor did not mention that I was a Jewish partisan. Simply and honestly he explained to me, "Whatever happens, Philip, it is better that they shouldn't know it."

※　※　※

The reverberating explosions of shells and bombs sounded closer now. From time to time the whole forest seemed to shake. Trees that were rotting at their roots collapsed suddenly. Animals wailed, yowled, ran in frenzy from place to place, from one cave to another, only to fly out again and speed across the ground, unable to find a place of safety.

In the hours of the day we sat scattered around, in small groups, keeping silent. The boughs of the trees gave us cover, and we no longer lit any fires to keep warm, so that enemy planes should not detect us. We made do with small portions of salted meat that we took out of the caves where they had been stored. The meat was full of ants, but the men were not overly fussy. The ants did not disturb them too much as they quieted their rumbling empty stomachs.

The Red Army kept coming closer and closer, yet no one knew what might still happen before its men actually entered the woods. We could not be certain if for some reason the Soviet forces might not halt their advance, so that we would probably have to stay here right behind the front, in territory that was still under enemy conquest. And we might be here together with the Germans who had spread out through the whole forest.

Overhead, air battles were going on. More and more Soviet planes appeared in the sky: heavy bombers whose steady drone sounded as if they were pounding and grinding the air. In the battles at night, before releasing their bomb loads over the enemy ground-forces, our planes would parachute down a whole series of lighted flares: brilliant man-made stars they seemed, that left heaven and descended, but never reached the earth. When these flares appeared in our sky, we forgot about sleeping. We climbed to good positions in the pine and oak trees, and gazed with satisfaction. It was a pleasure to watch the bombs dropping from our planes onto the destructive manpower and equipment of the enemy.

From afar we blessed those who were bringing closer the victory over the retreating German army. In our spoken thoughts we sent our fervent good wishes to our Soviet flyers. We gave them our heartfelt thanks for the happiness we felt over every German airplane we saw falling to earth or exploding in midair. We reckoned that our flyers did not see any sign of us. It would quite certainly never occur to them to think that in the very moments when they were carrying out their bomb attacks, their fellow fighters behind the lines were sitting in the trees and looking on, wallowing in delight and wishing them full triumph and victory till the end, till the enemy would be erased.

The Soviet planes also dropped human beings, Russian fighters who parachuted down into our region — generally at night, but in the daytime as well. Some of them came dressed in civilian clothes and mingled with the masses who were retreating with the Germans, as though they too were ordinary people in flight from the advancing

Russians. At a suitable time, when the Red Army was fiercely on the attack, they would join forces with it and strike out at the Germans, stirring confusion in their ranks.

In one of these groups that were parachuted down to mingle unnoticeably with the retreating Germans, there was a Jewish lad named Izak, from the hamlet of Kossov. In the past he had fought as a partisan in one of the units in our forests. Then he got through the battle lines and joined the Red Army as a regular soldier. After fighting in many encounters with the enemy, he somehow managed to get back to the forests that he had left two years earlier. People saw him and even exchanged a few words with him, before he rushed on. After all, he was in a hurry, "retreating with the Germans from those dreadful Russians."

In a few days, however, we learned that Izak was no longer among the living. We asked and asked, anyone and everyone we could — and there was nothing more we could find out. No one knew where or how death had overtaken him.

❧ ❧ ❧

I dreamt a nightmare, and woke. It was the second time I had dreamt it, and both times exactly the same: I spat out a few teeth into my hand. In search of help I told it to whomever I met, and they all gave me the same look: As far as they were concerned, I was a doomed man. Fate had marked me down for the grim reaper, and I had not much longer to go — perhaps a few hours. By their reckoning, I was finished — not worth a rubbed-out penny.

I found myself laughing at them. Frightful as it was, the dream did not trouble me at all. I didn't believe it. I knew, and know, that there is a higher Authority over us poor mortals, who gives life and takes it back only when He decides; and no dream could change that.

Meanwhile the Germans began retreating along the roads of the forest, with all their weapons and armaments. At several points we mined bridges. When the retreating forces went up on them with their heavy equipment, they plunged to their doom. Our fighter planes pursued them, continuing to drop their bombs steadily — till whole clumps of earth and uprooted trees, falling into the pits that the bombs gouged out, hid the fleeing enemy from sight.

We stopped counting the days that still remained, by our reckoning, till our liberation. We were certain that the end was literally on our doorstep. Days and nights went by, however, and our liberators did not arrive. And meanwhile the woods became filled with Germans. Their tanks and cannon moved along the dirt roads as they sought a quick way out of the woods, so that our forces should not overtake them. German bomber and reconnaissance planes accompanied their retreating armies, to give the ground forces protection. So from time to time the conflict became fierce, till the battlefront virtually became located in the woods, right in our area.

Finally forced to move our base, we penetrated into a very dark and swampy woods, where even in full day we could hardly recognize one another at any distance. To know what was going on in the forest around us, we climbed the tall tangled trees, and from there we could observe all that was happening.

Another night went by and a new day rose, and we were ordered to leave our hiding place and attack isolated groups of enemy soldiers that had become detached from their units, as well as any Germans moving on out-of-the-way side paths. We scattered along the edges of the paths and lanes, and capturing Germans alive became a competitive sport among us. Those we caught we turned over to our superior officers, and took no further interest in them. When we stopped individual German soldiers fleeing on bicycles, however, we dragged them back to our base; and there our men finished them off quickly, without any long, drawn-out questioning or investigation. In the situation, no other "treatment" for them was really possible. And everything we did, Anna Petrovna kept reporting on her transmitter at top speed to our armed forces, who were now only a number of kilometers away from us.

One operation of ours was particularly successful. Having finished off more than twenty German soldiers, we put on their uniforms, including their medals and decorations of honor. We took along some of their automatic weapons, of which we had a generous supply by now, and out we went on the roads, to mingle with the isolated groups of enemy soldiers still in retreat. Then we guided them to safer roads, because, as we told them, we knew the area. We led them straight into the hands of our men, whereupon they really became safe — removed from all further harm in this world.

Other partisan units split up into small groups, to operate in similar ways; and we had to be very careful that none of the men disguised as Germans should shoot at one another.

♛ ♛ ♛

At last the day we had been anticipating, waiting for, longing for, arrived. Liberation became a fact, a living reality. It was here.

On a late afternoon it happened. Someone arrived in a hurry at the spot where we were now concentrated, and informed us that Soviet tanks were making their way through the woods. The men out there, he said, wanted information about the partisans.

We were reluctant to believe the messenger. We were afraid it might be a ruse by the Germans, in a last-minute attempt to eradicate us, perhaps. There was no way of verifying then and there if this messenger had told us the truth. So the command staff decided to send out a few men to reconnoiter the area till they came in sight of the main roads on which the armies were moving, and there they were to get a good notion of what was happening.

In a little while the men were back from their reconnoitering, breathing and perspiring heavily, their mouths foaming helplessly. They couldn't utter a word, but they nodded their heads — and we understood. We didn't need a single word from them. We simply started dancing, prancing, going wild, crying out into the forest at the bellowing top of our lungs, "They're here, they're here! Our men, here, in the forest! We're free ... free ... fre-e-e-e ... fre-e-e-e-e!"

We just didn't know what to do, how to live those first moments of total, absolute liberation, release, release, total release, when we knew at last that this hell was over, done with, *kaput*. They were moments of confusion, bewilderment, disorder and chaos, out of time, out of this world.

❀ ❀ ❀

Before our eyes, in our woods, two mighty armies met and clashed. We partisans, who had ruled the forests till now, were no longer partners in the raging battle. We stood aside, but with our firm, considerable share, our indisputable contribution to the great victory. No one needed our rifles any more, nor our rusty, damaged bullets to put into them. We had fulfilled our missions and done our task; and now, when the great moment came, we were released from duty and set free.

Many of us had a strong wish to go on fighting, to join in and take part in the duration of the war, as long as it might still last, till the full victory would come, with the enemy in total, abject surrender, *kaput*. These partisans wanted to go on shooting their rifles and machine guns ... but alas, no one took them into account; they went unnoticed — for only the regular, powerful forces of the Red Army were in action now. They hit out at the enemy with their full might, and there was nothing left for us to do but look on and watch what was happening. We weren't accustomed to being no more than spectactors, and to a certain extent the feeling in our hearts was quite unpleasant. It was not easy to get used to this drastically different situation.

The nightmares of war went on before our eyes: corpses without number, wounded men in every piece of ground; and destruction:

Whatever we had not managed to demolish in the almost three years we spent in the forest, the massive Red Army finished off in passing, as it rolled by our watching eyes. How many, many trees writhed and fell from fragments of exploding shells, or from the munitions dropped by bombers overhead. The earth of the forest was overturned; enormous craters and pits were formed; but above all, blazing fires were started, and no one took the trouble to put them out.

There was another development, of which we knew nothing: With their families, thousands of farmers left the neighboring villages in these last few days and came milling into the woods. They abandoned homes and property, and came to find shelter among the partisans. These people pushed their way through, en masse, to climb up on the Russian tanks and cannon that were making their way along the forest — so that they could embrace the Russian soldiers in thanks for coming to liberate them. Many farmers wanted to go along with the soldiers to their homes, not realizing that the Red Army had not yet finished its job — that the enemy was only retreating, and it still had to be pursued, still had to be struck hard again and again, till it would know that the German wave of the future was finished, *kaput*.

One way or another, however, whatever was going on, the happiness was tremendous: so great that people kept wiping tears from their eyes and weeping again, from the sheer joy.

For some three years this territory had been under the dominion of foreigners. Inhuman brute conquerors ruled the land and its people. Day in and day out, night after night, only German planes had been seen in the sky, flying at high altitude to and from the front. Now ground and sky were freed from their dominion. Gone was the dread, the fear, the terror. We experienced our first night of freedom, our first night of release from hell. How were we to be? What should we be feeling? What should we be doing? We were still bewildered, dazzled and dizzied by freedom's glowing light.

From every corner of the forest they came, streaming into a "bald patch" of the woods, that had been cleared of its trees, till it looked like a kind of village square. Apart from our squad, other partisan units, that had come into our woods in recent days, gathered with us. We came to take part in a formal meeting between liberated partisans and representatives of the Red Army: a meeting between brothers-in-arms.

We stretched out on the ground, as the moon sailed on overhead, bright and clear and smiling. It had evidently invited itself to our happy gathering. At any rate, it was the first time in the forest that we were not afraid this piece of glowing silver might reveal us to the enemy.

The brilliant moon lit up another meeting as well: a gathering of the remnants of the Jewish fighters in the forests. We embraced one another and wept, but ours were not tears of happiness. All the wounds, all the anguish and pain we had suffered, all the hurt we had known through this whole period, opened up and rose to the surface; and the tears came.

We took stock of ourselves, and found we numbered seventeen: exactly seventeen Jewish partisans among the many hundreds, perhaps thousands, of non-Jewish fighters in the ranks of the forest fighters, gathered now in this "village square" in the woods, to march together, with the rising dawn, into the liberated city of Slonim.

Our lips stayed closed. For so long a time we seventeen had been scattered among the various partisan units, each with his own load of ache and pain to bear. Every one of us had his own story to tell, but we were still not ready to talk about ourselves. We couldn't — not till much later that night, as we sat together. Then we began remembering the names of fellow-fighters, other Jews who had been with us at the very beginning, when the partisan brigades and activities first took form in the forests, but had not come through to this moment in our lives.

So long was that list of Jewish names, so very long, that we found neither the time nor the ability to remember them all.

⚘ ⚘ ⚘

In the small hours of the night the top Soviet general appeared: The one who commanded all the forces that had liberated our regions. From the improvised platform that had been hastily constructed out of tree branches, he spoke with fiery, blazing words in praise of the mighty Red Army. He described the acts of murderous brutality that the Germans had committed against the Russian people under their domination. He called to mind the millions of Poles and Frenchmen, Russians and Byelorussians, Ukrainians and others, who had been put to death till now by the Germans, while others were still dying day after day in the death camps that the enemy maintained in various captive countries and in Germany itself.

We did not know much about the death camps; but we were astounded and shaken to hear nothing from this top Soviet general, not a single word, about what the Germans had done to the Jews, the people and the communities everywhere — as though it was not our people, ours specifically, who had been massacred and thrown into the huge open pits.

We stanched the tears that rose to our eyes, and simply stood there stunned. All, all were against us, and we could only keep silent. We could only be broken and crushed, miserable, mute.

With the rise of morning we went out on the road to Slonim. Fields of wheat stretched out before our eyes on both sides of the route along which we marched. The kernels were full, yellow in color. A clear summer day rose around us, without a shadow of a cloud. The golden rays of the sun accompanied us all the way, casting their sheen over soldiers' dead bodies, Germans and Russians alike, gilding them. Some bodies were whole; others were shattered; others, torn apart. Limbs and pieces were strewn about, some human, some animal. We passed by cannon and tanks: some damaged, some burnt, and a few of those had swollen parts of bodies attached to them — stuck to the steel, from the conquered casualties and victims.

And we had a whole army band escorting us. Our feet marched to the beat of patriotic Russian melodies. But if we didn't want to spoil the fine marching rhythm, with all the fine singing and playing, once in a while we had to go off the road or squeeze to the side: Whole bodies and parts had fallen spang in the middle of the road, as some ill-fated humans had ended their war right there.

Officially we were still under orders: We still had to obey our superior officers. But slowly, steadily, the discipline grew lax. Local partisans left their ranks, left the fine march, and went off home, for some long-awaited happiness with their parents, or with wives and children.

We, however, the little bunch of Jewish partisans, had nothing for which to hurry away. We did not leave the ranks. We marched on, but a little bent over, wrapped in ourselves, looking like mourners on the way back from a funeral in the family.

Arm in arm we marched, watching over one another like brothers. We couldn't talk. Words were beyond us. Only, the silence tore at our hearts and pressed down.

As the day moved along, the heat grew stronger. The sun blazed down, heating the ground under our feet. The full ears of wheat in the fields bowed low to us without any reason, and in so doing, shed their ripened kernels.

As we reached the city, the band's playing grew louder, and the mass singing of the partisans was deafening. Only we were still silent, we seventeen: The only Jewish partisans who came out of the forest alive. We did not sing along.

We walked on the main roads of the city and crossed into the narrow side streets, that had once been alive and full with Jews. We went into the courtyard of the synagogues, the warm houses of prayer, that had once stood there, next to the stores in the shopping center of the Jewish market place. And there we broke down. The tears would not stay back any more. They welled up in our eyes and poured, as the dams of emotion broke. We didn't talk, but now we all found ourselves out of the march. We sat down on the stones by the roadside and turned into mourners who could find no consolation.

❧ ❧ ❧

Wildly I ran over the sidewalks of the half-scorched roads, till I reached the house that had been my home before we were given a German-made ghetto to move to. I found the place a shambles inside. Outside, on the grounds, one wall still stood of what had once been the *beis medrash*, the homey, congenial house of prayer and study of our *rebbe*, our local chassidic spiritual leader. There was the wall, with its eternal light (a lamp of holiness that should never be allowed to go out) still attached to it — but with the light in the lamp gone out long ago. Parts of other walls also remained, complete with window frames. The roof was gone, but the smoke-blackened brick chimney was there, lying helter-skelter. The moment I arrived there, a small bird perched on its top; but as it saw me approaching, it flew off swiftly, as if frightened — as many non-Jews in the city actually were — at the appearance of a figure that had been trodden on and trampled into the ashes: A Jew who seemed to have risen back to life straight from the pits dug long ago for the massacres.

Having seen enough, I fled — and headed for the Jewish cemetery. I looked for the structure that had been built over the grave of our well-known chassidic rabbi. When I had been a member of the work crew compelled to remove the tombstones for our German masters, we had not had time to deal with this structure, before the Nazis decided to end the work crew's existence. It should still have been there. Yet no trace of it remained. Evidently the Germans themselves had dealt with it.

I left the cemetery and ran to the hills of Petrolovitch, to the pits themselves, where some three fourths of the city's Jewish population had been thrown, including thousands of refugees who had fled for their lives from other locations and come into our city to escape death.

Arriving at the pits, I found the group of Jewish partisans already there. We had entered the city together, but while I went on my other visits, on their own they had sought out the spot where the great majority of the city's Jews had been thrown.

We stood there together now, in pain, heartbroken, miserable. Each one of us picked a spot for himself, to stand alone in contemplation, imagining himself at the graves of his own kin, his own beloved relations, to unite himself with them in his thoughts.

In a choking voice someone among us began the *kaddish:* "Yisgadal ve-yiskadash sh'mey rabboh (Magnified and hallowed be His great name) ..." In its wings the soaring wind gathered the tears of our weeping, as we listened to our age-old prayer for the dead, and it scattered them over the large terrain of the pits, rolling them everywhere, from one spot to another, and finally carrying our tears upward, to the heavens above.

Forlorn, abject, we responded to the *kaddish:* "Ye-hey sh'mey rabboh mevorach le-olam ule-olmay olma-yo (Be His great name blessed forever and ever and ever)."

Was I dreaming, or was it reality? It seemed to me that an ocean of tears flowed from our eyes, spread over the green grass that covered the pits, and filtered down into the ground.

With our throats choking up, each of us said the *kaddish* in turn, and the others responded. We wanted the trembling words and the weeping that overwhelmed us to wend their way into the forest we had just left, to search and find the burial places of all the Jewish partisans who had fallen in combat, or had been deliberately killed by their non-Jewish fellow fighters — so that they would know that the *kaddish* we were saying in the hills of Petrolovitch was for them too; that the tears which came bursting from our hearts were being shed for them as well, for the tragic, confounded deaths that had cut them down.

There was one thing more we wanted them to know. Standing here, at the mass grave of our fellow-Jews, that included perhaps some beloved kin of theirs, we — seventeen Jewish partisans — swore an oath to remember them. If they could live on in our memory, this much life we would give them.

We would never forget them.

Never.